The Art
Screwball Comedy

ALSO BY DORIS MILBERG

World War II on the Big Screen: 450+ Films, 1938–2008 (McFarland, 2010)

The Art of the Screwball Comedy

Madcap Entertainment from the 1930s to Today

DORIS MILBERG

McFarland & Company, Inc., Publishers
Jefferson, North Carolina, and London

LIBRARY OF CONGRESS CATALOGUING-IN-PUBLICATION DATA

Milberg, Doris.
    The art of the screwball comedy : madcap entertainment
from the 1930s to today / Doris Milberg.
        p.   cm.
    Includes bibliographical references and index.

    ISBN 978-0-7864-6781-5
    softcover : acid free paper ∞

    1. Comedy films—United States—History and criticism.
I. Title.
PN1995.9.C55M52 2013
791.43'617—dc23   2013001097

BRITISH LIBRARY CATALOGUING DATA ARE AVAILABLE

Cover photograph: Katharine Hepburn as Susan Vance, Cary
Grant as Dr. David Huxley with Nissa as Baby, the leopard in
Bringing Up Baby, 1938 (Photofest)

Manufactured in the United States of America

McFarland & Company, Inc., Publishers
    Box 611, Jefferson, North Carolina 28640
    www.mcfarlandpub.com

To Ted,
my husband and best friend,
who was a tremendous help in this endeavor.
With all my love.

Table of Contents

Preface

In the pages that follow, we will trace the journey of the screwball genre from its inception in the 1930s to its present incarnation. We will meet some of the most famous people in the entertainment business, past and present, and we will understand why, as Irving Berlin put it so well, "There's No Business Like Show Business."

In the early 1930s, a group of moviemakers gave birth to a film genre which evoked smiles, chuckles and downright guffaws from a public desperately trying to emerge from the depths of an economic depression which lasted, in various forms, throughout the decade and into the second world war.

The history of this "birth" is an interesting one. With the collapse of Wall Street on that October day in 1929 and with men and women standing on breadlines or selling pencils and apples on street corners, the mood of the country was one of despair, emanating out of a hopelessness from which they were receiving no respite. In 1933, however, the tide slowly began to turn. The year before, to the strains of "Happy Days Are Here Again," Franklin Delano Roosevelt had become the 32nd president of the United States. Under his leadership, the New Deal began. His economic policies and social reforms, his ideas and ideals and, most of all, his confidence were like a tonic. A growing sense of optimism took hold in the land. People dared to hope once more, to dream once more and to move up and out of the dark valleys.

Hollywood, on the other hand, seemed to be plunging into some "dark valleys" of its own. During the Roaring Twenties, it was charged that the movie capital was to blame for the nation's lapse in morality. Lurid film titles such as *Forbidden Fruit* from Paramount, *Sinners in Silk* from Metro-Goldwyn-Mayer and *A Shocking Night* from Universal, just to name a few, did not help matters. Added to this were the scandals involving several well-known figures in the industry. Roscoe "Fatty" Arbuckle, accused in 1921 of the rape and subsequent death of a Hollywood party girl/actress (the comedian was later acquitted, but the stigma remained); the unsolved 1922 murder of director William Desmond Taylor, in which popular stars Mabel Normand and Mary Miles Minter were involved; the drug addiction of actor Wallace Reid—these were only a few of the scandals in which Hollywood was mired.

Before long, Congress got into the act. To paraphrase a United States Senator: Hollywood was a place where riotous living, drunkenness, dissipation and free love seemed to be conspicuous and contagious. The august Senator concluded his remarks with this nugget: "Looks like there is some need for censorship."

The film moguls evidently took the Congressman's words to heart. In 1922, the Motion Picture Producers and Distributors of America was formed in order to coordinate industry policies and practices. The organization, under the stewardship of former United States postmaster Will Hays, devised a Production Code to police the studios in their moviemaking endeavors. It set general standards of good taste and more specific guidelines for each film made.

The main thrust of the Code was that presenting evil on the screen is often essential, but it should not be presented alluringly. In the film, the evil must be punished commensurate with the crime.

The moviemakers eventually were not as careful with their product as members of the clergy, educators and the various groups of "reformers" would have wanted. As a result, in 1934, strict censorship became a reality. A group of Roman Catholic bishops formed the National Legion of Decency; its stated aim was to review all films. Those deemed "objectionable" were to be boycotted. The Legion attracted a nationwide following.

Frightened by a projected loss of revenue, Hays had the old Code expanded. He then entrusted its enforcement to Joseph Breen, a Catholic newspaperman. The Breen Office soon became the industry's chief censor. They had the authority to license films for screening. Scripts had to be submitted to a board of censors before cameras could roll. Comparing the films of the present day with those of the 1920s and 1930s—today, when movies play "Show and Tell All" in every genre—it is hard to believe, when seeing these golden oldies, that there were so many restrictions governing them. Taboos included open-mouth kisses, double beds (twin beds were *de rigueur* and if a man kissed a woman in a bedroom scene, one of his feet had to be firmly planted on the floor) and any form of blasphemy. Virtue was to be rewarded and vice punished.

Even the titles were scrutinized. Mae West's *It Ain't No Sin* became *I'm No Angel* (Paramount, 1933) while Jean Harlow's opus *Born to Be Kissed* was released by MGM in 1934 as *The Girl from Missouri*. During this era, when the Code reigned supreme, producers, directors and writers were constantly trying to outwit and circumvent its restrictions.

In this frenetic atmosphere, the screwball comedy came into existence. Many films of this genre are being enjoyed by this generation via television and on DVDs.

The first part of this book discusses the stars, producers, directors and writers who were there at the beginning and were responsible for some of the greatest comedies ever made.

The films discussed in my last two chapters are modern incarnations of the genre. Some of today's producers and directors of comedies have learned their craft by harkening back to the 1930s and 1940s and use many of the techniques of that era.

The second half of this book is made up of what I call the subgenres of the screwball comedy. I have written at length about certain films which I consider more interesting than others. Scattered throughout are anecdotes and trivia relating to both stars and films. Also noted and discussed are the remakes of several of these productions.

Some films that I've written about may overlap into other subgenres but I've placed them where I think it most appropriate.

There are probably many films in the genre that have been overlooked in these pages—for this I apologize. There are going to be fans and students of film who will not agree with the choices and placements within my subgenres, but as the French say, "Vive la difference."

PART I : THE ESSENCE OF SCREWBALL

Chapter One

Cut and Print:
The Anatomy of Screwball

Madcap heiresses, zany families, opportunistic newspaper people, off and on marriages, murders with a twist plus other unusual situations—these are the characters and plotlines which make up the body of motion pictures known as screwball comedies. The films that are part of this valuable heritage burst the bubble of pomposity and make us laugh at the antics of those involved while gently mocking an artificial social structure. They also poke innocent and not-so-innocent fun at the sacred institutions of love, marriage and family.

Screwball comedies are at once warm and healing, lighthearted and off-beat. Most of the characters are warm-blooded and human, with good and bad traits—exaggerated, yes, but human just the same. The films of this genre, when first seen in the 1930s and even now, when modern screwball comedies have taken their place, appeal to all types of people, to rural America and to urban America; to the haves, of which there were and are too few, and to the have-nots, of which there were and are all too many. These films, however, at that time and this, tend to unify the people in one important way: They enable the viewer to laugh and display a sense of humor peculiar to this nation. To see the eternal battle of the sexes played out on the screen in a humorous and often slapstick fashion gave the population just what it needed at that time and also gives people what they need in the hazardous times of today—an escape from their troubles, for at least a little while. It was, then, and perhaps now, in its way, good for America.

The screwball comedy began during the height of the Depression and after a fashion, is still ongoing. Several of the most popular Hollywood stars of that bygone era let their hair down, engaged in broad slapstick and made some great contributions to the art of moviemaking.

I also think of stars who have followed in later generations: Streisand,

5

Midler, Zellweger, Roberts, Gere *et al.* They have also made *their* contributions to the genre.

I am not a purist in any sense of the word when it comes to defining the screwball comedies. Many comedies in this narrative may not be screwball for some readers, but to my way of thinking, they have enough of the essential elements to warrant inclusion. No one can tell me that such films as *For Pete's Sake, The Main Event, Pretty Woman, The Runaway Bride* and *Down with Love* do not contain elements of the screwball comedy. This premise will be examined as I end my narrative.

The dictionary defines the word "screwball" as an erratic, eccentric and unconventional individual and "comedy" as a series of light and humorous incidents. Put both words together and we have the essence of screwball comedy: light and humorous incidents involving erratic, eccentric and unconventional individuals. Comedy and romance are intertwined in the films discussed in the following pages, giving way to what I call the screwball romantic comedies.

What made the screwball comedies of the 1930s and '40s (and even the present) so popular? Dialogue, for one thing. Lively or satirical, some of the most delicious lines ever heard on the screen are part and parcel of the genre. "Waiter, will you serve the nuts? I mean, will you serve the guests the nuts?" This line, as delivered with off-handed aplomb by Myrna Loy as Nora Charles in *The Thin Man* (MGM, 1934), simply crackles with humor. She knows, and the audience does too, that she's gotten her point across the first time.

"I'm more or less particular about whom my wife marries" is a line spoken by Cary Grant to Ralph Bellamy in *His Girl Friday* (Columbia, 1940). This is only one of the lines in this fast-paced newspaper yarn delivered with impeccable timing, a raised eyebrow and just the slightest hint of mockery by the peerless Cary, a master of the double entendre.

"Doctor," says Merle Oberon to Alan Mowbray in *That Uncertain Feeling* (United Artists, 1941), "I'm absolutely certain there's nothing wrong with me." Retorts the sardonic Mowbray, "I'm sure you'll feel differently when you leave this office." This is a light mix of truth and satire.

In *The Bride Walks Out* (RKO, 1936), Barbara Stanwyck asks a constantly bickering couple why they got married in the first place. Their answer to this age-old question: "Well, it was raining and we were in Pittsburgh."

Irrational? Yes. Screwball? *Definitely!*

These are only a few classic examples of dialogue to be found in a genre known for some of the most hilarious ever committed to film.

Another key element in screwball comedy is the conflict to be resolved before THE END is flashed upon the screen. Irene Dunne and Cary Grant, as the battling Warriners in *The Awful Truth* (Columbia, 1937), stage a classic scene in a divorce court as they fight over the custody of their pet pooch Mr.

Smith (played by Asta, Hollywood's top dog of the 1930s). Dunne cheats and the canine trots over to her. The lady has a triumphant smirk on her face.

In screwball comedy, all's fair in love and war, with love ever triumphant.

And speaking of fighting, a different kind of warfare can be seen 40 years later: In *That Old Feeling* (Universal, 1977), Bette Midler and Dennis Farina, divorced for many years, having a battle royale at their daughter's wedding, prompting one guest to remark: "It was a perfect wedding except for two things — the bride's parents."

Merle Oberon and her peripatetic husband (Dennis Morgan) have been divorced as *Affectionately Yours* (Warner Brothers, 1941) begins. He will use any ruse to get her back. The fact that she is set to marry another man fazes him not one iota. The battle is on.

And speaking of "battles," we come to another aspect of screwball comedy: its physicality. Comedy came out of the drawing room in the mid–1930s and became more physical, adding the element of slapstick to many of its situations. In *Breakfast for Two* (RKO, 1937), boxing gloves are used by Barbara Stanwyck as she tries to knock some sense into irresponsible playboy Herbert Marshall (before she marries him). Carole Lombard, engaged in combat with Fredric March in *Nothing Sacred* (Selznick International-United Artists, 1937), whimpers, "Lemme sock you just once — just once and I won't care what happens." Instead, *she* is the recipient of a Sunday punch.

Fast forward 40 years: At the end of 1979's *The Main Event* (Warner/First Artists), Ryan O'Neal and Barbra Streisand are the ones wearing boxing gloves. She is the victim of an embezzlement. The one asset she has left is a has-been boxer. Upon meeting him, she remarks, "Why couldn't I own something that doesn't eat?"

The finale of *The Moon's Our Home* (Paramount, 1936) finds Margaret Sullavan at an airport in a straitjacket, being whisked away by Henry Fonda and two men in white, while in *Bluebeard's Eighth Wife* (Paramount, 1938), the reverse occurs, with Gary Cooper in a straitjacket fighting on the floor with Claudette Colbert. In *Cafe Society* (Paramount, 1939), the glamorous Madeleine Carroll falls into water while arguing with Fred MacMurray.

The last three films are marital mix-ups — more sights and sounds of the screwball comedy. They and others will be discussed at length in later chapters.

The stars mentioned above are only a small part of the passing parade who participated in the early days of the beginning of this body. They and their peers are a most important reason for the popularity of the early screwball comedies. Easily recognizable, they are still able to evoke pleasant memories in many of us.

Let's take a look at some of these never-to-be-forgotten players and in later chapters take a look at the new generation of "screwballers."

Chapter Two

Screwball Personnel: The Stars

When discussing the screwball comedies of the 1930s and early 1940s, we think of several performers, superstars of that era, still fondly remembered today. Although adept at drama, they were able to project the qualities inherent in the best of the screwball genre: a sense of the outrageous, a feeling for comedy, an ability to satirize and the chutzpah to engage in slapstick. All of this, while preserving their style and glamour. This chapter is dedicated to these masters of the screwball comedy. Also mentioned are several major stars who went against type and performed in some of the lesser-known films of the genre.

When most people reminisce about the early screwball comedies, the first names that come to mind are Carole Lombard and Cary Grant. The two made only two films together, both dramas, *The Eagle and the Hawk* (Paramount, 1933) and *In Name Only* (RKO, 1939).

Blonde, beautiful and spirited, Carole Lombard was, and still is to some, the finest satirical comedienne the screen has ever known, the embodiment of screwball comedy, the queen of the genre. A native of Fort Wayne, Indiana, she was a working actress by 1929. A stint with Mack Sennett, the acknowledged "king of comedy" during the silent era, taught her the impeccable timing which was at the heart of her comedic genius. In 1934, a golden opportunity arose for her: She took a trip on a train with the great John Barrymore, playing a bombastic actress born with the improbable name of Mildred Plotka. *Twentieth Century* (Columbia) scored a resounding hit at the box office. Barrymore was once quoted as saying that Lombard was one of the greatest actresses he had ever worked with.

Though the blonde star mixed drama and comedy and did both with equal skill, the screwball comedy became her signature genre. Her films include *Hands Across the Table* (1935) and *The Princess Comes Across* (1936), both from Paramount, *My Man Godfrey* (Universal, 1936) and *Mr. and Mrs. Smith* (RKO, 1941)—a cross-section of the genre.

Tragedy struck when her life was snuffed out in a plane crash while she was on a bond tour in her home state of Indiana during the early stages of World War II. Ended was a career that had given much to the industry and also to her legion of fans. For many students and fans of film, there is only one Carole Lombard.

And only one Cary Grant. There was an elegance and casual charm about England's Archie Leach who became the matinee idol Cary Grant. An upwardly mobile eyebrow, a faint air of cynicism, an athletic grace, an impeccable sense of timing and a sublime sense of the ridiculous—is it any wonder that, like Lombard, who shared many of these characteristics, he became a leading exponent of the screwball genre? Though his two Academy Award nominations came for showing the darker side of his persona (about which much has been written) and talent, many of his fans preferred to see him in the light and airy fluff at which he was a master. His gallery of screwball screen characters in the classics *Topper* (Hal Roach, 1937), *The Awful Truth* (Columbia, 1937), *Bringing Up Baby* (RKO, 1938), *His Girl Friday* (Columbia, 1940) and *My Favorite Wife* (RKO, 1940) have become immortal with time—different, each one of them, but all imbued with the charm and talent which helped to make their portrayer a household name.

The Awful Truth and *My Favorite Wife* rank among the best screwball comedies. Both are marital mix-ups involving divorce and reconciliation. Premises like these are made to order for the genre and for Cary's co-star, Irene Dunne. With an elegance and panache matched only by Carole Lombard and Claudette Colbert, whom we'll meet in a bit, the Louisville (Kentucky) Lady was able to do broad comedy in a deliciously lighthearted way which enchanted both critics and fans and still does, decades later, when her films are shown on television. Catch her at a meeting of a literary society in *Theodora Goes Wild* (Columbia, 1936), doing a hilarious song-and-dance routine in *The Awful Truth* or talking endearingly about Randolph Scott in *My Favorite Wife* and you have the screwball comedy in all its brilliant manifestations. All this plus a lovely singing voice.

Another alumnus of the "Cary Grant Co-star Club" is Katharine Hepburn. With the urbane actor, she made three comedies that are still a joy to behold when seen on the small screen at home. *Bringing Up Baby* is pure screwball while *Holiday* (Columbia, 1938) and *The Philadelphia Story* (MGM, 1940), considered by many to be romantic comedies, contain enough screwball elements to warrant a mention here. In all three productions, Hepburn is cast as an eccentric, offbeat heiress. Bringing into play an aristocratic bearing and an odd Bryn Mawr pattern of speech, she is able to inject into each portrayal her own personality and independent spirit. With these comedic performances under her belt, the actress went on to co-star in several films with Spencer Tracy at MGM, among them *Woman of the Year* (1942), *Without*

Love (1945), *Adam's Rib* (1949) and *Pat and Mike* (1952), romantic comedies all. Each one contains elements of the screwball comedy: eccentric characters and humorous incidents.

Like Hepburn, Loretta Young was a versatile actress, successfully starring in both comedic and dramatic fare. Her appearances in several screwball films including Fox's *Love Is News, Second Honeymoon* (both 1937) and *Wife, Husband and Friend* in 1937, and Columbia's *Bedtime Story* (1941) and *A Night to Remember* 1943), are all good reasons as to why the lovely Loretta should be counted among the screwball immortals. (Behind an ultra-feminine and glamorous facade was a razor-sharp mind and an excellent sense of timing. Ms. Young went into television with an anthology series aptly titled *The Loretta Young Show* and made a fortune opening a door and gliding into a smartly arranged close-up as the program's hostess and occasional star.)

Viewers of early television programming will no doubt remember another Young coming into their living rooms on a weekly basis. Robert Young starred in TV's long-running *Father Knows Best* and was also seen as the kindly title character on *Marcus Welby, M.D.* Before his tenure on the small screen, the popular actor enjoyed a long and profitable career as a handsome leading man and starred in several screwball comedies, both major and minor. Two of his early comedic performances are in *The Bride Comes Home* (1935) and *I Met Him in Paris* (1937), both Paramount releases. In the first film he loses Claudette Colbert to Fred MacMurray; in the second feature, the lovely Claudette winds up in the arms of Melvyn Douglas. In *Red Salute* (United Artists, 1935), however, he does "get" Barbara Stanwyck in the final fadeout (and, as his star ascended in the Hollywood firmament, he usually got the girl). He also gets the girl in two minor screwball comedies made at MGM: *Married Before Breakfast* in 1937 and *Married Bachelor* in 1941.

Armed with a gift for sardonic humor, a debonair manner and an ability to charm the ladies, the aforementioned Melvyn Douglas was another important exponent of the screwball comedy. He was an actor of great depth, as he proved in the dramas in which he appeared and, in the later phase of his career, when he won the 1963 Best Supporting Actor Oscar for his work in *Hud*. He was, nonetheless, able to convey a lighthearted and often zany quality to his performances, complementing the antics of his leading ladies, among them Jean Arthur, Joan Blondell, Joan Crawford, Claudette Colbert and Rosalind Russell. His screwball comedies at Columbia include *She Married Her Boss* (1935), *I Met Him in Paris* (1937), *There's Always a Woman* (1938), *Too Many Husbands* (1940) and *They All Kissed the Bride* (1942).

Fans familiar with the era will, however, remember more than any other film his teaming with Greta Garbo in *Ninotchka*. The vintage romantic comedy, released by MGM in 1939, contains many screwball elements. Its publicity ads proclaimed, in large letters, "Garbo Laughs." It is Melvyn Douglas, at his best, goading her on. (*He Stayed for Breakfast*, a 1940 screwball comedy from Columbia with Loretta Young, has the actor in a reversal of his *Ninotchka* role.) Douglas also co-starred with the enigmatic actress in her last film, MGM's 1941 production *Two-Faced Woman*.

In his later career, Joel McCrea enacted mature, stoic Western-type heroes, but as a young leading man he was seen in both comedies and dramas, partnering with some of Hollywood's most famous leading ladies. Among his screwball successes are *The Richest Girl in the World* (RKO, 1934), *Three Blind Mice* (Fox, 1938), *The Palm Beach Story* (Paramount, 1942) and the World War II comedy *The More the Merrier* (Columbia, 1943). He was not a great actor by any means, but he was none the less able to hold his own.

A frequent co-star of McCrea's is Miriam Hopkins. Although not well-known today, she was one of the top stars of her era. The talented blonde actress appears in such delightful screwball comedies as *Trouble in Paradise* (1932), *Design for Living* (1933), *Wise Girl* (1937) and *Woman Chases Man* (1937).

Like McCrea, Henry Fonda typified the earnest, stoic, straight-talking film hero of his era. Though his most famous roles came in such stark melodramas from Fox as *The Grapes of Wrath* (1940), *The Ox-Bow Incident* (1943) and *My Darling Clementine* (1946), he was more than agreeable in his screwball appearances. Three of his best co-starred Barbara Stanwyck: *The Mad Miss Manton* (RKO, 1938) and two 1941 films: *The Lady Eve* (Paramount) and *You Belong to Me* (Columbia). An earlier screwball comedy, *The Moon's Our Home*, paired the much-married Fonda with his first wife, Margaret Sullavan.

In the mold of Grant and Douglas is David Niven. The suave Englishman is hard to place in these pages due to the fact that he plays second lead in some screwball comedies, while starring in others. In *Three Blind Mice* and *Bluebeard's Eighth Wife*, his roles are secondary to those of Joel McCrea and Gary Cooper, respectively, while in two 1939 releases, *Bachelor Mother* and *Eternally Yours*, he is the star. He also appears in several later film ventures which contain elements of the screwball comedy plus a 1957 remake of *My Man Godfrey* co-starring June Allyson.

What set the Lombards, the Grants, the Dunnes and their ilk apart from the hundreds of hopefuls who took Horace Greeley's advice to "go west" during the film industry's early days? Luck and the studio system which gave them ample opportunity to show their wares, yes, but in the final analysis, it was more than that. A look, a gesture, a voice, a style, something unmistakably individual. It took longer for some than others, but all of them paid their dues.

The last statement is certainly true of the sublime Jean Arthur. Noted for one of the most distinctive and expressive voices of the era, childlike in quality, yet warm and reassuring, the petite blonde actress seems to have been put upon this Earth for the screwball comedy, as we shall see in the ensuing chapters.

In the profession since the mid–1920s, she spent a good ten years plying her trade before she hit her stride in such films as *Mr. Deeds Goes to Town* (Columbia, 1936), *Easy Living* (Paramount, 1937), *You Can't Take It with You* (Columbia, 1938), *Too Many Husbands* and *The More the Merrier* (for the last named, she received an Oscar nomination). Once she got these plums, she more than made up for the time spent doing lesser roles.

So did many of her peers. Another case in point is Ginger Rogers, who paid her dues on both stage and screen before her big break came along with Fred Astaire in RKO's 1933 *Flying Down to Rio.*

Though she is mainly remembered for that musical and the ones she subsequently made with Astaire, she was a definite cog in the screwball machine. With a sparkle in her eyes, a toss of her blonde mane and a voice which smacks of independence, she typifies the working girl in the genre, hoping for the best, but ready to take on the world: a nightclub entertainer in *Vivacious Lady* (RKO, 1938), a department store clerk in *Bachelor Mother* (RKO, 1979), a homeless girl looking for work in *Fifth Avenue Girl* (RKO, 1939), a telephone operator in *Tom Dick and Harry* (RKO, 1941) and a manicurist in *The Major and the Minor* (Paramount, 1942).

Another lady typifying the working girl in both comedy and drama is Rosalind Russell. Except for different leading men and a switch in title, the roles she plays are stamped out of the same mold: sharp, crackly dames until the films' final few minutes. Her screwball comedies include *Hired Wife* (Universal, 1940), *No Time for Comedy* (Warner Brothers, 1940), *His Girl Friday* (Columbia, 1940) and *Take a Letter, Darling* (Paramount, 1942). A crisp delivery and a great sense of timing make many of her films seem even better than they are.

Of the all-time greats discussed in this chapter, only Clark Gable, Claudette Colbert and James Stewart won Academy Awards for their screwball comedies: Gable and Colbert for *It Happened One Night,* (Columbia, 1934) and Stewart for *The Philadelphia Story* (MGM, 1940).

Apple-cheeked, with saucer eyes and a throaty laugh, Paris-born Claudette Colbert served her apprenticeship both on Broadway and on the sound stages of Hollywood. Her big break came in a dramatic film, *The Sign of the Cross,* a 1932 Paramount release; from then on, showing her versatility, she switched from comedy to drama and then back again to comedy with grace and ease. The screwball characters that she created in *I Met Him in Paris, Bluebeard's Eighth Wife, Midnight* (Paramount, 1939), *It's a Wonderful World* (MGM, 1939) and *The Palm Beach Story* remain among her best-known and most delightful, in a career which lasted for over 60 years.

Claudette's co-star in *Bluebeard's Eighth Wife* is Gary Cooper. Winning his two Academy Awards for his portrayals of baseball great Lou Gehrig in *The Pride of the Yankees* (RKO, 1942) and the stoic sheriff of *High Noon* (UA, 1952), he also appears in such classic screwball comedies as *Design for Living, Mr. Deeds Goes to Town* and *Ball of Fire* (Goldwyn, 1941). His "yup" and "nope" style of delivery are admirably suited to the comedies in which he appears.

A lesson in longevity is the career of Fred MacMurray. "Steady" and "dependable" are not the sort of characteristics you usually find in the screwball genre, but MacMurray was just that sort of actor. A shrewd businessman who saw the possibilities of television long before many of his peers, he is today perhaps best known for the long-running *My Three Sons* sitcom.

His screwballs gave him several of his most popular roles and the enviable task of playing opposite some of the top Hollywood actresses, among them Lombard, Russell and Colbert.

For Paramount, as leading man to those three lovely ladies, MacMurray appears in six great screwball comedies. With the divine Lombard, he stars in *Hands Across the Table, The Princess Comes Across* and *True Confession*; he partners with Russell in *Take a Letter, Darling* and with Colbert in the comedic delights *The Gilded Lily* (1935) and *No Time for Love* (1943). It was MacMurray's appearance, against type, in the starkly dramatic *Double Indemnity* (Paramount, 1944) which brought him the best notices of his career. Co-starred with Fred is Barbara Stanwyck, whose performance in that film remains one of the most incisive portrayals of greed ever recorded on the screen. Though much of her career lies in the realm of the dramatic, the talented Brooklyn-born actress found a niche for herself in the screwball comedy. *The Mad Miss Manton, Ball of Fire, The Lady Eve* and *You Belong to Me* are ample proof of this. Like Fred MacMurray, Stanwyck saw the possibilities of television and for some time starred in the series *The Big Valley*.

Few actors in the fickle world of entertainment had longer careers than James Stewart, last in our list of screwball superstars. In his eighties, he was writing poetry, doing television commercials and speaking out against the colorization of the classics. The beloved Stewart was once described by a director as "so unusually usual." His roles in *Vivacious Lady, You Can't Take It with You, It's a Wonderful World, No Time for Comedy* and his Academy Award–winning performance in *The Philadelphia Story* serve to make him an immortal in this (or any) genre.

The screwball comedy was so immensely popular during the 1930s that several others of the era's most famous motion picture personalities tried their hands at it, in sharp contrast to what the public had come to expect of them.

Some readers will be surprised to note that Bette Davis and James

Cagney, who achieved lasting fame in highly charged dramatic fare, were teamed in two Warner Brothers films that are considered screwball: *Jimmy the Gent* (1934) and *The Bride Came C.O.D.* (1941). Davis also stars in three others for Warner Brothers, *It's Love I'm After* (1937), *The Man Who Came to Dinner* (1941) and *June Bride* (1948). In 1938, Cagney appeared in a devastating satire on Hollywood scriptwriters titled *Boy Meets Girl* (also from Warners).

Margaret Sullavan, she of the unforgettably husky voice, also kicks up her heels in screwball comedies, starring in the previously mentioned *The Moon's Our Home* plus two others, both from Universal: *The Good Fairy* (1935) and *Appointment for Love* (1941).

Others not known for comedy also ventured into the genre. Among the stars and the screwball comedies in which they appear are Herbert Marshall in *If You Could Only Cook* (Columbia, 1935), *Breakfast for Two* and *The Good Fairy*, Fredric March in *Design for Living* and *Nothing Sacred*, Robert Montgomery in *Mr. and Mrs. Smith* and *June Bride*, Joan Crawford in *Love on the Run* (MGM, 1936) and *They All Kissed the Bride* and Olivia de Havilland in three for Warner Brothers: *Call It a Day* (1937), *Four's a Crowd* and *Hard to Get* (both 1938). Clark Gable did two more screwballs for MGM, *Love on the Run* and *Comrade X* (1940), the latter film with a *Ninotchka*-like premise. Even John Barrymore got into the act with the aforementioned *Twentieth Century*, plus *Midnight* and *True Confession*.

Anyone familiar with the screwball genre will note the omission of two of its most endearing practitioners, William Powell and Myrna Loy. Because of their teaming in the *Thin Man* series and other films in the genre, I have left the delightful duo for later and star them in a chapter of their own.

Chapter Three

Screwball Personnel:
They Also Serve

Sandwiched in between Rin Tin Tin and Lassie, each a top animal star of its era, is Asta, the lovable wire-haired fox terrier who appears in the *Thin Man* series.

We begin our discourse on Screwball Supporting Players with the clever canine who made the decade of the 1930s his own, "acting" in the memorable detective series as well as in three top screwball comedies: *The Awful Truth, Topper Takes a Trip* (Hal Roach–United Artists, 1939) and *Bringing Up Baby*. A "bone" of contention in some films and a partner in mayhem in others, the precocious pooch justly deserves to be considered as one who also serves, an integral part of the screwball comedy.

Let us continue with the "male animal" and take a look at the men below the title. Franklin Pangborn's name is probably unrecognizable to all but the true movie buff. One look at his face, however, and the comment invariably is, "Oh, I know him." Pangborn appears in more screwball comedies than many of his peers. His patented style of comedy—fussy, flustered and temperamental, while trying to preserve a modicum of dignity—makes for much hilarity in some of the finest productions in the genre: *My Man Godfrey, Easy Living, Bluebeard's Eighth Wife, Mr. Deeds Goes to Town, Vivacious Lady* and *The Palm Beach Story*, to name just a few.

Walter Connolly is a better-known screwball staple, playing more substantial roles than many of "those who also serve." His presence makes a delightful addition to the classics *Twentieth Century, It Happened One Night, Fifth Avenue Girl, Libeled Lady* (MGM, 1936) and *Nothing Sacred*. These are just a few of the in which he appeared during his rich and varied career.

The puckish Eric Blore parlayed playing a "gentleman's gentleman," along with several other character types, into a long and happy life in the movies. His droll brand of acting enhances the genre favorites *The Ex-Mrs.*

Bradford (RKO, 1936), *It's Love I'm After, Breakfast for Two, Joy of Living* (RKO, 1938), *The Good Fairy* and *The Lady Eve*.

The cherubic Charles Coburn began his film career after many years on the legitimate stage. Armed with a monocle and a mischievous glint, he is best remembered for his role in *The More the Merrier*, which won him a Best Supporting Actor Oscar at the age of 66. He is also to be seen in *Vivacious Lady, Bachelor Mother, The Lady Eve* and *The Devil and Miss Jones* (RKO, 1941). Movie fans are always in for a treat when the production features Mr. Coburn, who made his screen debut in 1938 at 61 years of age.

Luis Alberni and Mischa Auer were versatile comedic actors who usually played roles calling for dialects. If a volatile Latin type was needed, Alberni got the role. *The Gilded Lily, Easy Living, The Lady Eve* and *The Gay Deception* (Fox, 1935) are some of his forays into screwball comedy.

When the script called for zany Russians or other comedic East European types, Auer was the likely choice to play them. His offbeat appearances in *The Princess Comes Across, My Man Godfrey, The Rage of Paris* (Universal, 1938), *You Can't Take It with You* and *Public Deb Number One* (Fox, 1940) rank among the classic performances of the day.

The delightful Roland Young was another popular character actor of the era. Best known for his role as the whimsical Cosmo Topper in *Topper, Topper Takes a Trip* (1939) and *Topper Returns* (1941), he also lends his comedic talents, in supporting roles, to such films as *Call It a Day, The Young in Heart* (Selznick International–United Artists, 1938), *He Married His Wife* (Fox, 1940) and, in a stand-out performance, *The Philadelphia Story*.

Playing butler to Young's Topper is Alan Mowbray, another in the line of versatile performers who served the studio system so well. This talented character actor toiled in the vineyards of most of the major Hollywood studios in dramas and in comedy. From villains to butler to supercilious psychiatrists, he played them all. His best remembered efforts in the screwball genre include the first two *Topper* films, plus two from Roach–United Artists: *There Goes My Heart* in 1938 and *Merrily We Live* in 1940, and from the same company *That Uncertain Feeling*.

Donald Meek's name was well-suited to his persona. The unique Mr. Meek had a virtual monopoly on timid, befuddled little men. His career began in 1929 and lasted until his death in the mid–1940s. His droll demeanor and performances in such comedic delights as *The Gilded Lily, The Bride Comes Home, Love on the Run, Breakfast for Two, You Can't Take It with You*, plus two 1940 entries from MGM, *Come Live with Me* and *The Thin Man Goes Home*, encompass a compendium of the screwball.

Another lengthy show business career was enjoyed by William Demarest, whom aficionados of the television series *My Three Sons* will remember as Uncle Charley. His crusty yet sentimental acting style put him in good stead in such screwball gems as *Hands Across the Table, Love on the Run , Easy Living, The Lady Eve, Christmas in July* (Paramount, 1940), *The Devil and Miss Jones, The Palm Beach Story* and two wartime comedies released by Paramount, *The Miracle of Morgan's Creek* and *Hail the Conquering Hero* (both 1944).

A well-known name below the title is that of Edward Everett Horton. In an acting career which began in 1918 and lasted through the mid–1960s, he is the eternal fussbudget, always trying to maintain his cool in the face of impending disaster. His screwball appearances include *The Front Page* (United Artists, 1931), *Design for Living, Bluebeard's Eighth Wife* and *Holiday*. It is interesting to note that in 1938, the actor recreated the role he had played in the 1930 version of *Holiday*.

The specialty of Charles Ruggles, an actor of much charm, was his ability to play genial blunderers for whom movie fans felt great affection. This skill he parlayed into a long and distinguished career. Among his better known comedic appearances are *No Time for Comedy, Bringing Up Baby, Public Deb Number One, The Doughgirls* (Warner Brothers, 1944 and *Model Wife* (Universal, 1941).

Another "Oh, I know him" actor, Raymond Walburn, scored in a variety of screwball films. The harrumphing performer makes memorable contributions to such golden oldies as *She Married Her Boss, Mr. Deeds Goes to Town, Eternally Yours, Christmas in July, Third Finger, Left Hand* (MGM, 1940) and *Hail the Conquering Hero*.

Edgar Buchanan will be remembered by fans of TV's *Petticoat Junction* for his role as Uncle Joe. Master of the "slow burn" school of humor, he also had a long and successful career in the movies. His screwball credits include *Too Many Husbands, Bride by Mistake* (RKO, 1944) and *You Belong to Me*.

A small fussy man in so many memorable films was Ernest Truex. In a career spanning almost half a century, he played second banana to the likes of Dick Powell, Ginger Rogers, Cary Grant and Claudette Colbert, among others. His screwball appearances help to brighten up *It's a Wonderful World, Bachelor Mother, His Girl Friday, Christmas in July, Twin Beds* (United Artists, (1942) and *True to Life* (Paramount, 1943).

Another well-known "name below the title" belongs to Eugene Pallette. A sandpaper voice and a pear-shaped figure made the actor a natural for comedy and he appears in several screwball productions as a gruff, rotund, bass-voiced character. Father, detective, business executive—he plays all of these and is always fun to watch. *My Man Godfrey, Topper, There Goes My Heart, The Lady Eve, He Stayed for Breakfast, Appointment for Love* and *The Bride Came C.O.D.* owe much of their success to this portly perennial.

There is much more typecasting to be found on the distaff side of screwball supporting players and several talented actresses did some of their finest and best known work in the genre. The fluttery female, carefully coiffed and matronly, was personified by Billie Burke and Spring Byington.

Three *Topper* films, *Merrily We Live, The Young in Heart, Eternally Yours,* and *They All Kissed the Bride* are only some of Billie Burke's excursions into screwball. The widow of famed showman Florenz Ziegfeld, the actress made her first screen appearance in 1918 and her last in 1960. Though her long career was highlighted by many fine performances, both comedic and dramatic, she will forever linger in our memories as Glinda the Good Witch in MGM's all-time classic *The Wizard of Oz* (1939).

Spring Byington's first film, RKO's *Little Women* (1933), established her motherly image for most of her successful tenure in motion pictures. Her contributions to screwball comedy include warm and appealing performances in *It's Love I'm After, You Can't Take It with You* and *The Devil and Miss Jones.* In 1936, she was cast against type in *Theodora Goes Wild* as the town gossip and in *Rings on Her Fingers* (Fox, 1942) as a motherly con artist. The younger than Spring-time actress spent a few years during the 1950s on television's *December Bride.* In the show, she portrayed a mother living with her daughter and son-in-law, always getting into scrapes. It was a senior citizen version of *I Love Lucy.*

Like Billie Burke, Alice Brady was a distinguished stage star before coming to Hollywood. Though she won an Oscar as Best Supporting Actress for the 1937 Fox drama *In Old Chicago,* she is mainly identified with giddy, lame-brained matron roles such as those she plays in *My Man Godfrey* (she is the perfect foil for Eugene Pallette as his ditsy wife), *Call It a Day* and *Joy of Living.*

In the latter part of her career, Mary Boland played a series of domineering, dimwitted matrons. Film buffs will remember her as the scheming but not too bright mother in *Pride and Prejudice* (MGM, 1940) and as the much married countess ("L'amor, l'amor—where love leads I always follow") in the all-star MGM production *The Women* (1939). *Three Cornered Moon* (Paramount, 1933), *There Goes the Groom* (RKO, 1937) and *He Married His Wife* are among her other screwball credits.

Other screwball ladies are not the ditsy type, but are masters of the putdown. The many genre back-talkers are memorably brought to the screen by some very talented performers, among them Helen Broderick, Margaret Hamilton, Hattie McDaniel, Ruth Donnelly and the one and only Eve Arden. Each lady was skilled in the delivery of the tart and sharply honed dialogue so much a part of the 1930s.

Stately Helen Broderick, mother of Academy Award–winning actor Broderick Crawford, portrayed many an acerbic and sharp-witted middle-aged lady. Her wry and cynical screen persona graces such screwball comedies as *Love on a Bet, The Bride Walks Out, The Smartest Girl in Town* (all 1936) and *She's Got Everything* (1937), all four made at RKO. In these last two films, Broderick appears with Ann Sothern. In the first, she is Sothern's older sister; in the second, she is Ann's aunt—so much for consistency in the screwball movies. Broderick's other credits in the genre include *The Rage of Paris, Honeymoon in Bali* (Paramount, 1939) and *Father Takes a Wife* (RKO, 1941).

Both *Nothing Sacred* and *The Moon's Our Home* feature former schoolteacher Margaret Hamilton as salty New England types. Though she is most famous for her role as the Wicked Witch of the West in *The Wizard of Oz*, she enjoyed a long and very satisfying career as a character actress, showing her versatility in both comedy and drama. Among her other screen credits are two more screwballs, *Four's a Crowd* and *Twin Beds*.

Hattie McDaniel, the memorable Mammy of *Gone with the Wind* and the first black actress to win an Academy Award, had been steadily employed since 1932. She made screwball appearances in *True Confession, The Mad Miss Manton, Affectionately Yours, The Bride Walks Out* and in a small bit in *Nothing Sacred*. Though most of her movie roles are as maids, the lovable Hattie plays them in a remarkable (for the era), free-spirited, feisty and independent manner, utterly devoid of any aspect of subservience.

An actress skilled in the delivery of a zinger in an off-handed manner is Ruth Donnelly. She was a no-nonsense type, in her younger days specializing in sassy secretaries and sharp-tongued friends of the heroine and in the later stages of her career as a "quick with a quip" mother. Donnelly's many screwball films include *Red Salute, Hands Across the Table, Mr. Deeds Goes to Town, The Amazing Mr. Williams* (Columbia, 1939), *Model Wife* and *You Belong to Me*.

The most famous practitioner of sarcasm, however, has to be Eve Arden. The statuesque blonde stage veteran played several screwball characters before attaining stardom in both radio and on television as the lovesick *Our Miss Brooks* of Madison High. Among her genre films are *Eternally Yours, Comrade X, That Uncertain Feeling, Bedtime Story* and *The Doughgirls*, in which she steals the show as a daffy Russian sniper who comes to wartime Washington on a government mission.

A couple of other statuesque actresses, Mary Astor and Gail Patrick, personify the glamorous "Other Woman of Screwball." Astor began her career during the early 1920s; by the mid to late 1930s, Astor, once leading lady to John Barrymore, was playing more character roles than leads and taking part in such comedic hits as the first screen version of *Holiday, There's Always a Woman, Midnight, Turnabout* (Hal Roach–United Artists, 1940) and *The Palm Beach Story*.

Her "comrade in arms," lanky brunette Gail Patrick, is known to fans of the *Perry Mason* television series as the show's executive producer. She is also known to screwball comedy buffs as the "other woman" in such frolics as *My Favorite Wife, Love Crazy* (MGM, 1941) and *The Doctor Takes a Wife* (Columbia, 1940) and the obnoxious sister in *My Man Godfrey*. The prototype for such roles, she came to Hollywood as a contestant in one of the thousands of beauty pageants held throughout the nation during the early 1930s. She lost the contest but, unlike many young hopefuls, stayed to carve out a long and successful career.

Astor and Patrick may have had much success as the "other woman" in films, but their male counterpart, Ralph Bellamy, typecast in the screwball comedy as the man who never winds up with the girl, beats both ladies. In fact, he is the most successful "other man" in the genre's history, losing Carole Lombard in *Hands Across the Table*, Irene Dunne in *The Awful Truth*, Rosalind Russell in *His Girl Friday*, Merle Oberon in *Affectionately Yours* and, in a minor screwball comedy, *Public Deb Number One*, Brenda Joyce. This may have been a blow to his movie ego, but professionally, these roles gave him the opportunity to appear in some of the finest films ever made. His biggest success, however, was on the Broadway stage portraying Franklin Delano Roosevelt in the acclaimed *Sunrise at Campobello*. In 1960, he recreated the role in the film version.

Most actors credit the success of their performances to their directors. The early screwball comedies were made under the guidance of some of the most talented men in the industry, several of whom are the subjects of our next focus. Besides directing, a few even produced their films. We'll also zero in on a group of writers, brilliant men all, who put pen to paper and came up with these gems. Their words are satirical, sophisticated, witty, warm, totally appealing and all wrapped in one package.

Chapter Four

Screwball Personnel: Behind the Scenes

Gable and Colbert may have scintillated on screen in *It Happened One Night*, but the blockbuster film was the baby of director Frank Capra and his favorite writer, Robert Riskin.

Under the guidance of producer-director Howard Hawks and with a great script by Ben Hecht and Charles MacArthur, *Twentieth Century* scored big at the box office and made Carole Lombard a star.

Capra and Riskin; Hawks, Hecht and MacArthur—these and other producers, directors and writers gave of their talents to create the screwball comedy genre. This chapter concentrates on the partnership between a producer, a director and a writer. As previously stated, many of the films mentioned herein will be discussed at greater length in Part II of this book.

In any discussion of the screwball comedy, a name invariably mentioned is that of Frank Capra, a premier director of the 1930s. His films glorify America and its rich heritage, while gently mocking its pomposity. Sicilian by birth, he was six years old when he arrived on these shores in 1903 and promptly began a love affair with his adopted land, one which never lessened with the passage of time. He was an assistant and also gag writer for both Hal Roach and Mack Sennett; his first feature film as a director came in 1926. In 1928, he joined Columbia Pictures and remained at that studio until 1939.

East met West when Robert Riskin, an alumnus of New York's Columbia University, and Frank Capra, who had graduated from the California Institute of Technology, discovered that they shared the same values and ideas about filmmaking. Thus began a friendship and a collaboration resulting in some of the finest films ever made, four of which are part of the screwball legend: *Lady for a Day* (Columbia, 1933), *Mr. Deeds Goes to Town* and the team's two Oscar winners, the aforementioned *It Happened One Night* and *You Can't Take It with You.*

Howard Hawks, an alumnus of Cornell University, spent summers in the prop department at Famous Players–Lasky (which later became Paramount Pictures) and by 1924 was in the movie business to stay, at first making several two-reel comedies. In 1934, he directed *Twentieth Century*, with a screenplay by Ben Hecht and Charles MacArthur based on the Broadway hit. The two writers had come into prominence via their stage hit *The Front Page*. Both Hecht and MacArthur (the latter married to the well-known actress Helen Hayes) had been Chicago journalists and their scathing commentaries on the Fourth Estate had brought them fame and fortune. Interestingly enough, the duo was not, however, hired to write the screenplay for *The Front Page*. While MacArthur concentrated mainly on drama, Hecht went on to write such screwball hits as *Nothing Sacred, It's a Wonderful World* and *Design for Living*.

Hawks' other ventures into screwball comedy are *Bringing Up Baby, Ball of Fire* and two post-war Fox releases, *I Was a Male War Bride* (1949) and *Monkey Business* (1952).

Both Capra and Hawks remade one of their biggest hits, but neither film reached the heights of the original. Capra's *Lady for a Day* became *Pocketful of Miracles* (United Artists, 1961) with a woefully miscast Bette Davis in the May Robson role while Hawks's *Ball of Fire* re-emerged as *A Song Is Born* (Goldwyn, 1948), a musical, with Danny Kaye in the role played by Gary Cooper.

In contrast to Capra and Hawks, German-born Ernst Lubitsch brought charm and sophistication to the American screen. Emigrating to the United States in 1923, he directed a film with Mary Pickford. For a time in the 1930s, he was chief of production at Paramount and among the films made during his tenure at that studio are *Trouble in Paradise, Design for Living,* and *Bluebeard's Eighth Wife*. After the Paramount stint, he moved over to MGM and the incandescent *Ninotchka*. It was Lubitsch who directed Carole Lombard in her last film *To Be or Not to Be* (United Artists, 1942).

After a varied career in Germany as a dancer, a journalist and a scriptwriter, Austrian-born Billy Wilder migrated first to Mexico and then to Hollywood. He began his long partnership with New York–born Charles Brackett in 1938. Brackett, a New Yorker, had an interesting background: While working as an attorney, he wrote novels and also articles for famous magazines. Going to Hollywood on a six-week Paramount contract in 1932, he remained with the studio until 1950. His meeting with Wilder gave the movie capital one of its best behind-the-screen duos. One of their most interesting collaborations is a comedy-drama titled *Hold Back the Dawn* (Paramount, 1941). The idea for the film came from Wilder's fertile mind; it is supposedly a fictional and romanticized version of the time he spent in Mexico awaiting his entrance into the United States.

For Ernst Lubitsch, Wilder and Brackett wrote the screenplays for *Blue-beard's Eighth Wife* and Greta Garbo's *Ninotchka*. At work for Howard Hawks, they penned the original story and screenplay of *Ball of Fire* and for Mitchell Leisen, the script for *Midnight*.

The Major and the Minor, co-authored by the talented duo, marked Billy's debut as a film director. He and Brackett went on to write, produce and direct several films together. Wilder was once quoted as saying that the reason he became a director was simple: "I wanted to protect my words."

Trained as an architect, Mitchell Leisen entered the film industry during the silent era and served as an art director for Cecil B. DeMille (one of the films he worked on is the 1923 silent version of *The Ten Commandments*). In the 1930s, he began to direct his own films. His screwball hits include *Hands Across the Table*, written by Norman Krasna, *Easy Living*, a story from the pen of Preston Sturges, whom we will meet shortly, *Take a Letter, Darling* and *No Time for Love*, both having an original story and screenplay by Claude Binyon, and *Practically Yours* (Paramount, 1944), with Krasna providing story and screenplay.

The prolific Krasna, New York City–born and bred, attended law school, then served as drama editor on two East Coast newspapers, before making the trek westward. After a stint in the publicity department at Warner Brothers, he focused on his writing. Besides those mentioned above, his contributions to the screwball genre include *The Richest Girl in the World, Mr. and Mrs. Smith* and *The Devil and Miss Jones*.

Claude Binyon also led a rich and varied professional life in Hollywood. Producer and director were two of the hats he wore, but he is best known for his credits as a writer. For several films, he teamed with director Wesley Ruggles. A native Californian, Ruggles, like his brother Charles, was an actor in silent films, learning much from his boss Mack Sennett. In 1917, he tried his hand at directing, but his budding career was interrupted by World War I (he served as a Signal Corps cameraman). After the cessation of hostilities, he returned to filmmaking. Switching from silents to talkies with ease, he worked for Universal during the 1920s, Paramount in the 1930s, and MGM and Columbia in the 1940s.

When screwball films became popular, Binyon became his head writer. The Ruggles-Binyon team produced such classics as *The Gilded Lily, The Bride Comes Home, True Confession, I Met Him in Paris, You Belong to Me* and *Too Many Husbands*.

Like many of his peers, Leo McCarey's career began in the early days of the film industry. After earning a law degree at the University of Southern California, he worked as an assistant director for Hal Roach. It was McCarey who first envisioned Stan Laurel and Oliver Hardy as a comedy team, subsequently directing several of their most famous films.

During his long tenure in Hollywood, he was a producer, writer and director, and received Oscars for *The Awful Truth* (Best Director) and for Paramount's 1944 *Going My Way* (one as Best Director, the other for Best Original Story). Besides *The Awful Truth*, his screwball hits include *My Favorite Wife* (producer and co-writer), *Ruggles of Red Gap* (Paramount, 1935) and *Once Upon a Honeymoon* (RKO, 1942). On the last film, a curious mix of drama and screwball comedy, with some elements of screwball thrown in, McCarey served as co-writer and director.

Like McCarey and several others in this chapter, George Cukor was probably expected to become a lawyer as had his father before him. Instead, the native New Yorker took an active interest in the theater, working as a stage manager on Broadway and as a director in summer stock. In the latter capacity, he came into contact with future stars Bette Davis, Miriam Hopkins and Robert Montgomery.

After a stint as a dialogue director at both Paramount and Universal, Cukor became a full-fledged director, noted for his ability to tame temperamental female stars. Two of his contributions to the screwball genre starred Katharine Hepburn and were based upon hit plays by Philip Barry: the second version of *Holiday* and the unforgettable *The Philadelphia Story*. Both screenplays were written by longtime Hepburn friend, Donald Ogden Stewart.

Cukor also directed *Two-Faced Woman*, the swan song for Greta Garbo. Though certainly not on a par with *Ninotchka*, the film is not quite the "turkey" of legend.

A good friend to both Hepburn and Cukor, Garson Kanin was a triple threat personality. A producer-director (and, in collaboration with his actress wife Ruth Gordon, a screenwriter), Kanin began his show business career as assistant to theatrical producer-director George Abbott and by 1938, he was directing on his own in Hollywood. Among his screwball ventures are *The Next Time I Marry* (RKO, 1938), a minor effort starring the queen of the RKO "B" films, Lucille Ball, and three major hits: *Bachelor Mother, My Favorite Wife* and *Tom, Dick and Harry*.

With Cukor directing, Kanin and his wife co-authored two highly entertaining comedies of the post-war era for Hepburn and Spencer Tracy, MGM's *Adam's Rib* (1949) and *Pat and Mike* (1952). Each contains elements of screwball. In 1971, Kanin wrote a memoir about his friends. It is a look into the relationship, both public and private, between the two great stars.

Michigan-born Norman Z. McLeod's formative years gave no indication as to his future choice of career. The son of a clergyman, he went to the University of Washington and served in the Royal Canadian Air Force during World War I. He then began a stint as a gag writer and soon gravitated into directing films. Between 1930 and 1946, he worked for Paramount,

MGM and United Artists. His screwball ventures include *Merrily We Live, There Goes My Heart,* and *Topper Takes a Trip.*

Some directors take an interminable amount of time in making a film, demanding take after take after take to achieve the desired results. Not so W.S. Van Dyke, a.k.a. "One Take Woody." A native of San Diego, Van Dyke performed in stock and in vaudeville. By 1915, he was a member of the film community, working as an extra in silent films. His apprenticeship in the burgeoning industry continued with a stint as an assistant to D.W. Griffith on the latter's monumental 1916 production *Intolerance.* As a full-fledged director, he freelanced at Fox and MGM; after 1929, he worked solely for the latter company.

Upon completion of the crime yarn *Manhattan Melodrama* (1934) which starred Clark Gable, William Powell and Myrna Loy, he put the last two named to work in a fast-paced comedy-mystery, *The Thin Man,* based upon characters created by popular writer Dashiell Hammett. The film was a runaway hit, prompting MGM to make a slew of sequels, five in all. Van Dyke directed all but the last two, which were filmed after his untimely death in 1943 at the age of 58. Besides the *Thin Man* series, he also directed the Powell-Loy duo in the delightful *I Love You Again* (MGM, 1940). His other screwball comedies are the zany *It's a Wonderful World* and *Love on the Run.*

Gregory La Cava did not make many screwball comedies during his long career, but he deserves mention here if only for the brilliant *My Man Godfrey* (he not only directed, he co-wrote the screenplay). An art student (The Chicago Institute of Art and New York's Art Students League), then magazine cartoonist, La Cava began his Hollywood career by drawing cartoon characters for Walter Lantz.

By the mid–1920s, he had turned to directing. His ventures into the screwball genre include Columbia's *She Married Her Boss,* filmed just before *Godfrey,* and RKO's *Fifth Avenue Girl,* released three years after his masterpiece.

William A. Seiter began directing silent shorts in 1918 and graduated to full-length features during the 1920s. His forays into screwball include *The Richest Girl in the World, If You Could Only Cook, The Moon's Our Home, Three Blind Mice* and *Hired Wife.*

A native of Philadelphia, William Keighley got his start by acting and directing on the Broadway stage. He came to Hollywood in the early 1920s and became a leading film director. In 1938, he married actress Genevieve Tobin, whom he directed in *No Time for Comedy,* Other screwballs under his belt include *The Bride Came C.O.D.* and *George Washington Slept Here* (Warner Brothers, 1942). Radio buffs will also remember Keighley replacing Cecil B. DeMille as host of *The Lux Radio Theater,* a weekly program which recreated films for the listening audience, often using their original stars.

Two writers who worked for Keighley share the distinction of being, thus far, the only set of twins in the fraternity of Hollywood scribes. Philip and Julius Epstein are better known, however, as the co-scriptwriters of the legendary *Casablanca* (Warner Brothers, 1942), for which they received an Oscar. The brothers' association with Keighley brought forth such screwball hits as the aforementioned *No Time for Comedy* and *The Bride Came C.O.D.*, also *The Man Who Came to Dinner* (the latter adapted from the Broadway hit by George S. Kaufman and Moss Hart). On his own, Philip wrote the original screenplay for the delightful screwball comedy mystery *The Mad Miss Manton*.

Last, but not in any way least, we turn our attention to Preston Sturges, the inventive genius behind several of Hollywood's finest comedies. In true screwball style, he had a sharp biting wit, his films satirizing many of our sacred cows and established institutions.

Chicago-born Sturges received his education in Europe and, while still in his teens, worked in his mother's cosmetics business. After serving in the Air Corps towards the end of World War I, he became a Broadway stage manager and was soon writing plays, among them *Strictly Dishonorable*, which was later filmed twice, once in the early 1930s and again in the 1950s. During the latter half of the 1930s, Sturges became a familiar part of the Hollywood scene, writing *The Good Fairy* and *Easy Living*.

Sturges' first opportunity as a director came at Paramount in 1940 with *The Great McGinty*, an assault upon American politics, for which he won an Academy Award for Best Original Screenplay. This was his first directing job and all of Hollywood was agog. In quick succession, he followed *McGinty* with the comedic gems *Christmas in July*, *The Lady Eve*, *Sullivan's Travels* (1941), *The Palm Beach Story*, *The Miracle of Morgan's Creek*, *Hail the Conquering Hero* (all Paramount) and *Unfaithfully Yours*, a 1948 Fox release.

By the early 1950s, Sturges had moved to France. The films made during this period of his life lacked the combination of sophisticated comedy and pratfall farce which had been his trademark. Gone since 1959, he is remembered with fondness by buffs and students of film.

Capra and Sturges—the beginning and end of this chapter. In between are the many producers, directors and writers who gave of their talent and, in some cases, their genius to the art of the screwball comedy.

It is time now to take a look at the finished products of these collaborations.

Chapter Five

Screwball Guys and Gals: Heirs and Heiresses

Young, attractive, spoiled, very rich, and prone to get into all sorts of zany situations—these are the screwball heirs and heiresses of the 1930s and early 1940s.

These high-toned ladies and gentlemen populate some of the most hilarious motion pictures ever made. Down deep, all of them crave happiness with the right mate. Armed with their looks and their wealth, they go about attaining their goals in various ways, from the ridiculous to the sublime. They range from Barbara Stanwyck's tough-minded Texan of *Breakfast for Two* and radical's girlfriend of *Red Salute* to the "decadent" count Melvyn Douglas portrays in *Ninotchka* to Tyrone Power posing as a member of royalty in *Cafe Metropole* to Robert Young's wealthy playboy in *The Bride Comes Home* and Katharine Hepburn's dizzy heiress of *Bringing Up Baby*. In between are the many others whose "lifestyles of the rich and famous" go from being mistaken as a maid, to posing as a secretary to find true love, to being the other man in a triangle. In most cases, it's the girl who has all the money.

The fact that there are problems inherent in being rich is made abundantly clear in the screwball comedies of the era. Depression audiences delighted in the shenanigans which gave them respite from their own woes. The icing on the cake was that they could watch some of the biggest stars (and stars-to-be) in the industry engaging in these antics.

To wit: Lucille Ball is the zany heiress of *The Next Time I Marry* (RKO, 1938) and is in a real bind: She must marry a working stiff in order to inherit $20 million. She devises a plan where she'll marry as stipulated. When the money is in her hot little hands, she will fly to Reno, get a divorce and then tie the knot with a poor but titled nobleman, played by American-born actor Lee Bowman.

She marries a good-looking government projects worker, a real "pick and shovel" man, played by James Ellison. (There is an element of realism in this as, by that time, President Roosevelt had initiated several such projects in order to create jobs.) His character is a man of principles and their initial battles are continued on a cross-country dash during which she realizes that she loves him. Exit the nobleman, who really isn't so noble after all.

The Next Time I Marry was more than a decade away from the lovable redhead's sensational television debut; for some of those years, she was a contract player at RKO, then at MGM, starring in both comedies and dramas.

Several screwball comedies in the runaway rich girl vein had their genesis in *It Happened One Night*. None achieved the everlasting fame of this classic, but a few are quite amusing. We will take a look at some others as we go further into this chapter.

A tougher image of the screwball heiress is to be found in Barbara Stanwyck's portrayal of Valentine Ransom in *Breakfast for Two* (RKO, 1937). She is a sharp, no-nonsense gal who meets a profligate playboy named Jonathan Blair (Herbert Marshall). His once prosperous business, a family-owned steamship line, is suffering and he is perpetually hung over from the revelries of a constant round of nightclubs, but he doesn't care. He thinks he's happy and he's even engaged to a gold-digging actress named Carol, played by Glenda Farrell.

Enter Valentine, the Texas Tornado. For some unfathomable reason, she has fallen for Jonathan and decides to "rehabilitate" him: "Men are like horses. Sometimes they need a whip to put some sense into them."

In this screwball, the man is the weak one; the woman is stronger and, in this case, brainier. Valentine secretly buys up all the stock in Jonathan's company, thinking that this will make him fight for what is his. He, however, does nothing. She takes over his household and only then does the tension begin to mount. Valentine picks up a pair of boxing gloves "conveniently" lying around and the struggle is on. He is now fighting to recoup his business *and* recover his life.

If Jonathan thinks that Valentine will soon be out of his hair, he is wrong. The resourceful gal has one more trick up her sleeve. Just as he is about to marry the brainless Carol, his butler (Eric Blore, in one of his patented roles) finds a marriage license in his employer's pocket. "That's bigotry," yells Carol, and she exits.

Of course, there is no real license; Valentine has planted a phony one in the pocket. At the film's "happy" ending, the two marry. As the judge, played by Donald Meek, pronounces them man and wife, he throws his hands above his head—and a boxing glove is on each.

An interesting star pairing. The dialogue between Stanwyck and Marshall and the scenes with Blore and Farrell make for a fun film.

In *Red Salute* (United Artists), Barbara is Drue Van Allen, the wealthy and badly spoiled daughter of an army general. She imagines herself in love with a radical student (Hardie Albright), and her dad (Henry Kolker) is afraid for her. He arranges to have her shipped (read "kidnapped") to Mexico in hopes that she will give up her extremist ways and equally extremist boyfriend.

South of the border, Drue meets up with a soldier named Jeff (Robert Young). He goes A.W.O.L. to help her get back to the States. Along the way, they argue about politics, but also fall in love. He lets her know that he is on to her, that she is not the radical she thinks she is. He then shows his political views by breaking up a rally of Liberal League of International Students, which has been organized by Drue's ex-boyfriend.

When the film was released in 1935, critics called it "a bad imitation" of *It Happened One Night*. At its New York City premiere, members of the leftist National Student's League picketed the theater, urging patrons not to see it. The majority of moviegoers seeing the film were not interested in any message; they were paying their money to see Stanwyck and Young in action.

On a similar theme, Brenda Joyce and George Murphy are the adversaries in *Public Deb Number One* (Fox, 1940). The film tells the tale of Penny Cooper (Joyce), the heiress of the Cooper Soup fortune. At the beginning of the film, the spoiled young lady is seen taking part in a rally taking place in New York City's Union Square. She and her leftist pals are picked up and hauled into court, but she is released.

Soon after her "arrest," Penny and her sometimes suitor (Ralph Bellamy) dine at The Red Samovar. She and a waiter, Alan Blake (played by top-billed future U.S. Senator Murphy), argue about Communism and also about her "friends"—he calls them "a bunch of people who want something for nothing." The two continue the argument until Alan suddenly decides to spank the deb and he does just that, to her utter humiliation. He is now the darling of the press.

Enter our ditsy heroine's uncle (Charles Ruggles), Mr. "Cooper Soups" himself. He offers Alan an executive position and encourages the enterprising young man's courtship of his niece. She realizes that in spite of, or perhaps *because* of what has occurred, that she really loves him. Penny is now a *former* Red Sympathizer; she has undergone a 180-degree change. Another victory for capitalism. An interesting premise, a lively film.

Along for laughs are Mischa Auer, Maxie Rosenbloom, Franklin Pangborn and America's foremost party giver of the 1930s and 1940s, Elsa Maxwell.

But wait, there are more triumphs ahead for the capitalistic way of life. After a spate of somber roles, Greta Garbo felt she needed a change of pace.

Ninotchka (1939): **Greta Garbo and her troika (Felix Bressart, Sig Ruman and Alexander Granach) are up to something.**

She wanted to star in a comedy and work with her fellow European, Ernst Lubitsch. The feeling was mutual on the part of the famed director, and the result was MGM's delightful *Ninotchka.*

The brainchild of Billy Wilder, Charles Brackett and Walter Reisch, the film concerns three Soviet commissars who are sent to Paris to recover jewelry taken out of the country by members of the White Russian nobility, led by Grand Duchess Swana (Ina Claire). Iranoff, Buljanoff and Kopolski, hilariously played by screwball veterans Sig Ruman, Felix Bressart and Alexander Granach, respectively, are seduced by the magic of this lovely city and are loathe to return to Mother Russia.

Enter special envoy Lena Yakushova (Garbo), whose assignment is to check up on the bumbling threesome. Through them, she meets Count Leon Dalgout (Melvyn Douglas), an elegant, debonair heir to a fortune. At first the man about town is amused by her and then finds himself falling in love with her. She is caustic, stoic and self-controlled. He talks about love, she talks about sewers and engineering. But gradually, she falls under his spell. He calls her "Ninotchka"—she smiles—she laughs—she is happy.

When she and her friends are summoned home, they go. Through a ruse, engineered by Leon, they are all reunited in Constantinople, Ninotchka slipping into the arms of her lover, the troika to open a restaurant, sponsored by Dalgout, featuring the specialties of the Russia they once knew and loved. In the supporting cast are George Tobias and 1930s bogeyman Bela Lugosi. Garbo, the film and its trio of writers were all nominated for Oscars, but as 1939 was the year of *Gone with the Wind,* none of them were winners.

A musical remake of *Ninotchka, Silk Stockings,* was released by MGM in 1957. It stars Fred Astaire and Cyd Charisse. Although Fred and Cyd are spectacular in the musical numbers, there is no comparison to Douglas and Garbo.

In a change of pace, Douglas is seen as a Communist agitator in *He Stayed for Breakfast* (Columbia, 1940). The setting is again Paris, where Douglas has shot a banker and unknowingly takes refuge in the apartment belonging to the latter's estranged wife (Loretta Young). From the lovely Loretta, the erstwhile Communist learns about life, love and luxury. Though the two stars struggle bravely, and there is a scene-stealing performance by Una O'Connor as Young's dizzy maid, the film is a minor one and has largely been forgotten by all but the most serious movie buffs. Others in the cast include Eugene Pallette, Alan Marshall and Leonid Kinskey.

Loretta is teamed with Tyrone Power in *Cafe Metropole* (Fox, 1937). Power, unlike the "hero" of *He Stayed for Breakfast,* is no Communist. He plays an American in debt to a nightclub owner. He is ordered by the owner to pose as a Russian nobleman and pursue heiress Young; the object matrimony and money. The plan backfires when the two fall in love. A nice solution to the problem, if there ever was one. The movie was a money-maker for Fox.

Posing as someone else is part of Miriam Hopkins' movie world as can be seen by two of the films she made in the 1930s. In *The Richest Girl in the World* (RKO, 1934) she plays the title role. Dorothy Hunter (Hopkins) is an unconventional heiress who thinks that every man who looks in her eyes sees dollar signs. This poor little rich girl poses as her own secretary in order to avoid publicity and possibly find a man who will love her for herself. This leads to several humorous complications.

Anthony Travis (Joel McCrea) makes no secret of the fact that he would like to be the richest guy in the world. He makes a play for Sylvia (Fay Wray, famous for her blood-curdling *King Kong* scream), the phony Dorothy, but is attracted to the real one. The latter pushes him away, but soon realizes that she's fallen for him—and now she is sorry that she started the whole thing. By film's end, when Travis tells the phony Dorothy that he loves her secretary, the masquerade is revealed. The guy is thrilled. And why not? He's hit the daily double. He has the girl he loves and all that lovely money. The film's original story and screenplay were written by young screenwriter Norman Krasna.

RKO remade *The Richest Girl in the World* in 1944 as *Bride by Mistake* with Marsha Hunt, Alan Marshal and, in the Hopkins role, Laraine Day. As in most cases, the remake is a "mistake" and does not have the verve of the original.

Hopkins portrays another heiress in *Wise Girl* (RKO, 1937). This time, the plot concerns her attempts to take the children of her dead sister away from their paternal uncle (played by Ray Milland), a Greenwich Village artist whom she considers unfit to raise the children. She has tried to get them by any means possible, but the artist is adamant that she cannot have the kids.

The two adults have never met so Hopkins devises a scheme: She passes herself off as a working girl, disowned by her family years before, and infiltrates the zany artists colony. When the two adversaries meet, there is a mutual dislike as the battle of the sexes begins. But in true screwball style, all is forgiven: Aunt and Uncle will marry and raise the children in tandem.

A Greenwich Village artist is also one of the central characters in *Live, Love and Learn* (MGM, 1937). An heiress (Rosalind Russell) leaves her cushy life to marry a struggling artist (Robert Montgomery). Through her connections, he becomes successful, but his newfound fame goes to his head. Wife leaves husband, his swelled head comes back to normal and the two get a second chance. They've lived, they've loved and he's learned. Heading a veritable "Who's Who" lineup of supporting players are Robert Benchley, Mickey Rooney and Billy Gilbert.

Greenwich Village could be a good place for a lady architect to attract a wealthy man to invest in her dreams. Joel McCrea is again leading man to Miriam Hopkins in *Woman Chases Man* (Goldwyn, 1937). In an about-face, it is McCrea, as Kenneth Nolan, who has all the money and is tight-fisted when it comes to matters financial. His father B.J. Nolan, engagingly played by Charles Winninger, and Virginia Travis (Hopkins), an architect, scheme to get him to invest in a building project.

The young woman is very serious about her profession. She tells a prospective client, "I know what you're thinking—that I'm a girl.... I've studied like a man and researched like a man. There is nothing feminine about my mind." In other words, she can prove that she is as good as any male in the profession she has chosen.

The son is reluctant to join the two in their project, so Dad pretends that he is the one rolling in dough. He and Hopkins arrange a party to raise money and get two movie usher friends, Judy (Ella Logan, who would later star in the Broadway musical *Finian's Rainbow*) and Hank (Broderick Crawford), to serve as maid and butler. These two do not know what they're doing and the result is hilarious chaos, a screwball staple.

McCrea finally surrenders as he is in love with the lady architect. At

Woman Chases Man (1937): Miriam Hopkins is not the delicate female she seems to be. Watch out, Joel McCrea!

film's end, she winds up in the arms of the millionaire, much to the delight of his father. She will definitely *not* give up her career.

Though some of the films discussed thus far may not be one hundred percent screwball, they contain enough of its elements to be included in this chapter.

In the main, the Misses Stanwyck and Hopkins are the more clever of the screwball heiresses: They know what they want, and their cleverness comes out through the antics they indulge in to get what they want. A couple of the ladies we are about to meet are just as pretty and just as rich, but there is one big difference: They are exasperating to their families and to the men in their lives, being eccentric and unconventional in various ways.

Exasperating is just the word to describe Susan Vance in *Bringing Up Baby*. The film, which stars Cary Grant and Katharine Hepburn, was considered an unmitigated disaster in 1938, the year of its release. While Grant was popular and his films were bringing money into the RKO coffers, the same could not be said for Hepburn. After a series of poor quality films, she had just been labeled "Box-Office Poison" by the Independent Theater Owner's Association (Fred Astaire and Marlene Dietrich were two other personalities making the list). Another problem besetting the film was that producer-director Howard Hawks allowed it to go over-budget. It lost over $360,000. All of this aside, *Baby* is pure screwball and is now considered a classic.

In the film, Grant plays David Huxley, a stuffy paleontologist. His life is sedate and orderly. He is trying to obtain a grant to keep his work ongoing. He is engaged to a dull, drab girl named Alice Swallow (Virginia Walker) who exhorts him to forget about their forthcoming honeymoon and keep going on with his project.

A far cry from Alice is Hepburn's Susan Vance, a giddy society girl. David meets her on a golf course where she uses his ball and then in the parking lot where she damages his car. He soon learns that it is her Aunt Elizabeth from whom he hopes to get his grant, so David is now irretrievably tied to Susan.

Susan's pets include George, a fox terrier played by the lovable Asta, and "Baby," a leopard who purrs in ecstasy upon hearing the song "I Can't Give You Anything but Love, Baby." This tune is heard throughout the film.

Susan asks David to help her transport "Baby" from her apartment to her farm in Connecticut. Her reasoning? "Imagine Aunt Elizabeth coming here and running into a leopard. That would mean an end to your million dollars." This is to say that she is the one who will help him to get the money.

At breakneck speed, the scenario finds the duo losing a priceless bone which the dog finds and buries, making them scamper after him in search of the burial spot. They also mistake a dangerous wild leopard on the loose for "Baby," after which they wind up in jail.

Some frantically funny scenes stand out. While at a nightclub, David tries to shield Susan, whose dress has been torn off in the back; David wears a frilly housecoat (Susan has sent his suit out to be pressed without his knowledge); the jail scene during which she pretends to be a gangster's moll. Aiding and abetting the two are May Robson as Aunt Elizabeth and Charles Ruggles as a big game hunter who specializes in imitating loons. Also in the cast are Fritz Feld, Jonathan Hale and Barry Fitzgerald.

At film's end, David is working on his project, the building of a brontosaurus skeleton. In comes Susan, who she has the lost bone and announces that Aunt Elizabeth has given her the money for him. She climbs on a rickety ladder that collapses and pushes her into David. The skeleton collapses and so do David's defenses. His last words are, "Oh dear, oh my." He will give up his strait-laced fiancée and opt for the uncertainties of life with the unpredictable Susan.

A change of pace role for Hepburn was her character in *Holiday*, made the same year as *Bringing Up Baby*, but for a different studio (Columbia) and again pairing her with Grant. It was based on the play by Philip Barry; the leading role had been understudied by Hepburn on Broadway. The first ver-

Bringing Up Baby (1938): Katharine Hepburn, Cary Grant and Baby. Cary is befuddled. Katharine is dizzy and what about the bone?

sion of *Holiday* was filmed in 1930 with Ann Harding, Mary Astor, Robert Ames and Edward Everett Horton in the principal roles. The second version, besides its two stars, features Lew Ayres, Doris Nolan, Jean Dixon and, reprising his 1930 role, Edward Everett Horton.

Johnny Case (Grant) is a cheerful non-conformist who has no money to speak of and really couldn't care less. His take on life is that a man should enjoy a "holiday" from regular employment while still in his prime so as to discover life and enjoy himself, then return to the work force in his later years.

He meets a socially prominent heiress, Julia Seton (Nolan), daughter of a wealthy banker, and becomes engaged to her. He is then introduced to her family: her father Edward Seton (Henry Kolker), whom she worships, her brother Ned (Ayres), who usually has a drink in his hand, and her sister Linda (Hepburn), an unconventional girl, exasperating to her father and her sister.

Seton Sr. has it all worked out: He will give them the wedding, he will build them a house and Johnny will work in a bank. All of this Julia applauds.

Johnny tries to explain to her that this is not at all what he wants, but he cannot change her mind. This begins a gentle battle of the sexes.

Johnny takes refuge with Julia's sister. Linda is very unlike her sibling: She is sympathetic to Johnny, agreeing with his philosophy of life. In her playroom, in contrast with a fancy dress dinner going on downstairs, he lets his hair down, joins in on the antics, plays games and really enjoys himself. They invite his friends, Nick and Susan Potter (Horton and Dixon), to spend time with them and Linda's brother Ned. Johnny is happy being himself.

The conclusion has Johnny breaking off with Julia and boarding a steamship to far-away places. Linda, having been tipped off to his plans by the Potters, joins him and the two realize that they truly belong together. The last scene shows Grant doing a backflip, an acknowledgment of his pre-acting career as an acrobat.

Holiday is a sharp and penetrating commentary on the values of the era's so-called upper classes, a screwball requisite and, in one way, a case of mistaken identity, as Johnny soon realizes that Linda, not Julia, is the girl for him. The film did well at the box office. Two years later, Grant and Hepburn scored a resounding hit in the movie version of another Philip Barry play (see Chapter Thirteen).

Hepburn's Linda of *Holiday* is very unlike her daffy Susan Vance in *Bringing Up Baby*, but the two are sisters under the skin in their relish for life and their quest for happiness. They just go about attaining their goals in different ways. And when the prize is Cary Grant in the guise of Johnny Case or David Huxley, anything goes.

Just as scatterbrained as Susan Vance is Irene Dunne's character in *Lady in a Jam*. In this minor 1942 Universal release, she is an heiress with a passion for numerology who has squandered away the fortune that her grandfather left her. She meets and falls in love with a psychiatrist played by Patric Knowles.

Enter Irene's feisty grandma (Queenie Vassar), who facilitates a happy ending by opening up an old but rich vein in an abandoned Arizona quartz mine. This feat allows granddaughter and the shrink the continuation of a lifestyle to which they are accustomed. Along for the ride are such screwball stalwarts as Eugene Pallette and Ralph Bellamy, the latter in his usual role as "the other man."

The film was not among Dunne's finest and neither was it a feather in the cap of director Gregory La Cava. He would make one more movie before his death in the early 1950s.

A discernible quality in many a screwball heiress is her stubbornness. The most famous example of this is Claudette Colbert's Ellie Andrews in *It Happened One Night*. Colbert and her imperious peers think they can get what they want just by crooking their little fingers, but in screwball comedies, it doesn't always work out that way (see Chapter Nine).

Socialite Merle Oberon wants barrister Laurence Olivier in *The Divorce of Lady X* (United Artists, 1938) and will do all in her power to get him. The film, using the theme of mistaken identity, was produced in England by Alexander Korda, whom Oberon married in 1939 and divorced six years later, and contains many of the elements that are to be found in the American screwball comedies so popular during that pre-war era.

As the story unfolds, Oberon is at a charity ball in an over-crowded hotel. She and another woman (Binnie Barnes) are wearing identical gowns. When a thick fog envelops the area and Oberon can't get home, she spends the night in the room of a young barrister. It is all very innocent and everything would be fine, except that a case of mistaken identity has taken place. A friend of the barrister's (Ralph Richardson) thinks that his wife, the woman wearing the same dress as Oberon, is having an affair—and he sees a woman coming out of a man's suite in the morning. He doesn't know who the man is and hires Olivier to represent him. The lawyer, upon hearing the story, knows that he is the man and concludes that Oberon is Richardson's wife. This comedy of errors is finally straightened out to everyone's satisfaction: The married couple are happily reunited and Olivier and Oberon wind up in a clinch. It's a well done comedy of errors.

In the same year, Merle appeared in UA's *The Cowboy and the Lady*, this time as an American. She is bored and rich, the daughter of a presidential candidate. One night in Palm Beach, she goes out with her maid (played by the always hilarious Patsy Kelly) and meets up with rodeo rider Gary Cooper. She tells him that she is a lady's maid. The two fall in love and elope. His plans are to quit the rodeo and settle down in Montana.

Prior to traveling west, she returns to Palm Beach to help her father with an important political dinner. Cooper, still unaware of his wife's true identity, unexpectedly shows up at the mansion as the dinner is about to begin. He discovers his wife's duplicity and, during the course of the evening, proceeds to tell the august stuffed shirts what he thinks of them. He goes to Montana; she is in tears. Dad comes through and, with his help, she goes to Montana to be a rancher's wife.

The film's attempt to poke fun at the rich and powerful is a weak one. A good supporting cast, including Walter Brennan and Fuzzy Knight as Cooper's rodeo pals, Harry Davenport as Merle's uncle and Thelma Todd as another maid, are wasted. Also, Oberon and Cooper are an incongruous pair. With another actress, an American, the film might have been somewhat better.

In *Maid's Night Out* (RKO, 1938), there is a double case of mistaken identity. Joan Fontaine is cast as an heiress whom leading man Allan Lane thinks is a maid. She, in turn, thinks that he is a milkman. He is nothing of the kind. He is as wealthy as she is; he is only delivering milk to settle a bet with his father. Dad doesn't think that his son can last for even a month in any kind of job, and Sonny is out to prove him wrong.

After a series of zany escapades, including a mad dash in a milk wagon, Fontaine and Lane discover the truth about each other and, as Shakespeare once wrote, "all's well that ends well." Also taking part in the goings-on are Billy Gilbert, Cecil Kellaway and Hedda Hopper. Fontaine went on to true stardom in dramatic fare and won a 1941 Oscar for her performance in Alfred Hitchcock's *Suspicion*.

Another Oscar winner, Bette Davis, plays Joan Winfield, a stubborn girl who usually gets what she wants, in *The Bride Came C.O.D.*, a Warner Brothers 1941 release. She is a temperamental oil heiress, about to elope with egotistical bandleader Allen Brice (Jack Carson) whom she has only known for four days. Her astounded father Lucius Winfield (rotund screwball veteran Eugene Pallette) hires charter pilot Steve Collins (James Cagney) to bring her home unmarried.

Joan is infuriated by this interference and tries to thwart Steve at every turn. Eventually, after several screwball escapades, including an escape attempt from a ghost town in which they have had to make a forced landing, she has fallen for the rough-hewn Steve who has taken her down a peg and given Brice the heave-ho. It's an enjoyable romp, with Davis and Cagney doing a good job of playing off each other with the laughs coming fast and furiously.

A truly perplexing problem facing several rich and beautiful screwball heroines is that of choosing between two eager swains. In *Love Before Breakfast* (Universal, 1936), Carole Lombard is sought after by both Preston Foster and Cesar Romero. Each pursue the lovely blonde avidly—their intentions are matrimony—and the fun is in the ways that they try to outdo one another. In the final reel, it is Foster, the older, wealthier man who puts the ring on her finger. In true Hollywood fashion, the guy who gets the gal was the more important actor at the time. It was a minor Lombard film.

Claudette Colbert, another highly skilled practitioner in the art of screwball, faces a similar dilemma, but with a difference, in Paramount's *The Bride Comes Home*. She plays Jeannette Desmareau, a recently impoverished society girl who is loved by both wealthy Jack Bristow (Robert Young) and his bodyguard, Cyrus Anderson (Fred MacMurray). She is constantly switching her matrimonial decisions back and forth and is about to elope with Young, but in the final reel, it is Fred who winds up with the curvaceous Claudette. As in the case of Preston Foster vs. Cesar Romero, MacMurray was a bigger star than Young in 1936. As the latter's star ascended in the Hollywood firmament, he got the girls (Stanwyck, Lana Turner, Hedy Lamarr and, yes, Colbert, among others).

Young is again a wealthy man in *Bridal Suite* (MGM, 1939). A playboy by nature, he proposes to women, but seldom appears at his own weddings. His new bride, played by French import Annabella, makes sure he will be beside her in the chapel. In this minor screwball scenario, the cast also includes Walter Connolly, the everpresent Billie Burke, Reginald Gardiner and Arthur Treacher.

Vivacious Ann Sothern was some years away from her MGM *Maisie* series and even further away from superstardom as television's *Private Secretary* when she appeared in RKO's *Walking on Air* (1936). In the film, she plays a rich girl whose father is outraged by her choice of husband: a slick fortune hunter (Alan Curtis). The resourceful young woman concocts an ingenious scheme to make Dad change his mind: She hires a struggling singer (Gene Raymond) to impersonate a suitor so obnoxious that her family will have to approve of her marriage. In the meantime, Raymond has decided that he wants Ann for himself and mounts a radio campaign to get her. In true screwball fashion, Curtis gets the "air" and Raymond will marry the girl. Also featured in the cast are Jessie Ralph as Ann's salty, no-nonsense aunt and Henry Stephenson as her bemused papa.

RKO was pleased with the results of the teaming and that same year paired them again in *The Smartest Girl in Town*. The plot line deals with a romance between a lovely model and a millionaire. This time it is Raymond who has the money. It's another case of mistaken identity as model Sothern thinks that the wealthy young man is a fellow model. She doesn't know that his butler (the irrepressible Eric Blore) is merely fronting the ad agency for his boss. In the end, she knows the truth and is happily nestled in the hero's arms. It was another hit for the studio. Also involved in this merry mix-up is veteran actress Helen Broderick as Sothern's sister.

There is an old saying, "Don't mess with success." So RKO bought a third story for its two stars, *She's Got Everything*. In this 1937 release, Ann is an heiress who is very much in debt. As the film opens, her aunt (Helen Broderick) and one of her creditors (Victor Moore) are trying to promote a marriage between Ann and a wealthy young coffee tycoon (Raymond—again it's the man who has the money), after which she will be able to pay off all that she owes.

Neither is aware that their strings are being pulled. When they do find out what their elders, Moore and Broderick, are up to, they are incensed and they separate. True to the code of Hollywood screwball comedy, they are reunited before "The End" is flashed on the screen. Aiding and abetting are Billy Gilbert and Jack Carson.

It must be remembered that the ladies and gentlemen we have met thus far are not the only "heroes" and "heroines" of the genre. Various types inhabit its several subgenres. Many work for a living and their jobs are integral to the screwball plot. It is time now to meet some of these working stiffs.

Chapter Six

Screwball Guys and Gals: The Working Stiffs

Ginger Rogers is Polly Parrish, a department store clerk in *Bachelor Mother*. Passing a foundling home, she finds an abandoned baby on the doorstep and spends much of the film's running time denying that the child is hers.

No one believes her, including her employer J.B. Merlin (Charles Coburn) and his son David (David Niven), whom the home has contacted. She is fired by Niven for being an unwed mother. But when the young man becomes intrigued with her and begins to take an interest in both her and the baby, even though at first she evinces none in him (it is a classic case of cross class relationships), old man Merlin begins to think that the little tyke is really his natural grandson. *We* know that the baby is not, but by the time the final credits roll, it is obvious Polly will become "Mrs. Young Millionaire" and that, in one fell swoop, the cherubic Mr. Merlin will have two new additions to his family.

The film turned a tidy profit for RKO in 1939. It is interesting to note that Rogers did not like the Norman Krasna script, but had to play the role because she was under contract to the studio. This delightful comedy was one of the best films in her long and varied career.

In 1956, RKO remade the film as a musical. *Bundle of Joy* stars the then-married Debbie Reynolds and singer Eddie Fisher, with Adolphe Menjou in the Coburn role. The public considered Reynolds and Fisher to be America's Sweethearts (this was, of course, before Elizabeth Taylor appeared on the scene) and the studio wanted to cash in on their popularity. The film does not compare to the original: This version plays up the slapstick scenes, and the added musical interludes (no song leaves a lasting impression) make a mockery of the subtle and witty elements so evident in the Krasna script.

The foregoing makes it clear that the characters in screwball don't always

Bachelor Mother (1939) with Charles Coburn, Elbert Coplen, Jr. (the baby), Ginger Rogers and David Niven. This lady is not the baby's mama. Why won't the men believe her?

have to be wealthy society types. A varied group populates the working class screwball subgenre—capricious, non-conforming, happy-go-lucky, scheming. All are offbeat personalities who either instigate or are the victims of the antics within.

The screwball working stiffs hold a variety of jobs. From shopgirl, office personnel, sandhog, cook and butler to con artists, their involvements in screwball fun and games are all in a day's work for them.

Alice Brady (two years away from her Best Supporting Actress Oscar for *In Old Chicago*) goes from construction worker's cook to society lady in *Lady Tubbs* (Universal, 1935). In a series of amusing events, she exposes the shallowness of some of her "new friends" while helping along the romance of a young couple (Anita Louise and Douglass Montgomery). It's a minor, but interesting film. Supporting the leading players are Alan Mowbray, Minor Watson and Hedda Hopper.

Model Wife (Universal, 1941) finds stars Joan Blondell and Dick Powell at work in the same place. They are married but, because of the strict conditions of their employment, must keep their marriage a secret. They would like to start a family but do not have the financial resources. And therein lie the screwball elements including their dilemma in trying to keep their secret from their disagreeable employer (Lucile Watson). At the time of filming, Blondell and Powell were indeed married. As Warner Brothers contract players, though they appeared in several of the same films, rarely were they teamed romantically.

Myrna Loy took some time off from being the perfect wife in the *Thin Man* series to being the object of working stiff Robert Montgomery's affection in *Petticoat Fever* (MGM, 1936). He is a United States wireless operator, stationed on a lonely Labrador outpost, who hasn't seen a woman in two years. Who should drop in unexpectedly but the lovely Myrna and her stuffy fiancé (Reginald Owen), whose plane has been forced down nearby.

When Montgomery makes a play for her, the lady isn't having any, but by the end of the film, Owen is the one left out in the cold: Myrna ditches him for the handsome smooth operator (who wouldn't?) and all is well in Screwball Land. The stars make this unusual film work.

In *Youth Takes a Fling* (Universal, 1938), handsome Kansas-born Joel McCrea has always craved a life on the sea. He comes to New York in pursuit of his dream. Because there are no berths available, he takes a job in a department store. Working at the same store is a beautiful young lady (played by Andrea Leeds) who, upon seeing Joel, is immediately smitten with him. His thoughts, however, are thoroughly water-logged. The storyline has Leeds doing anything and everything to make him a landlubber. She does succeed. Also in the cast are Frank Jenks, Virginia Grey, Grant Mitchell and Willie Best. The minor comedy lacks a strong female star who possibly would have been able to draw fans to the ticket window.

McCrea expresses a desire to see those faraway places with the strange-sounding names. Fred MacMurray lives on one in *Honeymoon in Bali* (Paramount, 1939). Finding life in the fast lane not his cup of tea, he has moved to the South Sea Island of Bali. On a subsequent trip to the States, he meets and falls in love with a beautiful but harried department store executive (Madeleine Carroll). She is attracted to him but is also involved with a handsome opera singer (Allan Jones). She has been seeing Jones for years, but they've never set a wedding date. During the course of the film, the lovely lady agonizes over her choice: the steady Jones and her career, or MacMurray and her chance to "smell the roses." At first, she opts for the fast lane, but changes her mind and sets off for a life with MacMurray amidst palm trees and pineapples. Supporting the stars are Helen Broderick, Akim Tamiroff and Osa Massen. The stars make the most of their roles and come up with a winner.

Life in the South Seas must have seemed like Heaven to a nation still suffering through a Depression and also witnessing the gathering storm in

Europe. By 1940, Paris was under the thumb of the Nazis. One year later, America would be in the midst of that storm.

The next film under discussion takes place in pre-war Paris. A native Parisian, Claudette Colbert, goes back to the city of her birth, if only on celluloid, in *I Met Him in Paris* (Paramount, 1937). She plays Kay Denham, a dress designer, bored with her life and her staid fiancé, who, on a much-needed vacation, sets off for that lovely city. There she meets and is wooed by George Potter, a cynical playwright (Melvyn Douglas), and Gene Anders, a married novelist (Robert Young). The latter is even willing to give up his wife (Mona Barrie) for her. Soon another complication sets in with the arrival of Claudette's fiancé (Lee Bowman). Which of the three does she choose? Simple. As Melvyn Douglas was the top-billed male in the film, the reader will readily guess that it is he with whom our heroine will bill and coo. Again, the three names on the marquee make it work. In the hilarious skiing scenes, Sun Valley doubles for the Alps.

Claudette's frequent co-star Fred MacMurray played leading man to several other top stars, among them Carole Lombard. With the beautiful blonde, he appeared in some of the most successful screwball comedies of the 1930s.

Carole literally has her *Hands Across the Table* in the Paramount 1935 film of the same name. Regi Allen is a manicurist out to snare a rich husband. She meets disabled millionaire Allen Macklyn (Ralph Bellamy, again the other man) and then Theodore Drew II (Fred MacMurray). Because of his name, Regi assumes that Ted is rich. She gives him a manicure, during which his fingertips begin to bleed from her "tender ministrations." Regi uses a nail file like a lethal weapon.

After a night on the town with him, she learns that Ted is also on the prowl (read: fortune-hunting) and is engaged to Vivian Snowden (Astrid Allwyn), whose father is "the pineapple king." She now knows that he is penniless and yet, against her better judgment, Regi is attracted to Ted. They have a romantic fling, which they enjoy so much that they ditch their respective love interests and vow to see life through in tandem.

Among many, one hilarious scene stands out: Ted calls Vivian, telling her that he is in Bermuda. Regi, trying to distract him with comical gestures and faces, pretends to be a long-distance operator. In other hands, both action and dialogue might seem trite and silly, but when Lombard goes into her act, it is a comedic gem. MacMurray matches her word for word, gesture for gesture. The two bring out every possible nuance in the scene. In his book *Screwball: Hollywood's Madcap Romantic Comedies*, Ed Sikov quotes director Mitchell Leisen describing the effect Lombard had on MacMurray: "Carole was a great help to Fred. She'd get him down on the floor and sit on his chest and say, 'Now be funny, Uncle Fred, or I'll pluck your eyebrows out.'"

Hands Across the Table was a resounding hit for Paramount. It was also another triumph for Norman Krasna, head of the film's script-writing team.

With Lombard and Colbert, MacMurray made some of his finest comedies. Paramount's 1943 production *No Time for Love* is a case in point. Claudette is again his co-star. She plays a photographer who, on an assignment, meets tunnel digger Fred. She is both attracted and repelled by him. At first he thinks of her as a "dame." The battle of the sexes is on. He becomes her "mentor" while she's on the job, giving her a tour of the tunnel and answering her questions. When the tunnel collapses with MacMurray in it, the now smitten lady shows her true mettle and tries to help out in any way she can—her face even gets dirty. He now realizes that she's the gal for him.

Like Lombard and Colbert, Ginger Rogers had become a major star by the late 1930s. In *Vivacious Lady* (RKO, 1938), a sparkling screwball comedy of clashing cultures, she plays Francey La Rochelle, a night club dancer. She is pitted against the family of Peter Morgan (James Stewart), professor of botany in a small college town. Francey has impulsively married Morgan after a whirlwind courtship. He explains his feelings for her in terms of chemistry. Peter had gone to New York to rescue his cousin, Keith (James Ellison), from the "perils" of big city life.

There is more than one fly in the ointment. For openers, Peter is engaged to a girl named Helen (Frances Mercer) who is respectable and dull. Secondly, he is the son of the stuffy president of the university where he works (Charles Coburn, who, a year later, in *Bachelor Mother*, is eager to have Ginger in his family). Peter is expected to one day take over for his father.

Peter has neglected to tell the members of his family that he is married. It is this inability to confront them that leads to some comical situations, including one in which Francey and Helen mix it up at a college dance, kicking, slapping and wrestling with each other. When the staid Coburn steps into the fray, he is socked in the jaw by Francey. The latter, unable to tolerate the situation, leaves. On the train, she meets her mother-in-law (Beulah Bondi) who, for years, has felt put upon by her husband. The wives' actions galvanize the two men. They meet the train and Coburn feigns illness. Both men show remorse and all is forgiven.

In one stroke, Francey has liberated both herself and her mother-in-law and in today's culture could be called a founding member of the woman's lib movement. She has also liberated Peter from the domination of his college president father. He will be his own man now. In the supporting cast are such screwball veterans as Jack Carson, Franklin Pangborn, Hattie McDaniel and Willie Best, the latter in a very funny scene on the train.

Clashing of cultures of a different sort are at the heart of *Tovarich* (Warner Brothers, 1937). Based on a stage success by playwright Robert E. Sherwood, it is the story of a couple of aristocratic Russians (Charles Boyer

Vivacious Lady (1938) with Ginger Rogers and James Stewart. Jimmy hasn't told his family that he is married. Why can't he?

and Claudette Colbert) who have fled to Paris after the Revolution. Finding themselves out of funds, they take jobs in the Paris household of Melville Cooper and Isabel Jeans—he as a butler, she as a maid. Much of the comedy comes from their unskilled labors.

All is going along fairly well until they are recognized by Basil Rathbone in the role of their employer's friend. Rathbone, in reality, is anti–Royalist— his appearance in the film gives it its bite. Audiences of the 1930s enjoyed the stars; they had come to expect a sparkling performance from Colbert. The surprise is Boyer, who usually played in dramas. He was by no means a comedic actor, but in *Tovarich*, he handles himself quite well.

Again without funds in Paris is Colbert's Eve Peabody in *Midnight* (Paramount, 1939). She has arrived there from Monte Carlo. When the train porter asks about her luggage, she replies that it is in a pawn shop in that gambling mecca. She is, however, dressed in gold lamé, with purse to match, souvenirs of better days.

It is raining when she steps onto the platform so she spends her last sou on a newspaper to keep her head dry. She is picked up by a cab driver named Tibor Czerny (Don Ameche), who is the true working stiff in this film.

Eve is up front with him, saying that there's no money to pay him. "What I need is a taxi to find myself a job and I need a job to pay for a taxi. No taxi, no job, no soap." He treats her to lunch and she airily tells him that she was paid off by a millionaire's family in Monte Carlo to leave their son alone. Obviously, this money has been left on the gaming tables.

After he pays for her meal, she dumps him, then crashes a party in order to keep out of the rain. She is spotted by Georges Flammarion (John Barrymore) whom she soon finds out wants to hire her to seduce his wife Helen's lover. In another room, she sees Helen (Mary Astor) and her lover Jacques Picot (Francis Lederer) at a bridge game. She introduces herself as the Baroness Czerny, taking the name of her cab-driving friend. Flammarion sees that Jacques seems interested in the "baroness." He buys her a stunning wardrobe, sets her up in a posh hotel suite and invites her to his home. Tibor, getting wind of the scheme, arrives at the Flammarion home, pretending to be the Baron Czerny.

The film is vintage screwball and vintage Colbert, with strong assists from the writing team of Brackett and Wilder and a supporting cast which includes Hedda Hopper and Monty Woolley.

Colbert and Ameche got on well during the making of *Midnight*. In their book *Hollywood Anecdotes,* Paul Boller and Ronald Davis reveal an amusing incident involving the duo. Ameche picked a very old extra on the set and sent him to Colbert's dressing room. When she opened the door, the man said, "Miss Colbert, I've adored you ever since I was a little boy." Guessing at once who the culprit was, the 35-year-old actress chased her co-star all over the lot.

A pallid remake of *Midnight* was released by the same studio in 1945 under a new title, *Masquerade in Mexico.* The stars were Dorothy Lamour and Arturo de Cordova (his character is now a bullfighter rather than a cab driver).

Claudette's con artist in *Midnight* is an amateur compared to Barbara Stanwyck in *The Lady Eve* (Paramount, 1941). Jean Harrington, like Colbert's Eve, is a working girl of sorts. She and her father, "Colonel Harrington" (Charles Coburn), are a couple of card sharps plying their trade aboard an ocean-going luxury liner. They meet their match in Charles "Hopsie" Pike (Henry Fonda), snake scholar and heir to the Pike's Ale fortune.

By sticking her foot out in his path, Jean meets Hopsie, and means to fleece him, but suddenly she finds that she cannot do this to him. She is strongly attracted to him and, to the consternation of her father, she is unwilling to go along with his plans.

Mugsy (William Demarest), Hopsie's friend and employee, soon discovers, by nosing around, that the Harringtons are crooks and informs his boss. The latter rejects her, not realizing that she is in love with him and is willing to give up her crooked ways for him.

Midnight (1939) with Don Ameche, Claudette Colbert and John Barrymore. A cab driver, an adventuress and an aristocrat. How do they fit together?

Smarting from this rejection, Jean vows revenge. With entree supplied to her by a phony lord (Eric Blore), she gains admittance to the Pike home as "The Lady Eve." Hopsie, in his wonderment about this lady, finds himself doing off-the-wall things: He trips over a couch and lands head first into a bowl of lobster dip and, when leaving the room, pulls the drapes along with him. Later, at dinner, a platter of meat is dumped on him. "Eve" succeeds in getting him to marry her. On their wedding night, she tells a truly preposterous story about all of her other "marriages." Repelled by this, Hopsie leaves. When he requests a divorce, she will give it to him only if he asks for it himself. He refuses and decides to go on another ocean voyage. Jean is there and trips him again. The romance is rekindled. He tells her that he can't understand it, that he adores her, but tells her that he is married. She answers, "So am I, darling, so am I." The End.

A sparkling script by Preston Sturges, who also directed, plus a cast of screwball veterans including Eugene Pallette and Luis Alberni, made the production a box-office smash. Paramount's 1956 remake *The Birds and the Bees* stars George Gobel, Mitzi Gaynor and David Niven. Gone is the sparkle of the Sturges script plus the Stanwyck-Fonda combo. It was not a profitable venture for the studio.

The Lady Eve (1941): A con artist father-and-daughter team (Charles Coburn, Barbara Stanwyck) seemed to have found a mark in rich man Henry Fonda, but love conquers all, even a card sharp.

Light years away from con artists and card sharps are the secretaries, the honest working girls, who make up a most important part of the screwball genre. In some films, they are the leading characters, in others, the name below the title, i.e., supporting players. Stars marry the boss, character people do not. The amusing and quite often unrealistic situations that crop up in the various films probably had the real Gal Fridays laughing into their steno pads while, at the same time, wishing that *their* bosses looked like the ones they saw in the movies (except for possibly one film, *Take a Letter, Darling,* in which Rosalind Russell is the boss and Fred MacMurray her "man" Friday; most men, however, would not have minded having that lady as their boss).

George Brent in *More Than a Secretary* (Columbia, 1936) is the publisher of a magazine called *Body and Brain*. He is also in constant need of good office help. A passing parade of capable candidates is furnished him by Jean Arthur, who owns and runs a secretarial school.

Why can't Brent hold on to his employees? Jean wants to find some answers to this perplexing problem. She goes to his office and is mistaken for a stenographer. After taking a look at the boss, she decides not to correct this error. While on the job, she changes not only his attitude towards office personnel and procedures, but also his thoughts on love and romance. In the supporting cast are Lionel Stander, Reginald Denny, Ruth Donnelly and Dorothea Kent as a ditsy blonde stenographer. A cute idea and a sparkling Arthur go far to make for an entertaining hour and a half.

Unlike hard-working Brent in the previous film, Robert Young is the opposite in *Vagabond Lady* (MGM, 1935). Evelyn Venable, a leading lady in "B" films of the 1930s, plays the secretary of a department store owner. She is coveted by both of her employer's sons, devil-may-care Young and staid, stuffy Reginald Denny. (The talented Denny was typecast in these roles throughout much of his lengthy career.) Naturally, it is the youthful, more exciting Young whom she chooses; presumably, she will straighten out her feet-of-clay hero. This minor flick probably did nothing for the careers of its players.

A twist to the old saw of the boss falling in love with his secretary is the basis for the plotline of *Take a Letter, Darling*. In this Paramount 1942 release, Roz is A.M. MacGregor, an advertising executive who hires male secretaries so that the wives of her clients don't get wrong ideas.

Enter Tom Varney (Fred MacMurray). Things go well at the beginning and the relationship is strictly business until they go to work on an account involving handsome, wealthy Jonathan Caldwell (Macdonald Carey). The latter is attracted to Russell and brings his man-hunting sister Edith (Constance Moore) into the picture to distract MacMurray. The British title of the movie, *Green-Eyed Woman*, is very apropos for Roz, who becomes jealous when she thinks there may be a relationship between her secretary and the beautiful Miss Moore. It turns out that Fred is not interested in the man-trap and in the natural progression of the screwball comedy, he winds up with Ros (he has been in love with her almost from the start). In the supporting cast are Robert Benchley as Roz's partner, who would rather indulge in his expensive hobbies, Cecil Kellaway and Dooley Wilson.

Jealousy may not be the word to describe Joan Blondell as Jenny Swanson in *Good Girls Go to Paris* (Columbia, 1939), but she is envious of the wealthy college girls who frequent the campus restaurant at which she works as a waitress. She dreams of money and travel, including a trip to Paris, hence the film's title, which originally ended with the word *Too*. The Hays office insisted that it be switched to protect "America's moral fiber."

The young lady sets out to find a rich mate. Alan Curtis plays Tom Brand, the collegiate son of tycoon Olaf Brand (Walter Connolly), and he seems to fit the bill. He proposes and invites his fiancée to meet the family. Jenny then takes a shine to Ronald Brooke (top-cast Melvyn Douglas), a visiting professor of Greek mythology, and decides that he is the man for her. By film's end, he agrees.

Will she get to Paris? As the film ends before this question is resolved, we can only guess at the answer. The zesty Blondell and the urbane Douglas were a delightful team and made other screwballs together.

Douglas plays a reporter in *They All Kissed the Bride*, but the story is more about a high-powered career woman (Joan Crawford) who has inherited a large trucking company than the Fourth Estate. The lady in question has no time for a private life. When marriage does intrude upon her, it is not her own, but that of her sister. At the ceremony, the details of which have been arranged by her, she meets reporter Douglas and literally goes weak in the knees, which we later find out is a family trait, signifying an attraction to the opposite sex.

He, however, is not attracted to what he sees on the outside. He sends her a bunch of violets with a note saying, "I debated before sending these. With them, you might be mistaken for a girl."

Once warmed up, however, this lady proves more than a match for him with words. She tells him that he runs scared, that he has always hidden behind his typewriter. She gets drunk and is involved in a jitterbug contest (Crawford had started her show business career as a dancer) and later, during a business conference with her staff, starts talking about flowers and babies. She even wants to learn to knit. (Remember folks, this was 1942.) In the end, this executive will give in to her feminine instincts and a life with the man who makes her feel weak in the knees.

The role that Crawford plays in *They All Kissed the Bride* was originally intended for Carole Lombard. As a gesture to Lombard's memory, Crawford donated her entire salary to the war effort.

Like Joan Blondell in *Good Girls Go to Paris*, Lana Turner goes the small town waitress route in *Slightly Dangerous* (MGM, 1943). Lana, however, has a far different and more complicated scheme for achieving the good life: She travels to the big city and feigns amnesia, pretending to be the long-lost daughter of a millionaire. All goes according to plan until her hometown boyfriend (Robert Young) is suspected of being involved in her disappearance. In the end, the ersatz heiress confesses all and goes into the sunset with her "Young" man. A supporting cast of well-known players, including Dame May Whitty, Walter Brennan, Alan Mowbray, Ward Bond and Ray Collins, are on hand to give this slight comedy a helping hand.

Waitress, shop girl, secretary, dancer, manicurist, executive and yes, even con artist and card sharp—they and their peers succeed, screwball-style, in the attainment of their goals in one way or another. For the final film in this chapter, we come to a production which celebrates one of the ultimate "screwballian" triumphs—that of the worker over the super rich.

The Devil and Miss Jones (RKO, 1941) stars Jean Arthur and Robert

Cummings. Third-billed Charles Coburn, Oscar-nominated for his performance, plays John P. Merrick, a flinty multimillionaire who goes undercover as Thomas Higgins at his department stores in order to find out why his employees are so disgruntled. In this guise he meets co-workers Mary Jones (Arthur), her hot-headed boyfriend Joe O'Brien (Cummings) and matronly Elizabeth Ellis (Spring Byington).

In the course of the action provided by Norman Krasna's Oscar-nominated script, Coburn learns a lesson in humility and humanity from the young and falls in love with the soft-spoken Byington, who has awakened feelings long dormant within him.

The fine supporting cast includes Edmund Gwenn as a smarmy section manager, S.Z. Sakall as Coburn's butler and William Demarest as the store detective.

The clash of the classes, the theme of mistaken identity and scenes of Coburn being irate in various stages (one of which, dressed in a bathing suit, being hauled off to a police station) all add to the atmosphere of the screwball comedy. An interesting sidelight to this production is that writer Krasna once worked in a department store similar to the one he depicts in this film.

By now, it should be abundantly clear that the working stiff is well-represented in the screwball comedy. What might almost be called a subgenre of this subgenre will be examined next as we come to the Cinderellas and Cinderfellas of Screwball.

Chapter Seven

Screwball Cinderellas and Cinderfellas

Cinderella was a poor but beautiful young girl whose fairy godmother (with the aid of a few mice and a pumpkin) brings her love, marriage and all the riches she could ever want.

Ginger Rogers doesn't need a fairy godmother in *Tom, Dick and Harry*. Her Janie is a telephone operator, living in the requisite small town with the requisite small town family. She is pert and vivacious and thinks she knows what she wants: steady and dependable car salesman Tom (George Murphy). Complications set in when she becomes involved with rich playboy Dick (Alan Marshal), who treats her like a princess, and non-conformist Harry (Burgess Meredith), a mechanic who hasn't a dime and couldn't care less. Janie imagines herself in love with all three of them.

There is a dream sequence, in real screwball style, during which Janie finds herself marrying all three men. The minister solemnly proclaims, "I now pronounce you the only solution." She wakes up with a headache, but thinks she knows what to do.

She has chosen rich, but at the last moment, she hops on Harry's motorcycle and they go off to who knows where. Why has she chosen the devil-may-care mechanic? Because she hears bells ring when he kisses her.

"Cinderella" Ginger could have chosen rich, but she finds her true "prince" in a mechanic. Love and marriage, but no riches. Well, two out of three isn't bad.

The 1941 release marked the end of Ginger's exclusive contract with RKO and was the last picture director Garson Kanin made before entering the armed forces.

Tom, Dick and Harry was remade as *The Girl Most Likely* in 1958. The RKO film stars Jane Powell, who is engaged to three men at the same time. Keith Andes is the rich prospective husband, Cliff Robertson the mechanic and Tommy Noonan a real estate salesman. In the end it is Robertson winding up with Jane, who even gets to sing a few numbers. The remake does not compare to the original. Powell, though a personality, is no comedienne.

Cinderella isn't always young, isn't always pretty and isn't always a she. Among others in our cast of Cinderellas and Cinderfellas are a typist, a fruit peddler, a tuba player, a struggling architect, an inventor, and a trio of young ladies who set out to find wealthy husbands. Most of the foregoing, like many of us, are searching for the proverbial pot of gold. Unlike most of us, they find what they are looking for.

Hollywood has devised several ways for a gal to find her Prince Charming. How about on a bus? Or on a park bench? It happens to Jean Arthur in both *Easy Living* and *If You Could Only Cook*.

In the first, the blonde actress plays Mary Smith, a typist, riding to work on an open-top bus. All of a sudden, a gorgeous fur coat flies down and envelops her. Unbeknownst to her, it has been thrown from a window by an irate tycoon (Edward Arnold) named J.B. Bull, "The Bull of Broad Street." The flighty Mrs. Bull (Mary Nash) has been overly extravagant, buying the coat even though she already has a closet full of furs.

The bewildered Mary walks back in the direction of where the coat has come from and meets Bull. During their conversation, he not only decides to let her keep the coat, he also takes her out to buy her a matching hat. The store owner, a fussy little man named Van Buren (Franklin Pangborn), has a change of attitude when he discovers the identity of his famous customer. Van Buren talks about Mary and Bull to his friend Louis (played to perfection by Luis Alberni), owner of the hotel that Bull is about to foreclose on. They wonder, why would J.B. buy a hat for such a young lady if she is not his mistress? Louis gives Mary the best suite in the house. Everyone in town wants to get into the act and Mary has clothes beyond her dreams—plus a matched pair of Russian wolf hounds.

In the meanwhile, Mary has met and fallen in love with Johnny Bull (Ray Milland), who has been ostracized by his father. He has taken a job at the Automat (where one could get meals from vending machines). A funny scene takes place there: Johnny asks Mary to meet him behind the grapefruits and is fired for this "infraction of the rules." He causes a riot in which food is thrown about, and all the lucky people in the place are treated to free food.

All ends well: Father and son are reconciled and lucky Mary will become a "Bull." With a script by the irrepressible Preston Sturges and direction by Mitchell Leisen, the film is a pure delight in every way.

The premise of *If You Could Only Cook* has the distinctive-voiced Arthur portraying a jobless blonde who befriends Herbert Marshall, whom she meets in the park. Unaware of the fact that he is a well-known millionaire automobile executive, she obtains jobs for them as cook and butler. She is also unaware of the fact that their bombastic boss, played by Leo Carrillo, is a gangster.

The latter immediately recognizes Marshall as a prime pigeon, ripe for the plucking, and stages a kidnap attempt. After a merry melee of police sirens and car chases, the millionaire reveals himself to the blonde. In true screwball style, this Cinderella will live happily ever after with her "prince." The hapless mobster is not so lucky.

When this 1936 film, directed by William Seiter, was shown in London, it was advertised as a Frank Capra production. The latter threatened to sue both Columbia and studio head Harry Cohn, the man responsible for the deception. Cohn apologized to Capra and promised to buy the screen rights to the Broadway smash *You Can't Take It with You* which the director wanted to do.

Arthur was Capra's only choice to play opposite Gary Cooper in *Mr. Deeds Goes to Town* (Columbia, 1936), a comedy with screwball elements, but at the same time containing a message. The feisty Cohn balked at using Arthur but the equally feisty Capra prevailed. Who could argue with one of the industry's most successful directors?

This time, it is a Cinderfella who is our subject: Longfellow Deeds (Cooper) is an unassuming tuba-playing Vermonter whose lifestyle undergoes a dramatic change when he inherits $20 million from an uncle he hardly knew. He leaves his hometown for New York City where he has to live in his benefactor's mansion (a condition of the inheritance).

As he leaves Mandrake Falls, he plays at his own going-away ceremony. In New York, he finds that a cynical press agent named Cornelius Cobb (played by Lionel Stander) has been hired to show the ways of the big city. He even has a valet (Raymond Walburn) he is not too thrilled about. Though he is thought to be naïve, he has the common sense not to be taken in by many of those around him and for this, gains the respect of Cobb.

Arthur is Babe Bennett, a hard-nosed reporter who is assigned by her paper to cover the newly rich man in every aspect of his life. She'll do it for a month's vacation, all expenses paid. She hangs around him (with photographers following them), observing his habits and what he has to say. She thinks he's a screwball, but keeps this thought from him. Within days, however, Deeds is in love with her.

She cannot believe that he's for real and ridicules him in every way possible. She has invented a new persona for herself and plays up his naivete and hick ways, not realizing that she is slowly falling for him.

When Deeds finds out who Babe really is and that what she's written about him has made him a subject of ridicule, he is disillusioned and vows to give his money away to any farmer in need. His conniving big city lawyer, John Cedar, well-played by Douglass Dumbrille, is fearful of losing his fat fees, so he maintains that this is a mark of insanity and imports two elderly ladies from Mandrake Falls to testify that he is "pixilated." Deeds doesn't seem to care about the courtroom proceedings, but when Babe admits her love for him, he decides to fight and fight he does, with the crowd gathered in the courtroom cheering him on.

Everyone should be as "pixilated" as Longfellow Deeds. The film echoes Capra's own belief that "a simple, honest man, when driven into a corner by predatory sophisticates, can, if he will, reach down deep into his God-given resources and come up with the necessary handfuls of courage, wit and love to triumph over his environment" (Hirschhorn, *The Columbia Story*, 68).

The film, Capra and Cooper were Oscar-nominated, but only the director received the coveted statuette, his second within three years. He always maintained that Robert Riskin should also have been honored, for his superlative script.

A not-very-good remake, *Mr. Deeds* (2002), starred Adam Sandler in the Cooper role and Winona Ryder as the reporter. In no way can it be compared to the Capra classic of 1936.

An earlier Capra version of the Cinderella saga, *Lady for a Day* was a 1933 comedy fantasy from Columbia based upon a story by famed New York writer Damon Runyon with a script by the aforementioned Riskin. This time, the lady in question is an elderly fruit peddler named Apple Annie. The role is played by character actress May Robson, who got the part when Columbia was unable to obtain the services of Marie Dressler from MGM.

It seems that Annie has a daughter whom she hasn't seen for years. Convent-educated in Europe, the girl, now grown and newly engaged, is under the impression that Mama is a rich dowager (she's been receiving letters written on expensive stationery which Annie has filched from a luxurious hotel).

The action heightens when the girl writes that she, her fiancé and his father will be in New York for a day's visit. What does Annie do? She appeals to Dave the Dude (Warren William), a superstitious gambler who never makes a bet without buying an apple from the old lady.

With Dave's help, Apple Annie becomes Mrs. E. Worthington Manville. She is beautifully gowned and living in a beautiful apartment. She sees her daughter and has the satisfaction of knowing that her little girl will be happy. When her "guests " have left, she goes back to selling apples, but has the memory of being a lady for a day.

The film is a gentle satire of class distinction. Do clothes make the person? Or is it that innate sense that makes Apple Annie into the mother of whom a girl can be proud? The film's supporting cast includes Jean Parker as the daughter, Walter Connolly as the fiancé's father and Guy Kibbee as a judge who has a soft spot in his heart for Annie and goes along with the scheme. Much of the comedy comes from the characters inhabiting Dave's world.

The film, Capra, Riskin and Robson were nominated for Oscars, but none were forthcoming. An incident at the awards ceremony has gone down in Hollywood lore: Capra was so sure that he had been named Best Director that when presenter Will Rogers said, "Come and get it, Frank," he bounded down the aisle only to realize that Rogers meant Frank Lloyd, director of *Cavalcade*. The next year, however, a triumphant Capra stepped up to the podium when *It Happened One Night* won all five major awards.

Bette Davis as Apple Annie? Unbelievable, but true. A miscast Davis plays the old lady in *Pocketful of Miracles*, a 1961 production from United Artists. Glenn Ford plays Dave the Dude and Hope Lange is Dave's girlfriend. Even with Capra (who should have known better) directing and a cast which includes Thomas Mitchell, Peter Falk, Sheldon Leonard and Ann-Margret, the remake does not in any way live up to the original.

Like May Robson and Bette Davis, Dick Powell's reign as a male Cinderella is short-lived in Preston Sturges' *Christmas in July*. Sturges was writer and director on this Paramount film, which satirizes the popular American custom of contest-entering. Powell plays a clerk who, in the mistaken belief that he has won $25,000 for a coffee slogan, goes on a shopping spree, paying for everything on credit—buy now, pay later, a forerunner of modern-day practices. He gets gifts for his girl (Ellen Drew), his mother and all of his neighborhood pals.

Pocketful of Miracles (1961): Bette Davis as Apple Annie in this remake of *Lady for a Day*.

When he learns the truth, and he is forced to return everything he has bought, he is sadder but much wiser, of course. All is resolved by the end of the picture, with Powell and Drew hopeful for a bright future by working for it. The two stars are ably supported by such Sturges screwball standbys as Raymond Walburn, William Demarest, Ernest Truex, and Franklin Pangborn.

Buying on credit figures largely in another Dick Powell film, *Hard to Get*, only this time he is not the one who says, "Charge it." He is a struggling architect who, unable to get a job in his field, is riding out the Depression by doubling as a filling station attendant and motel manager. While on the job, he meets Olivia de Havilland, a spoiled heiress. She seeks revenge after he refuses to extend her credit for the gas she has bought (she has no money with her) and then further humiliates her by making "Her Highness" work in the motel to pay off what she owes. The battle of the sexes has begun.

Powell, thinking that Olivia is a maid in the home of a millionaire (who, in reality, is her father), dates her and talks about an architectural project for which he needs financing. The spiteful girl, with the help of her doting daddy (Charles Winninger) and moronic maid (Penny Singleton), sends the poor guy on a fool's errand in pursuit of his dream.

Meanwhile, she tries to fight her growing feelings towards him, which complicates matters. Powell soon catches on to the scheme and wants nothing to do with her or her family, but before "The End" is flashed upon the screen, you know that Cinderfella has won both the girl *and* the money to finance his project. Also in the cast are Thurston Hall as the family butler, Bonita Granville as Olivia's sister, Isabel Jeans as Winninger's wife and Allen Jenkins as Powell's assistant at the filling station.

The film, released by Warner Brothers in 1940, is not one of the better-known screwball comedies, but the premise is a clever one and it does have its moments, especially when the engaging Winninger and the peppery Singleton take center stage. The scene in which the latter impersonates Olivia is a howl. (Singleton, born Dorothy McNulty, went on to fame and fortune as the carnation of Chic Young's lovable cartoon character Blondie on radio and in films.)

If buying on credit is an American tradition, what can we call the millions of dollars we spend each year on lottery tickets? And what about sweepstakes? Hardly a novelty—we all dream the impossible dream. In 1940, Ginger Rogers and Ronald Colman made an RKO film called *Lucky Partners*, a gentle satire on these impossible dreams. It opens with Greenwich Village sketch artist Colman calling out from a window wishing a pretty passerby (Rogers) good luck.

When the girl is suddenly gifted with a brand new ensemble after this chance encounter, she becomes the artist's partner in a sweepstakes ticket and, through it, comes into money. Though she is engaged to a somewhat nerdy insurance salesman (Jack Carson, who gives the movie several very amusing moments in pursuit of his fiancée), she goes to Niagara Falls with Colman, falls in love with him and then finds out that he is a famous painter. He winds up with Ginger, and Carson goes to bed with his policies.

Adapted from a French story by Sacha Guitry ("Bonne Chance"), the film features Spring Byington as Ginger's aunt and Harry Davenport as a small town judge.

Inventor Tom Wakefield gets a lucky break in *Married Before Breakfast* (1937), a minor MGM film. A leading razor company has given him a huge sum of money not to publicize his latest invention, a hair-removing shaving cream that would make razors obsolete. To celebrate, Tom wants to take his fiancée on a cruise. While booking the trip, he meets Kitty Brent. She is engaged also. Her fiancé needs to sell one more insurance policy so that he can get promoted and they can get married. Tom decides to help and, in doing so, embarks on an adventure with Kitty involving cops, cab drivers, firemen and gangsters. He even lands in jail. Before this is straightened out, Tom has lost his lady, which is fine: He has fallen in love with Kitty and she with him. Amazingly, all this has taken place in one day and the two are indeed married before breakfast. Robert Young is Tom and Florence Rice is Kitty. June Clayworth plays Tom's fiancée and Hugh Marlowe is Kitty's intended.

Our next film tells the story of a Cinderella *and* a Cinderfella *and* a fairy godfather: In *The Good Fairy* (first a 1931 Broadway play with Helen Hayes starred), Margaret Sullavan made one of her few forays into screwball comedy and came up with a winner. With a script by Preston Sturges and direction by her then husband William Wyler, she turns in a beguiling performance as a naive young girl with the unlikely name of Luisa Gingle-busher.

Luisa meets a wealthy lecher named Konrad (Frank Morgan) who is attracted to her. To fend off his amorous advances, she invents a husband. Konrad tells her he will help her spouse; the old roue will do this to keep hubby busy, so busy that he, Morgan, will be able to pursue Luisa.

She resists, he persists. She has to produce a husband and does this by picking a name at random from the nearest telephone book. Her choice is struggling lawyer Max Sporum (Herbert Marshall). Rich in *If You Could Only Cook*, in this one, he's as poor as the proverbial church-mouse. By the final reel, Luisa and Max have fallen in love, much to the consternation of Konrad, who now knows the truth. Even so, he will be giving Max the "business": The younger lawyer will be handling the older man's legal affairs. The latter has become the couple's "fairy godfather."

Max is the Cinderfella and Luisa is both the Cinderella and the good fairy who, innocently at the start, has made it all possible. She will marry her "prince" and, with fairy godfather Konrad's help, they will struggle no more. Adding to this scenario are Reginald Owen, Alan Hale, Beulah Bondi, Eric Blore and Cesar Romero.

Deanna Durbin plays the Sullavan role in *I'll Be Yours*, a 1947 Universal remake of the foregoing with Tom Drake as the lawyer and Adolphe Menjou as the philanderer. Six years earlier, Durbin starred in an interesting screwball

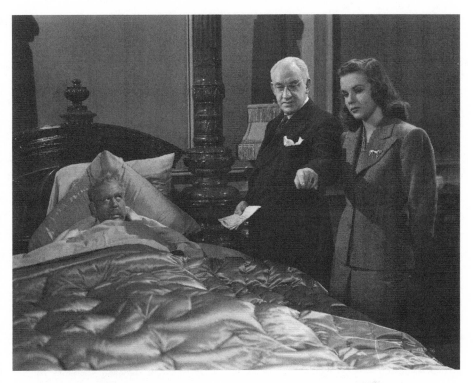

It Started with Eve (1941) with Charles Laughton, Walter Catlett and Deanna Durbin. An ailing grandfather wants to meet his grandson's fiancée; she's not available and Deanna substitutes, with predictable results.

for Universal titled *It Started with Eve*. In this version of the Cinderella story, as in the previously discussed film, there is a fairy godfather, Charles Laughton, seen here in a change-of-pace role: He plays a cantankerous old millionaire whose deathbed wish is to meet his son's fiancée.

The lady in question is unavailable at the moment, so the son (Robert Cummings) brings in the first replacement he can find (Deanna). He introduces her to Dad, who instantly takes a shine to her. Complications set in when the old codger suddenly gets better and when the real fiancée (Margaret Tallichet) is set to arrive on the scene. The Norman Krasna script resolves the "conflict" by the final reel: exit fiancée, enter Durbin, all under the benevolent gaze of Papa Laughton.

It Started with Eve was remade almost a quarter of a century later as *I'd Rather Be Rich* (Universal-International, 1964). In a reversal of the sexes, Sandra Dee plays the Cummings role, Robert Goulet the one enacted by Durbin and Maurice Chevalier is Papa Millionaire. It was not a bad imitation of the original.

As has already been seen, the plotline of many a screwball comedy turns on a case of mistaken identity. In *Easy Living*, Jean Arthur is thought to be Edward Arnold's sweetie, in *If You Could Only Cook*, she thinks that Herbert Marshall is as down-and-out as she, and in *Hard to Get*, Dick Powell mistakes Olivia de Havilland for her own maid. In a 1938 release from Universal, the heroine takes part in a scheme which involves her being mistaken for a wealthy heiress: Danielle Darrieux, a French actress unfamiliar to many American movie-goers, is top-cast in *The Rage of Paris*. She is paired with two well-known leading men of the era, Douglas Fairbanks, Jr., and Louis Hayward, plus a pair of screwball veterans, Helen Broderick and Mischa Auer.

Mlle. Darrieux plays Nicole de Cortillon, who loses her job in the Casino de France, a posh hotel, and finds another as an artist's model. She goes to the wrong address and starts to disrobe in front of Fairbanks, who immediately suspects blackmail.

The plot thickens when, after extricating herself from this mess, she agrees to a "get rich" scheme thought up by her friends Broderick and Auer (who could be thought of as her fairy godparents). Cinderella/Nicole will take up residence in an expensive hotel and set her cap for millionaire Louis Hayward.

The mixture boils over when Fairbanks, a friend of Hayward's, reappears. He tries to save his buddy from the "imposter" only to fall in love with her himself. There is another screwball happy ending: Fairbanks and his French pastry are in a clinch as Broderick and Auer look on approvingly.

Three Blind Mice (Fox, 1938) features Loretta Young, Marjorie Weaver and Pauline Moore as sisters seeking their destiny in California. They have a small inheritance and, upon their arrival on the West Coast, use their money to register in a fancy hotel.

Loretta poses as a rich socialite, while the other two pretend to be her staff. They meet Joel McCrea, whom they think is rich (he is not), David Niven, who has some money, and bartender Stuart Erwin, who is actually a millionaire. After several screwball misunderstandings, the girls find out that McCrea is not wealthy, but by now, Loretta realizes that he is the one she loves. Niven doesn't know it, but his true love is Weaver, while Moore and Erwin round out the sextet. The film was enjoyed by audiences during those hectic years before the outbreak of war and served as a blueprint for other productions to come.

Two remakes, both musicals, were filmed at Fox, one in 1941 and the other in 1946. First came *Moon Over Miami* starring Betty Grable, Carole Landis and Charlotte Greenwood as the plotters, while Don Ameche, Robert Cummings and Jack Haley play the men in their lives. The film was a hit during the war years when Grable was the pin-up darling of the armed forces.

The later film, *Three Little Girls in Blue*, is set in Atlantic City in the early 1900s and stars June Haver, Vivian Blaine and Vera-Ellen. Enticed by them are George Montgomery, Frank Lattimore and Charles Smith.

And then there is Adolphe Menjou, who becomes a "bachelor father" in the 1948 United Artists production *The Bachelor's Daughters*. The plot again involves Cinderellas in search for rich husbands, but this one has an interesting twist. Menjou plays Mr. Moody, a distinguished-looking department store floorwalker who, with his assistant Molly (Billie Burke), is persuaded to become the "parents" of four beautiful young salesclerks on the lookout for suitable husbands. Playing the ladies are Claire Trevor, Jane Wyatt, Ann Dvorak and Gail Russell. The quartet rent a nice home on Long Island and pretend to be rich heiresses. Three of the girls get married, as do Menjou and Burke.

Chapter Eight

Show Business Screwballs

Several screwball comedies use the world of show business as a backdrop. From the time of the Barrymores (Lionel, Ethel and John), Mary Pickford and Douglas Fairbanks, Charlie Chaplin and the Gish Sisters (Lillian and Dorothy) up to the present, the public has been interested in the glamour surrounding the entertainment industry.

Unlike the electronic age in which we get to see and hear all the news and chit-chat fit (or not so fit) for our eyes and ears, 1930s audiences usually got their gossip laundered to fit each image. Hedda (Hopper), Louella (Parsons), Walter Winchell and others covered the celebs in newspapers and on the radio.

Since the public was so fascinated with the comings and goings of their favorites, the petted and pampered "haves" of the era, the lifestyles of these rich and famous icons became cannon fodder for the ever-grinding cameras and also ripe for satire. Enter the screwball comedies to be discussed in this chapter. Each contains the basic elements of the genre: the battle of the sexes, broad satire and some bits of purely physical comedy.

One of the funnier battles of the sexes is to be found in the theatrically oriented *It's Love I'm After*. Take two tempestuous performers with colossal egos who, underneath all the bombast, love each other, but have postponed their nuptials several times for one reason or another. Mix lightly with a young heiress who imagines herself in love with the male half of the team and let it come to a boil when the actress decides to take matters into her own hands. Voila—we have the premise of a screwball classic.

Bette Davis and Leslie Howard star as the petulant performers who, as the film opens, are snarling and hissing at each other during a scene from *Romeo and Juliet* (he accuses her of over-playing while she says he's showing off to a pretty girl at every performance they give). Their grievances, of course, are more imaginary than real. The fun begins when one of the pretty faces (Olivia de Havilland) becomes a fly in the ointment by feeding Howard's vanity

It's Love I'm After (1937) with Bette Davis and Leslie Howard: Temperament vs. love, Broadway style. Which will win out?

and professing her love for him. Her fiancé (Patric Knowles) asks the actor to disillusion her and Howard agrees. As a house guest of Olivia's family, Howard is boorish and nasty, but not until Davis shows up portraying the wronged wife, complete with children, does the impressionable Olivia go back to where she belongs—into the arms of Knowles, while Howard is back where he belongs—with Bette. Also in the cast are Spring Byington, Eric Blore and Bonita Granville.

The acting couple of *It's Love I'm After* are, in a sense, aristocratic, albeit of the theater. In *Fools for Scandal* (Warner Brothers, 1938), French actor Fernand Gravet, a now forgotten personality whom Hollywood tried and failed to make a major star, portrays Rene Viladel, an impoverished nobleman who meets Hollywood film star Kay Winters (Carole Lombard) on a street in Paris. She is unaware of his social status and is intrigued by him, but is engaged to stolid insurance salesman Philip Chester (Ralph Bellamy, so fans of screwball will know how *this* scenario ends). A scene ensues wherein Gravet is to meet Lombard, but he must first get his suit from the pawn shop. It comes late and he dashes to her dressed in two rugs which are grabbed off him by two passing women. She goes to London, still unaware of his title, and he follows.

At a party, his friends make Gravet cook a dinner and, as a joke, Lombard says she'll hire him. To her chagrin, he turns up next morning in her bedroom serving her breakfast, breaking into a song bearing the film's title. There are many more screwball scenes before the marquis reveals his true identity and he and the movie star wind up together. Also in the cast are Allen Jenkins as Gravet's American sidekick and Marie Wilson as Lombard's maid. The musical team of Richard Rodgers and Lorenz Hart was hired to provide this film's songs but most of them were cut from the final print.

Many movie stars yearn for all the publicity they can get on their way to the big time. Once there, they talk about preserving their privacy, but are somewhat miffed when they are not recognized. A true dichotomy, Hollywood style.

Ginger Rogers certainly knew the feeling in real life and in 1935, RKO assigned her to a project titled *In Person*. The storyline revolves around an exhausted actress who tries to escape her adoring public by assuming outlandish disguises and hiding out in the country. While in hiding, she meets George Brent who at first doesn't know that she is a star. When he finds out, he says he couldn't care less. This, of course, piques her interest and she wants to get to know him better. By the final fadeout, they have fallen in love.

An actor who was considered by most film critics to be a second-tier star, George Brent made a career out of being leading man to many female leads, including two actress wives, Ruth Chatterton and Ann Sheridan.

In the decade of the 1930s, Lucille Ball was a rising young player in "B" films at RKO. By 1938, she had status enough to star in several minor films for that studio, among them two in which she plays a daffy actress who has a big problem on her hands, an off-the-wall press agent (Jack Oakie). Both she and her agent have one goal in mind: stardom for her. He devises several hare-brained schemes for getting her name in the papers and, reluctantly, she goes along with them. In *The Affairs of Annabel*, she hires out as a maid, falls into the hands of a pair of wanted criminals and lands in jail. In the supporting cast are Ruth Donnelly, Fritz Feld and Thurston Hall. Before the year had ended, the follow-up *Annabel Takes a Tour* had been released. In this film, the ditsy one makes a round of public appearances organized by her zany press agent to revitalize her flagging career. In her travels, the actress meets a nobleman (Ralph Forbes) who is an author of romantic novels. She falls for him, dreaming of retirement, and finds out that not only is there a wife, there are also children. Her castle in the air has evaporated and all she can do is look forward to more wheeling and dealing from her agent. The

Annabel films had been envisioned as a "B" series but after the release of the second film, the project was discontinued.

As an RKO contract player, Lucy did appear in some "A" pictures, one of which stars Irene Dunne. *Joy of Living* tells the tale of an overworked and repressed Broadway musical comedy star whose acquisitive family is taking advantage of her earning power and living it up. Among the members of this grasping family are Alice Brady, Guy Kibbee, Frank Milan and the peripatetic Miss Ball as Dunne's younger sister.

Enter shipping tycoon–playboy Douglas Fairbanks Jr., who teaches the young woman all about doing zany things and the "joy of living" plus the equal bliss of getting her shiftless family off her back. Though the 1938 release contains some melodies by Jerome Kern and Dorothy Fields and has good performances from such screwball stalwarts as Eric Blore, Franklin Pangborn and Billy Gilbert, it did not fare as well at the box office as some other Dunne films and can be considered one of her few screwball misses. Where were Cary Grant or Melvyn Douglas?

When musical movies of the 1930s are mentioned, the name of teenage Deanna Durbin is fondly remembered. In 1940 at the age of eighteen, she ventured into screwball comedy with *It's a Date* from Universal. Pamela Drake (Durbin) is a precocious teenager blessed with a beautiful voice. Georgia, her mother (Kay Francis), is a famous stage star. The latter is given a part she is dying to play and goes to Hawaii to rehearse.

Little does she know that after she's left, the writer of the play, Carl Ober (S.Z. Sakall), has given the part to Pamela. The latter now sails to Hawaii to work on her lines. On board, she meets John Arlen (Walter Pidgeon), an attractive, wealthy businessman who comes to the wrong conclusion: He thinks she's an unhappy girl who may be trying to end it all. They fall overboard in a true screwball scene. He spends a lot of time with her and she imagines herself in love with him.

While docking, Arlen meets Georgia and they are attracted to each other, he not knowing that she is Pamela's mother. They meet again at a dinner planned by the youngster. In another screwball scene, he arranges with a waiter to get him out of his "predicament," but seeing Georgia, he doesn't need any excuses to leave, to the befuddlement of the waiter.

The end of the tale has Pamela telling Mama she wants to marry John. They go to the Governor's Ball and the governor (Eugene Pallette, in a small but very funny bit) helps Arlen by announcing that Pamela will sing so that Arlen can make his case with Georgia. Not to be believed is the inane way he finally proposes to her. (As we have seen, anything can happen in screwball.) She accepts, which leaves the way clear for her daughter to get her big break. Of course, in between laughs, Durbin sings four songs.

It's a Date was remade by MGM in 1950. *Nancy Goes to Rio* stars Jane

Powell in the Durbin role with Ann Sothern and Barry Sullivan taking over the adult roles. Supporting the trio are Louis Calhern and Hans Conried. The film is almost as good as the original with the advantage of Technicolor and Powell's singing.

Because of Him (Universal, 1946) shows a grown-up Deanna as a stage-struck waitress intent upon a career in the theater. By singing an old Irish melody, she persuades an aging actor (Charles Laughton) to give her a job, much to the chagrin of the show's playwright. Seen in this role is Franchot Tone. It's another battle of the sexes, Broadway style.

All is resolved when the fledgling actress triumphs and the playwright realizes that he is smitten. In the cast are veteran screwballers Helen Broderick and Donald Meek. It's a likable film, mainly for fans of its singing star.

The Moon's Our Home (Paramount, 1936) is just as notable for its star team as for its delightful screwball screenplay.

In the late 1920s and early 1930s, Margaret Sullavan and Henry Fonda had been members of the Princeton Players, an East Coast repertory theater group which was not only the jumping-off point for their careers, but spawned that of a tall lanky actor named Jimmy Stewart. By the time filming started on *The Moon's Our Home*, Fonda and Sullavan had been married and divorced. A bit of dialogue in the film is very apropos in light of this:

HE: Haven't I seen you somewhere before?
SHE: Possibly—I'm the girl you married once.
HE: I knew it! I never forget a face.

The two stars played off each other rather nicely in the film and for a while, rumors persisted that they would remarry. Nothing of the sort occurred, but the resultant reams of publicity boded well for the story of an impulsive romance between a movie star and a famous travel writer, each of whom has never heard of the other.

Sullavan is Cherry Chester, a temperamental movie star, born Sara Brown into a wealthy family. Fonda is Anthony Amberton, real name John Smith. They are on a train bound for New York and when he hears that Cherry Chester is on the train, he wonders aloud whether a Cherry Chester is a new kind of soft drink. She, on her part, is reading his latest travel guide: "'Mr. Amberton and his camel,'" she reads. "Oh, I see. He's the one with the hat on." But they are soon reluctantly attracted to each other.

They land up in New England, and Cherry falls into a snow bank. Amberton pulls her out and they make a bet: She will marry him only if she fails to stand up with a pair of skis on. She falls and they marry, but separate soon after.

They are miserable apart and Amberton tries to make up to no avail until the madcap final scene, which takes place at an airport. He has Cherry put into a straitjacket and kisses her until she gives in to him. Does Screwball *have* to make sense?

The film, adapted from a *Cosmopolitan* magazine serial by Faith Baldwin, contains several bits of witty dialogue contributed by Dorothy Parker and her husband, Alan Campbell, and has an excellent supporting cast including Walter Brennan, Beulah Bondi and Margaret Hamilton.

In *No Time for Comedy* (Warner Brothers, 1940), the aforementioned Jimmy Stewart is playwright Gaylord Esterbrook, husband of actress Linda Paige (Rosalind Russell). He is known for his comedies, but yearns to write an important serious drama. What now flows from his pen is really awful.

Linda knows how bad the work is and tries to let him down easy, but a flirty patroness of the arts (Genevieve Tobin, in real life the wife of the film's director William Keighley) encourages his endeavor. Her husband (Charles Ruggles) loves her and indulges her in every way possible. He doesn't think much of the play, but goes along with his wife.

Esterbrook and Paige almost split up over this but all works out well when he finally realizes that his flair for making people laugh is a gift given to a select few and is to be cherished. Moviegoers of 1940, anxiously following the course of the war in Europe, got the message and the film did well at the box office.

Another Broadway playwright figures prominently in *Bedtime Story* (Columbia, 1941). This fellow (Fredric March) has written several successful plays for his wife, played by Loretta Young. They are the toast of Broadway, but after seven years of "The Business," she decides to leave the stage for the domestic life on a farm in Connecticut. "Nay, nay to that," says March. This battle of the sexes leads to irreconcilable differences and she leaves him. She then meets a banker (played by Allyn Joslyn), the direct opposite of her husband.

March tries every which way to get her back to where he thinks she belongs. After several screwball mishaps, including a funny car chase, he accomplishes his goal. The finale finds Miss Loretta taking bows. Adding to the festivities are such genre veterans as Robert Benchley and Eve Arden.

In 1938 a team of real Broadway writers, Bella and Sam Spewack, sold the rights to their stage hit to Warner Brothers. What emerged was the satirical *Boy Meets Girl.* James Cagney and Pat O'Brien star as two wacky writers who love to play practical jokes. Just for the fun of it, they dream up a Western for the studio's egotistical cowboy star (played by Dick Foran) in which he will be playing second fiddle to an infant. Cagney and O'Brien are very ably supported by a cast which includes Ralph Bellamy, Frank McHugh, Marie Wilson and an up-and-coming young actor named Ronald Reagan. With rapid fire dialogue and terrific performances from its stars, *Boy Meets Girl* bounces from one absurdity to another with the resilience of a rubber ball.

Originally, the film was to star the popular team of Olsen and Johnson, plus Marion Davies in the role eventually played by Marie Wilson, but the casting went awry, so the second string was called in. No matter—the film did a brisk business at the box office.

The action of *Stand-In* (United Artists, 1937) takes place at a mythical film studio in Hollywood. Leslie Howard is top-cast in this spoof of studio politics and Joan Blondell is seen in the title role. Howard plays Atterbury Dodd, a stuffy accountant who has been sent to Hollywood by his New York office to balance the books of an almost bankrupt Colossal Studios. He meets all sorts of personalities on the lot including perky stand-in Lester Plum (Blondell), who teaches him about life and love and helps him save the studio from almost certain disaster.

Humphrey Bogart is third-billed as Doug Quintain, an eccentric, cynical but basically honest director who gives his basic philosophy to Howard in one concise sentence: "In Hollywood, when you turn the other cheek, they kick it." Others in the cast include Alan Mowbray as an unscrupulous director, Jack Carson as a shady public relations man and Marla Shelton as the studio vamp, once married to Bogart's character.

Sylvia Sidney plays a stand-in of a vastly different sort in *Thirty Day Princess* (Paramount, 1934). An aspiring actress looking for work, she is hired to impersonate a princess who has suddenly taken ill. In the fulfillment of her "royal" duties, Sylvia is sent on a good-will tour of the United States. Her comings and going are duly reported in newspapers; one reporter assigned to her is the good-looking Cary Grant. The bogus princess falls for this member of the Fourth Estate and when all is revealed she ends up in his arms. Veteran character actor Edward Arnold is featured in this fairly early example of the screwball comedy. With a script by Preston Sturges and Grant as the leading man, this gentle satire on theatrical royalty was a hit.

MGM starred Jean Harlow in two early screwballs with show business backgrounds, *Blonde Bombshell* (1933) and *The Girl from Missouri* (1934). By 1937, the studio's platinum blonde sensation was dead. At the age of 26, she had much to live for: money, a fabulous career and the love of her life, actor William Powell. She was considered one of the biggest and brightest stars in Hollywood; one can only guess as to what she might have accomplished had she lived.

Blonde Bombshell is a devastating satire on the inner workings of Hollywood and the fabled studio system. Harlow is seen as a hard-working actress who goes from picture to picture without any time off. She is also under the thumb of a studio publicity agent (played by Lee Tracy) and put upon by her screwball family who are grasping and unfeeling. Tired of being exploited by those around her, she skips out and meets a man she thinks she's in love with, but finds out he's been hired by Tracy to lure her back to Hollywood.

She does go back and chases the agent around the studio lot, but is a little wiser than before. The two stars are ably supported by Franchot Tone as the unscrupulous suitor, Frank Morgan, Pat O'Brien, Isabel Jewell and Louise Beavers.

In *The Girl from Missouri*, Jean is a chorus girl with principles. Still and all, she is on the make for a rich husband. She will not, however, sacrifice her principles and integrity to attain her goal. She doesn't have to: She meets handsome, wealthy Franchot Tone. (Type casting in this role: Tone, in real life, had a wealthy East Coast background.) In support of the two stars are Patsy Kelly, who supplies most of the laughs, Lionel Barrymore, Lewis Stone and Alan Mowbray.

This chapter would not be complete without two show business screwballs that take place on a train. The first is one of the greatest comedies of all time, the second a highly amusing but not very well-known film.

Twentieth Century (Columbia, 1934), an inspired bit of lunacy, stars a scenery-chewing John Barrymore as egomaniacal Broadway producer-director Oscar Jaffe. Oscar saw a small time actress with the improbable name of Mildred Plotka and recognized talent. Under his tutelage, she became Lily Garland and is soon the toast of Broadway. The role is played by Carole Lombard, who matches her co-star in every way, line for line, shout for shout, quip for quip.

When Lily appeared in Oscar's play before her climb to fame, she enacted the role of a Southern belle. When the scene called for a scream, Oscar was not satisfied with the way she projected, so he stuck a pin into her rear. The film's director, Howard Hawks, then cuts to Lily accepting flowers from her adoring fans.

Two tempestuous, headstrong personalities are bound to go toe to toe on more than one occasion; Lily and Jaffe are no exceptions. She feels he has a stranglehold on her career and he thinks she should be grateful to him for the rest of her life. The two bicker and snarl at each other with such intensity that she decides to declare her independence from his manipulations and goes to Hollywood. When Oscar hears of her departure, he wails, "She's left me." His partner, Oliver Webb (screwball veteran Walter Connolly), aware that he is being theatrical, retorts, "Say the word and I'll kill myself."

Lily-less now, Oscar's next artistic endeavors come to naught. Down and out in Chicago, being pursued by creditors, he sneaks out of town and boards the Twentieth Century Limited, bound for New York. And who is coming East on that same train? Why, none other than Lily Garland with a boyfriend (played by Ralph Forbes) in tow. The latter is not around for long.

It is inevitable that these two bombastic "lovebirds" wind up with each other. In the film's final scenes, they are doing a play together. He patronizes and she screams.

Twentieth Century (1934) with Ralph Forbes, Carole Lombard and John Barry-more. A Broadway producer makes an actress a star, loses her and gets her back. Barrymore is at his outrageous best, goading Lombard. This film made Carole a major star.

Ben Hecht and Charles MacArthur, who had co-authored the successful stage hit, also collaborated on the screen version. It is interesting to note that the play begins on the train, whereas the film goes back in time to show how Jaffe has transformed Mildred into Lily Garland. Both writers felt that opening up the narrative would give more scope to the film. They were cor-rect.

United Artists–Hal Roach Productions released *their* train screwball in 1941. *Broadway Limited* stars Leonid Kinskey as a zany Hollywood director on a cross-country publicity tour with the star of his latest production. The latter is played by Marjorie Woodworth. Kinskey insists that she pretend she is a mother to make her seem less frivolous in the eyes of her fans. She has found a baby who they think is the kidnapped child of a wealthy family. Woodworth and Kinskey keep the baby hidden and then announce that he is the child everybody's been looking for.

Aiding and abetting the two are Dennis O'Keefe as a doctor who falls for the star, Victor McLaglen as the train engineer, Patsy Kelly as Kinskey's put-upon secretary and ZaSu Pitts as a truly peculiar passenger. Though a minor production, there are many screwball incidents including McLaglen reading "The Three Bears" to the baby, the antics involved in hiding the child from the police and anything in which Pitts is involved.

The last scene shows that the baby is not the kidnapped child and Kinskey tearing his hair out—he has lost his star to matrimony while secretary Kelly goes off with McLaglan.

Chapter Nine

The Screwball Literati:
Anything for a Story

Before the advent of television, even before radio was a part of the American scene, newspapers gave us all the news that was fit to print. People devoured their morning papers along with their breakfast coffee, and the evening edition was what Dad curled up with while Mom put the finishing touches on dinner.

That the Fourth Estate was an integral part of American life and had a powerful influence upon an avid reading public is a given. The newspaper industry was ripe for satirizing, and that's just what Hollywood did. Some of the finest films of all time were the result.

Newspaper editor Walter Burns is trying to stop his star reporter, Hildy Johnson, from getting married and quitting the profession. The conniving, sneaky Burns will do anything to lure Hildy away from his prospective bride, so when an anarchist is sentenced to be executed, the editor assigns the story to the groom-to-be, telling him that this could be the scoop of his career, hoping the bird dog in the reporter will make him forget about wedded bliss and stick to what he knows best. Such is the premise of *The Front Page* (United Artists, 1931).

The film is based upon the 1928 Broadway hit by the aforementioned team of Ben Hecht and Charles MacArthur. It is a satire on political corruption, which runs rampant even today, and journalistic ethics, which have often been somewhat questionable.

Before becoming playwrights, both men had been reporters in Chicago, and the characters of Burns and Johnson had their basis in real life. Reporters would do anything for a scoop, from misquoting to stretching the truth and changing the facts in a story.

The film stars Adolphe Menjou as Burns and Pat O'Brien as Hildy, and they parlayed the rapid-fire, wisecracking script into a box office hit. Its action takes place in the press room of a courthouse with different characters wandering in and out of the setting. They include George E. Stone as Earl Williams, the condemned man (he has been convicted of killing a policeman and is scheduled to be hanged) and Mae Clarke, famous for having half a grapefruit pushed in her face by James Cagney in *The Public Enemy*, as Molly Malloy, a prostitute friend of the prisoner; also Edward Everett Horton, Frank McHugh and Slim Summerville as news hounds in search of "the story of a lifetime." The film, director Lewis Milestone and Menjou picked up Oscar nominations, but there were no winners among them.

Although *The Front Page*, like some other films mentioned in this book, predates the "official" beginnings of screwball comedy by a couple of years, it must be included here, not only because it *is* screwball in every sense of the word but also because of its relationship to one of the most celebrated films of the genre, *His Girl Friday* (Columbia, 1940). The latter production is unique in that, as a remake, it has surpassed the original in both critical and popular acclaim and is still fondly remembered many decades later by older moviegoers. Younger generations can watch and enjoy it on television stations replaying the "Golden Oldies" or on a DVD.

The genesis of *His Girl Friday* lies in the genius of Howard Hawks. The veteran filmmaker, wearing two hats as both producer and director, saw the project as a kind of love story and made Hildy a woman. With this new development a *fait accompli*, the storyline had to be altered: It now becomes a newspaper story plus a battle of the sexes with the right players assembled.

The casting of Cary Grant as the scheming editor was easy but getting an actress for the role of Hildy was not. According to legend, the list of female stars who turned down the role includes Katharine Hepburn, Irene Dunne, Jean Arthur, Margaret Sullavan, Carole Lombard and Claudette Colbert. But Connecticut-born Rosalind Russell jumped at the opportunity. She and her co-star, responding to Hawks' fast pace and frenetic direction, including overlapping dialogue, turn in inspired performances.

As the film opens, Burns, once married to his star reporter, wants her back, but Hildy is engaged to stodgy insurance agent Bruce Baldwin (Ralph Bellamy—who else?). Hoping to change her mind, Burns assigns her to a major story, the same one as in the earlier film (Earl Williams, the condemned man, is played in this film by John Qualen). Burns practically salivates over the story, which will be a coup for him and the paper—a story so hot that it could help to bring down a corrupt city administration. He also thinks that the newsprint that runs in Hildy's veins will not allow her to become a *hausfrau* in Albany (living with her mother-in-law, no less).

And it doesn't. After several very funny mishaps, Bruce and Mama go back to Albany. Hildy and Walter will try to make a go of it again. As they

His Girl Friday (1940) with Cary Grant and Rosalind Russell, a remake of *The Front Page.* This is one remake that turned out better than the original.

make plans for a honeymoon at Niagara Falls, there is a breaking story coming out of Albany. Walter is gleeful. Albany is on the way to the Falls.

Jack Lemmon and Walter Matthau are Hildy and Walter in the 1974 Universal production of *The Front Page.* An ever more up-to-date version titled *Switching Channels* was released in 1988, by Rank/Ransohoff Productions. It stars Burt Reynolds, Kathleen Turner and Christopher Reeve. Like *His Girl Friday*, the reporter is a lady; however, the action takes place in a television studio. The two films were somewhat popular in their day, but who could touch the Grant-Russell combo?

In between *The Front Page* and *His Girl Friday* RKO put out a film with a similar plot: *There Goes My Girl* (1937) stars Ann Sothern with her frequent leading man, Gene Raymond. Character actor Richard Lane is the Walter Burns–like editor who tries to sabotage reporter Sothern's wedding to Raymond, her opposite on a rival paper. (Their battle of the sexes has always been who can get the scoop first.) Ever the schemer, Lane even invents a murder and in a very funny scene, Ann, true to her calling, abandons Raymond at the altar in pursuit of the hot story.

Another 1937 newspaper plot is featured in Universal's *A Girl with Ideas.* Wendy Barrie stars as a young woman who inherits a newspaper which had once printed unfavorable things about her. She is successful, much to the chagrin of its former owner (Walter Pidgeon). He tries to even the score by faking the kidnapping of her father and giving the story to a rival paper. This battle of the sexes continues until both realize that they can work in tandem, professionally and romantically. Aiding the stars are Dorothea Kent, Samuel S. Hinds and George Barbier.

Anything for a story? How about Loretta Young as June Cameron in *The Doctor Takes a Wife*, a 1940 film from Columbia. She plays an unattached author and feminist to boot. Marriage is the last thing on her mind.

After a chance meeting with medical instructor Dr. Timothy Sterling (Ray Milland, who already has a fiancée), the two are mistaken for husband and wife. The lady, sensing a best seller in the offing, and the man, wanting a full professorship which he can only get if he's married, agree to the deception. The bickering starts, but after a screwball scene involving the fiancée, doctor and author realize that they are in love; the phony marriage will become a reality. Also in the cast are Reginald Gardiner, Gail Patrick and Edmund Gwenn.

"Oh what a tangled web we weave, When first we practice to deceive": These words of William Shakespeare describe in essence the plotline of *Nothing Sacred,* Ben Hecht's 1937 satire on the press and its credulous readers. The opening words of the film reveal what Hecht thinks of his chosen profession: "New York, skyscraper champion of the world, where the slicker and know-it-alls peddle gold bricks to each other, and truth, crushed to earth, rises more phony than a glass eye."

Fredric March and Carole Lombard were at the top of their careers when making this film. Hazel Flagg, deliciously portrayed by Lombard, is a small town girl mistakenly diagnosed as having radium poisoning by her alcoholic doctor (screwball veteran Charles Winninger). A reporter named Wally Cook (March) has been assigned to the obituary page after having pulled a fast one on the public as well as on his newspaper: He had hired a Harlem man to portray "The Sultan of Mazipan" at a lavish banquet. The man's wife (Hattie McDaniel) appeared at the hall with several children, yelling, "That's my husband." Cook's editor Oliver Stone (Walter Connolly) was incensed—therefore the obit page assignment.

Cook sees the Flagg story and persuades Stone to let him cover it. Stone agrees and Wally is off to Warsaw, Vermont. He meets Hazel and is quite sympathetic when she expresses a last wish, to go to New York City. Seeing what a great human interest story this will make, he tells the girl that the paper will grant her wish.

She subsequently finds out that she is not going to die, but delays telling

Wally and Stone. She allows herself to be given the royal treatment. When the reporter and editor find out that they have been taken, there is a battle and Cook takes a sock at Hazel. Then he asks Stone where his sense of chivalry is. How could he allow him (Wally) to hit a defenseless woman? Stone replies to this by saying, "My sense of chivalry? You hit her." To which an exasperated Wally replies, "That's entirely different. I love her." The feeling is mutual. In spite of the "fisticuffs," the film ends with the radium poisoning story petering out and Hazel and Wally on their way to getting married.

The original screenplay by Ben Hecht was so corrosive that producer David Selznick ordered a rewrite and handed the job over to a group of writers headed by Dorothy Parker. The film, an early example of the Technicolor process, premiered at New York's Radio City Music Hall and ran there for four successful weeks. There was a 1954 remake of this classic with Dean Martin and Jerry Lewis, *Living It Up*. This version has Lewis in the Lombard role, Martin as the doctor and Janet Leigh as the reporter. Why mess around with a great film? Answer: The popularity of Dean and Jerry.

Fredric March, as Bill Spencer, is again a reporter in *There Goes My Heart* (United Artists, 1938). He is assigned to track down runaway heiress Joan Butterfield (Virginia Bruce). The latter is befriended by Peggy O'Brien (Patsy Kelly) who doesn't know who Joan is. Peggy gets her new friend a job in Butterfield's department store. There Spencer finds and recognizes Joan. Though he initially seeks to expose her in print, he finds himself falling for her and by the final fade-out, they are on an island he uses as a getaway. The original story was written by newspaper columnist-television host Ed Sullivan.

Others in the supporting cast include Marjorie Main as a shopper harassing the department store clerks, Eugene Pallette as March's editor and Arthur Lake (later typecast as Dagwood Bumstead) as a bumbling photographer.

Several scenes stand out: Patsy Kelly demonstrating a vibrato to anyone who will listen, her rapport with her boyfriend who for years has been studying to be a chiropractor by mail, and Bruce trying to sell a "fireless cooker" to the stubborn Marjorie Main.

Virginia Bruce in *There Goes My Heart* can do without publicity. So can Rosalind Russell in *Design for Scandal* (MGM, 1941). She is Cornelia Potter, a judge who sculpts as a hobby. She has ruled against newspaper tycoon Judson Blair in a costly divorce case. The latter is irate and assigns Jeff Sherman, his top reporter, to humiliate her and get her disbarred. Of course, a battle of the sexes goes on until newsman and judge find mutual agreement and the tycoon is forced to pay the full settlement, a not inconsiderable amount for that era. Walter Pidgeon and Edward Arnold co-star as reporter and boss while the supporting cast includes Lee Bowman, Guy Kibbee, Jean Rogers and Mary Beth Hughes.

Wedding Present (Paramount, 1936) stars Cary Grant and Joan Bennett as rival reporters who are either in love or out of love. When he becomes an editor, she is somewhat angry and decides to marry someone else. Grant disturbs her wedding with police cars and fire engines and, in the confusion, kidnaps her. All turns out for the best and the couple are together in the end. This was a minor film in the careers of both Bennett and Grant.

Another film involving a male-female reporter combo stars Bette Davis and her frequent co-star of the era, George Brent. In *Front Page Woman* (Warner Brothers, 1935), Davis and Brent are rival newshounds determined to scoop each other. The fact that they are romantically involved leads to the familiar battle of the sexes. They are both assigned to the same case which causes comic complications. Featured in the cast are Roscoe Karns and J. Carrol Naish. *Front Page Woman* is a minor venture in the illustrious career of Bette Davis.

A strikingly handsome actor was Tyrone Power, who by 1937 had become a major star. One of his few forays into screwball comedy is *Love Is News*. Supported by a cast including old friend and frequent co-star Don Ameche, Power plays reporter Steve Layton, who continually prints scathing remarks about heiress Tony Gateson (Loretta Young). Annoyed and angered by what he has been doing, she turns the tables on him and announces their engagement. It is now his turn to be annoyed and angered. The two pick at each other until they realize that their theme song should be "You Were Meant for Me."

The same script, tailored to fit the talents of Betty Grable, emerged in 1943 as *Sweet Rosie O'Grady* with Robert Young as the reporter, and in its original form as *That Wonderful Urge* (1948). Both remakes were released by Fox. Eleven years after his first stint as the breezy newsman, Power is at it again, this time with the lovely Gene Tierney as the subject of his barbs.

The year 1935 saw the emergence of Fred MacMurray as a major star. His debut vehicle was Paramount's *The Gilded Lily* in which his "quarry" was Claudette Colbert. MacMurray is Peter Dawes, a popcorn-eating, bench-sitting reporter who in a series of articles makes fellow bench-sitter Lillian David (Colbert), a typist, into a celebrity. She meets Charles Gray (Ray Milland), an unemployed Englishman, and offers to help him. She soon finds out that he is really a wealthy nobleman named Charles Granville, becomes romantically involved with him and follows him to England.

There she is exploited and, because of her celebrity, is offered a singing job—but she is no singer. She is humiliated and returns to America and her popcorn-munching reporter. For this film, MacMurray was brought to Hollywood from New York where he had appeared in the Broadway hit *Roberta*.

English actress Madeleine Carroll plays a bored socialite in *Cafe Society*. Her heiress is in the same boat as Tony Gateson in *Love Is News*. In the first of four films made with the lovely blonde star, Fred MacMurray is a reporter who constantly heckles Madeleine and her crowd for their dilettante ways. On a bet, the young woman weds her "tormenter," intending to be an embarrassment to him. Instead, in true screwball style, this battle of the sexes becomes a love match and she is brought down from the glitz of her life to the reality of his.

After her 1940 hit on Broadway in *The Philadelphia Story*, Katharine Hepburn could write her own ticket at MGM. Which she proceeded to do. *Woman of the Year* was the result. Hepburn asked for and got Spencer Tracy as her co-star. Their legendary meeting has since been recorded for posterity:

> She, upon meeting him for the first time said, "I fear, Mr. Tracy, that I'm a bit tall for you." For years it was presumed that Tracy retorted, "Don't worry, Miss Hepburn, I'll cut you down to size."

It is now thought that writer-producer-director Joseph Mankiewicz was the author of that famous putdown.

Take a sportswriter named Sam Craig, match him up with political columnist Tess Harding and you have the plotline of *Woman of the Year*. Their courtship (he takes her to a ballgame and watches her in fascination as she proceeds to ask one inane question after another) and subsequent marriage are strained by opposing ideas and temperaments and he walks out. After she is given a talking-to by her wise aunt (Fay Bainter), Tess (who knows nothing about a kitchen) tries to make breakfast for Sam. Both realize that they belong together and that there is compromise in a marriage and that radical changes are not necessary for happiness together.

The film, produced by Mankiewicz and directed by George Stevens (the latter by order of Hepburn in a communiqué to MGM studio head Louis B. Mayer), was a resounding hit and paved the way for more of that special Tracy-Hepburn magic. The husband-and-wife team of Renee Taylor and Joseph Bologna starred in a 1976 TV-movie remake. There is no magic in it.

Designing Woman (MGM, 1957) is somewhat similar to *Woman of the Year* in that a sports reporter (Gregory Peck) marries a woman (Lauren Bacall) who is not a part of the world he knows (she is a well-paid fashion designer). They try to compromise and therein lies the screwball aspects of the film. The couple goes to a sports event in which she is out of her element. Other screwball scenes have Peck and his cronies involved in a poker game while Bacall is entertaining her friends in another room; Peck in his former girlfriend's apartment, hiding when Bacall comes marching in; and Peck being confronted by screwball gangsters. Directed by Vincente Minnelli, the cast features Dolores Gray as the ex-girlfriend and Chuck Connors as a shady character gunning for Peck.

The screwball comedy great Sheridan Whiteside is the central figure in *The Man Who Came to Dinner* (Warner Brothers, 1942), the film version of the Broadway hit co-authored by Moss Hart and George S. Kaufman. As played by Monty Woolley, who had created the role in the play, Whiteside is irascible, cantankerous, overbearing, self-absorbed and hilariously funny.

Based upon an actual personality (Alexander Woollcott, acerbic wit, critic and charter member of the famous New York Algonquin Hotel Round Table), Whiteside speaks before a literary club meeting in a small Ohio town at Christmas time, breaks his hip and must remain at the home of his hostess, Mrs. Stanley. On what he considers his best behavior, he proceeds to take over the household and the lives of the Stanley family, wreaking havoc all around him.

The screen rights to the play were purchased by Warner Brothers at the request of Bette Davis, who envisioned it as a vehicle for herself as Whiteside's secretary with John Barrymore playing the title role. When the latter proved incapable of remembering his lines, the juicy role went to the bearded Woolley, who almost walked away with the picture.

Besides parodying Woollcott, the script has fun with several other notables of the era. Weaving in and out of the scenario are Ann Sheridan as Lorraine Sheldon, Jimmy Durante as Banjo and Reginald Gardiner as Beverly Carlton, doing devastating take-offs on Gertrude Lawrence, Harpo Marx and Noël Coward, respectively. Davis as Maggie Cutler and Richard Travis as small town newsman Bert Jefferson inject a bit of romance into the proceedings. This turn of events does not make Whiteside happy. He tries to meddle, but is cut off at the pass. Hilarious scenes include Whiteside getting a present of penguins, Lorraine being locked in a mummy case and Banjo making his entrance into the scenario.

Heading the supporting cast are such veterans as Billie Burke and Grant Mitchell as the Stanleys, Whiteside's host and hostess, and Mary Wickes as Miss Preen, the much put-upon nurse. Her dialogue as she leaves the Stanley home is a classic:

> I am not only walking out on this case, Mr. Whiteside. I am leaving the nursing profession. I became a nurse because all my life, ever since I was a little girl, I was filled with the idea of serving a suffering humanity. After one month with you, Mr. Whiteside, I am going to work in a munitions factory.
>
> ... If Florence Nightingale had ever nursed you, Mr. Whiteside, she would have married Jack the Ripper instead of founding the Red Cross.

June Bride (Warners, 1948) has enough of the screwball element to warrant inclusion in this chapter. Bette Davis' leading man is Robert Montgomery. They are a typical screwball couple—sophisticated, adversarial and in

The Man Who Came to Dinner (1941) with Ann Sheridan, Richard Travis, Bette Davis and Monty Woolley. A devastating satire. What mischief is the bearded one up to?

love, though they fight it. The film lampoons the magazine industry, playing up the "anything for a story" angle until things begin to unravel.

Davis plays a high-powered magazine editor and Montgomery a writer and her former lover who jilted her for the life of a roving correspondent. The only job he can find when he returns to America is on her magazine. He would like to resume their relationship, but she is adamant in her refusal: "I had measles once. Now I'm immune," she tells him.

Their first assignment as a team is to cover a small town wedding in Indiana. The only catch is that the bride and the groom are in love, but not with each other. The bride's kid sister (played by Betty Lynn) loves the intended groom and, with Bette's help, snares him, while her older sister goes off with the one *she* really loves. There is a June Bride for the magazine to cover, not the original one, but no matter, it's all in the family. Bette, with stars in her eyes, agrees to follow Montgomery around the globe if that's where he chooses to go. Funny scenes include the bride's mother getting a massage and Montgomery getting drunk on apple cider (spiked, of course). In the cast as the older sister is Barbara Bates while her parents are played by Tom Tully and Fay Bainter.

Ten years before, Montgomery made a screwball comedy for MGM titled *Three Loves Has Nancy,* co-starring Janet Gaynor and Franchot Tone. Gaynor, as Nancy, is a jilted bride who comes to New York in search of her fiancé. She meets a famous author (Montgomery) on the train and, after a series of funny incidents, winds up in his apartment during a party. His girlfriend is not too thrilled with this and departs saying, "I've had a lovely evening, but this wasn't it."

Third-billed Tone plays Montgomery's publisher who falls in love with Nancy and wants to marry her. Finally realizing that *he* loves Nancy galvanizes the author into action and the last scene finds him racing to catch the honeymoon ship.

Another writer in *Honeymoon for Three,* a Warner Brothers 1941 production, has troubles of his own. George Brent is Kenneth Bixby, a famous novelist, and Ann Sheridan (who in real life was Brent's wife at the time) plays Anne Rogers, his long-suffering secretary. Julie Wilson (Osa Massen), an old flame of Kenneth's who thinks she's been the inspiration for his latest book, tries to rekindle a romance with him though she is married to a man named Harvey (hilariously played by veteran screwballer Charles Ruggles).

Anne is not thrilled by this turn of events and with the help of Julie's cousin (Jane Wyman) tries her best to throw a monkey wrench into Julie's plans. Because of this ever-loyal secretary, the novelist avoids a nasty legal situation and winds up with her—she has always loved him.

Warren William as the novelist, Joan Blondell as the secretary and Genevieve Tobin as the flirtatious wife, appear in an earlier version of this film in 1933. Its title is *Goodbye Again,* also from Warner Brothers.

Jealousy rears its ugly head in *The Feminine Touch* (MGM, 1941) when professor John Hathaway (Don Ameche) writes a book on that very subject and takes his wife Julie (Rosalind Russell) to New York on a public relations trip. Julie soon suspects him of having an affair with another woman, played by the glamorous and sophisticated Kay Francis. Van Heflin plays John's publisher who casts amorous glances at Roz. Her husband insists he is not jealous. But then the triangle becomes a quadrangle when Roz uses the publisher to make Ameche jealous. The finale has the men engaged in a fistfight with Roz backing Ameche and Kay helping Heflin, with whom she has always been in love.

A triangle of a sort is the premise of the 1941 MGM film *Married Bachelor.* It can be readily seen from the title that this is a screwball comedy. Robert Young stars as Randolph Haven, who goes into partnership with a bookie and, in order to cover a bet, submits a manuscript on how to stay single. The book is successful. However, there is a catch: Randy is happily married, so for publicity purposes he has to pose as a bachelor.

When his wife Norma (Ruth Hussey) announces that they will be welcoming a blessed event, they need to get a substitute husband (book sales are at their height). Enter the unsuspecting Eric Santley (Lee Bowman), Randy's publisher, who does not know that Randy is married. Of course, this is all ironed out in the end, but getting there is entertaining.

There is a mixture of art and literature of a kind in both *Theodora Goes Wild* (Columbia, 1936) and *Third Finger, Left Hand* (MGM, 1940). In the former, Theodora Lynn, a prim New Englander delightfully played by Irene Dunne, has written a scandalous (by 1936 standards) best seller titled *The Sinner* under the pseudonym of Carolyn Adams. Only her publisher Arthur Stevenson (Thurston Hall) knows her secret. The editor (Thomas Mitchell) of her hometown paper *The Lynnefield Bugle* has serialized the book and the town literary society, of which Theodora is a member, condemns it. Charter members of this society are Theodora's maiden aunts (played by Elisabeth Risdon and Mary McWade) who have raised her from childhood.

Upon traveling to New York to see Stevenson, she meets her book's worldly illustrator, Michael Grant (Melvyn Douglas). She takes an immediate dislike to him and when she and the publisher dine at a restaurant, the artist comes in uninvited and makes a nuisance of himself. Michael convinces Theodora to have a drink, one of many, and they wind up in his apartment. She is uncomfortable and rushes out.

Michael, curious about Theodora's double existence, follows her back to Lynnefield. His unconventional manner and thoughts about life make her fall in love with him, but she gets a shock upon discovering that he is married, albeit unhappily. His politician father

Theodora Goes Wild (1936): What happens when a staid New Englander (Irene Dunne) falls for an unconventional artist (Melvyn Douglas) who already has a wife?

demands that there be no divorce in the family until his term of office as lieutenant-governor is over. Theodora goes into action, moves into Michael's place and confesses that she is the author of *The Sinner*. She is named co-respondent in a divorce suit initiated by Michael's wife.

The town gossip, Rebecca Perry (Spring Byington), is ready to pounce on Theodora until the latter shows up carrying a baby, which she reveals is the grandchild of Mrs. Perry. The good lady faints, but Michael and Theodora are happily together. He is free from an unhappy marriage, she from the restraints of a narrow-minded town. Irene Dunne was Oscar-nominated for her performance, but lost the coveted award to Luise Rainer of *The Great Ziegfeld*.

In *Third Finger, Left Hand*, Melvyn Douglas is again an artist. This time the object of his affections is fashion editor Myrna Loy. The lady, thinking she's too busy for love and romance, fends off all suitors by telling them that she is already married. She is in shock when commercial artist Douglas turns up, claiming to be her husband. She marries him to avoid embarrassment and humiliation. Then, in a true "screwballian" twist, Myrna becomes engaged to Lee Bowman. In time, as in all films of this kind, she realizes that she loves her husband. In the expert hands of its stars, plus a supporting cast which includes Donald Meek, Bonita Granville, Sidney Blackmer, Felix Bressart and Raymond Walburn, the film plays out much better than it sounds.

Warner Brothers assembled a four-star cast for the aptly titled *Four's a Crowd*, a 1938 screwball comedy. Rosalind Russell, two years before her triumph in *His Girl Friday*, plays ace reporter Jean Christy, working for publisher Patterson Buckley (Patric Knowles). The latter is engaged to Lori Dillingwell (Olivia de Havilland), a zany heiress whose father (Walter Connolly) glories in being hated by everyone who knows him. When Robert Lansford (Errol Flynn) is fired as the editor of Knowles' paper, he opens a public relations firm. And who is his most difficult client? Through Olivia, he gets Connolly.

To soften the crusty tycoon's image, Flynn romances Olivia, though he is in love with Roz. There are several complications, plus a true screwball ending.

Harry Cohn, Columbia Studio's head, upon hearing the plot line of *It Happened One Night*, is reported to have made a remark which has come down through the years in Hollywood lore: "Who wants to see a picture about a bus?"

Based upon a *Cosmopolitan* magazine short story titled "Night Bus" by Samuel Hopkins Adams, the project was the brainchild of director Frank Capra and his head writer Robert Riskin. Much of Hollywood agreed with Cohn's assessment but Capra was the darling of the studio. Casting, however, presented a problem. The male lead was turned down by Robert Montgomery, while Constance Bennett, Myrna Loy, Miriam Hopkins and Margaret Sullavan "passed" on playing the female lead.

To "punish" Clark Gable for some recalcitrance on his part, MGM mogul Louis B. Mayer loaned him out to Cohn's "Poverty Row" studio. Claudette Colbert undertook the feminine lead only after her demands were met: Columbia had to pay her asking price, which was double what she was getting at Paramount per picture, and also had to guarantee her no more than four weeks work.

To paraphrase Cohn, much of the action in *It Happened One Night* does take place on a bus (a Greyhound to be exact, which thrilled that company). Reporter Peter Warne (Gable) meets Ellie Andrews (Colbert) traveling incognito. Ellie is the rich, spoiled daughter of millionaire Alexander Andrews (Walter Connolly). Because Daddy disapproves of her quickie marriage to notorious playboy King Westley (Jameson Thomas), she has fled. Peter soon recognizes the runaway heiress and sees her as "the biggest scoop of the year" and his ticket to fame and fortune. At first they are adversarial, constantly trading barbs, but soon each feels an attraction toward the other. He sees her as someone who needs looking after, while she regards him as the one man she cannot wind around her little finger.

When Ellie mistakenly thinks that Peter has abandoned her, amid much publicity, she decides to marry Westley in an official and elaborate wedding, but confesses to her father that she still loves Peter. The latter, thinking that Ellie has run away from him on a whim,

Four's a Crowd (1938) with Patric Knowles, Olivia de Havilland, Rosalind Russell and Errol Flynn. The finale finds the four married but there is a mix-up. Who winds up with whom?

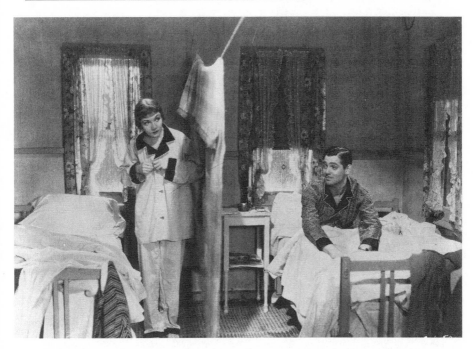

It Happened One Night (1934) with Claudette Colbert and Clark Gable. The film won all five major Academy Awards.

goes to her home on the day of the wedding and hands her father an itemized bill for $39.60. Mr. Andrews knows that Peter is right for Ellie and tells her to go to him, which she does.

Several scenes stand out: Gable teaching Colbert how to properly dunk a doughnut; she showing him her hitchhiking technique; Gable removing his shirt and revealing a bare chest (to the delight of the ladies in the audience, but the consternation of the underwear industry whose sales took a sharp drop); and the "Walls of Jericho" scene in a motel. (At the beginning of the film, they had spent the night there when the bus had to make an unscheduled stop. "The Walls of Jericho" was a blanket put up in between their beds. In the final scene, a trumpet is blown and you know what has come tumbling down.)

The film opened to mixed reviews in New York City, but in the vast hinterlands it was a tremendous hit. The 1934 release won the five major Academy Awards and Capra again could write his own ticket.

From the same studio that had given us that classic came *You Can't Run Away from It* (1956), a musical remake. Directed by Dick Powell, it stars his second wife June Allyson, Jack Lemmon and Charles Bickford. Same names, same plot, but there the similarities end. The musical numbers are inane and the stars, though adequate, cannot compare to the originals. Robert Riskin, who had written the original screenplay in 1934, collaborated with Claude Binyon on the updated version.

In a variation on *It Happened One Night*, *Love on the Run* (MGM, 1936), Gable is again a reporter hot on the trail of a runaway heiress about to be married. This time the lady is his frequent co-star Joan Crawford. Two is company, three is a crowd, the third party being Franchot Tone (at that time married to Crawford in real life) as Gable's pal, a rival reporter. It is Tone who, showing a flair for comedy, supplies the screwball touches when he is constantly being outwitted by his so-called "pal."

The trio becomes involved with a trio of international spies when Gable and Crawford steal their plane. When the plane, containing a valuable map, crashes, they find themselves in France and stay for a night at the Palace of Fontainbleau where they meet, in another screwball touch, an eccentric care-taker (delightfully played by Donald Meek). The spies are foiled and Gable and Crawford will marry.

Although *Cross-Country Romance* (RKO, 1940) does not involve writing *per se*, I have placed it here because of its theme: the spoiled runaway heiress finding true love. The film features Gene Raymond as Larry Smith, a bac-teriologist who becomes involved with a runaway rich girl named Diane North (Wendy Barrie) when she stows away in his trailer while he's on a trip from New York to San Francisco on his way to China. There he will work under an eminent scientist with an eye toward possibly publishing their findings.

Stopping off to deliver a plaque to her mother, he interrupts Diane's arranged marriage. She doesn't want to marry her stuffy fiancé so she stows away, clad in only a slip. Larry finds her and doesn't believe her story so she concocts a phony one and the fun begins. In the usual screwball ending, the two wind up together. The supporting players include Hedda Hopper and Billy Gilbert.

Chapter Ten

Love on the Rocks:
Marital Mix-Ups, Screwball Style

There are several emotions to be felt besides love and hate during the course of a marriage. Joy, sorrow, pride and jealousy are only a few of them. Conflict is something else that arises between two people who share bed and breakfast and when it does, said couple experiences a state of wedded blitz instead of the much sought-after wedded bliss.

An appreciation of this fact of life is apparent in the screwball comedies that are devoted to marital mayhem. Exaggerated though the emotions and conflicts in the film may be, they are the ones that we ourselves know to be true. When we laugh at the couples on the screen, we may well be laughing at ourselves and if that can be done, it is a healthy sign.

Mistrust and jealousy all too often rear their ugly heads. In many cases, there is no basis for these feelings; they are, however, two of the essential elements in screwball comedies.

Cary Grant and Irene Dunne, two of screwball's most accomplished practitioners, star in *The Awful Truth* (1937). (It had already been a play in 1922, a silent in 1925 and an early talkie in 1929.) It's the story of two people who, in their ongoing battle of the sexes, mistrust each other to the nth degree, but have such strong feelings towards one another that even a divorce cannot stop them from eventually coming together again.

Lucy and Jerry Warriner divorce on grounds of (presumed) marital infidelity. He says he's been in Florida with a group of buddies (who are willing to swear to it) but gives her a gift orange clearly stamped *California*. Lucy, on the other hand, is not there when he gets home—she comes breezing in, all dressed up, with her music teacher in tow, explaining that she is late because his car broke down. Neither believes the other and they wind up in divorce court. By a ruse, Lucy gets custody of their pooch Mr. Smith (Asta) and Jerry gets visitation rights. The divorce will be granted in 60 days.

The Awful Truth (1937): **Irene Dunne and Cary Grant are divorcing. Both want custody of the pooch (Asta).**

She meets Daniel Leeson (Ralph Bellamy), a wealthy oil man from Oklahoma, and Jerry becomes involved with both nightclub singer Dixie Belle Lee (Joyce Compton) and debutante Barbara Vance (Marguerite Churchill).

Jerry and Lucy get in each other's way, a development reflected in some standout scenes: Grant and Asta staging an impromptu concert, with Cary on piano and canine on vocal; Cary breaking up Dunne when she is in the midst of a recital; and she barging into the home of his socialite girlfriend saying that she is his sister and doing a devastating take-off on Dixie Belle.

By film's end, they are in her aunt's country home. At twelve o'clock midnight, their divorce is to become final. In this last scene, two mechanical figures march out of their separate stations on the clock to begin the chiming. Then, instead of returning the way they came, the boy is seen chasing the girl. The audience is wise to what will happen next.

Academy Award nominations went to the picture itself, director Leo McCarey, Irene Dunne and Ralph Bellamy. Only McCarey took home a statuette. A remake with music, *Let's Do It Again*, starring Jane Wyman, Ray Milland and Aldo Ray, was released by Columbia in 1953.

In 1940, Cary and Irene combined for another popular screwball comedy. In *My Favorite Wife* (RKO), she plays Ellen Arden (a take-off on the Enoch Arden tale of bigamy by Alfred Lord Tennyson) who has been shipwrecked on a deserted island for seven years but returns home on the day that her husband Nick (Grant) has had her declared legally dead. He has, also on this day, taken unto himself a brand new bride, Bianca (Gail Patrick). Ellen is shocked upon hearing this bit of news.

All bodes well for the newlyweds until Nick bumps into wife number one at the resort to which he has taken wife number two. He is all set to tell Bianca about the return of Ellen, but mistrust enters the picture: Ellen wasn't alone on that deserted island! He-man Stephen Burkett (Randolph Scott) kept her company for that long stretch of time. If that's not enough, Ellen calls him Adam and he has given her the nickname of Eve. He remarks that they have nothing to be remorseful over. But is this the unvarnished truth?

By the end of the film, Nick and wife number one are together again, but not before several screwball incidents have entertained the audience, among them a scene at the Yosemite National Park Hotel where a manic Grant dashes from one wife to another; one in which Randolph Scott is entertaining a bevy of bathing beauties poolside much to Cary's disgust and chagrin; and another wherein Ellen, knowing that Nick's wedding to Bianca has already been annulled, tells him that he has to wait until the full 60 days has elapsed before they can resume being man and wife. She says that they will get together around Christmas. A few minutes later, he comes through the door dressed as Santa Claus.

The remake *Move Over, Darling* was released by Fox in 1963. It was originally penciled in as a vehicle for Marilyn Monroe just before her death in 1962; the role was taken over by Doris Day, James Garner, Polly Bergen and Chuck Connors co-star.

The Enoch Arden saga is also the theme of *Too Many Husbands*, a 1940 Columbia film which was adapted from a Somerset Maugham play. When Bill Cardew (Fred MacMurray) is reported a victim of drowning, his widow Vickie (Jean Arthur) marries Henry Lowndes (third-billed Melvyn Douglas). A year later, Bill, who like Ellen Arden in *My Favorite Wife* has been living on a deserted island, returns.

Vickie is now on the horns of a dilemma—Bill or Henry? Which husband should she choose? She cannot make up her mind and plays one against the other, enjoying every moment with the two men vying for her until an exasperated judge sends her back to hubby number one.

The trio of Arthur, MacMurray and Douglas carry off the film in grand style with the aid of a stellar supporting cast which includes Harry Davenport as Arthur's father, Melville Cooper and Edgar Buchanan.

Betty Grable starred in a musical remake of *Too Many Husbands*: In

Three for the Show (Columbia, 1955), Jack Lemmon and Gower Champion play the men in Betty's complicated life. Of course, Lemmon is the guy who gets her in the fadeout. Also featured in the cast is Marge Champion, then married to Gower. Grable and Lemmon fans will enjoy the film, which does not compare with the original. Very often it is the casting which can make a movie and in this case, the Grable-Lemmon-Champion trio cannot compare to the Arthur-MacMurray-Douglas threesome.

Complications of a somewhat similar sort confound Dennis Morgan in *Kisses for Breakfast,* a 1941 Warner Brothers release. Morgan plays Rupert, who has just married his Juliet (Shirley Ross). About to go on his honeymoon, he is accosted by an old flame who threatens to blackmail him about their past together. They get into his car and, when he refuses to pay, he is hit over the head and the car goes into a river. Rupert manages to escape and the blackmailer is never seen again. He now has a classic case of amnesia. In his pocket, he finds a name and address. He doesn't know that it belongs to Laura (Jane Wyatt), Juliet's cousin, who was unable to attend the wedding. He meets her, falls for her and in time Happy (Rupert has chosen this name from a billboard) and Laura are married and go to visit her cousin who faints when she sees him. A hypnotist restores his memory but since his first marriage has not been consummated, he tricks Laura into hitting him and he is "Happy" again.

Melvyn Douglas is the star of *And So They Were Married* (Columbia, 1936), whose plot concerns a widower (Douglas) who meets a widow (Mary Astor) at a winter holiday resort. After initially taking a dislike to each other, they fall in love and marry. It takes a while for "They Lived Happily Ever After" to come about as their respective offspring (Edith Fellows and Jackie Moran) are not thrilled with the marriage. The kids do anything and everything to keep the newlyweds apart. When they finally realize the error of their ways, they stage a fake kidnapping to bring the couple together.

Douglas, who really got around some in the screwball genre, is top-cast in *Our Wife* (Columbia, 1941). He's a composer who loves Ruth Hussey and wants to marry her, and she feels the same way about him. Her love has inspired him to complete his finest work. There is a fly in the ointment: Ex-wife Ellen Drew is very jealous of the success her former husband has achieved and schemes to get him back. In a series of comical incidents, Hussey catches the opportunistic ex at her skullduggery and shows her up for what she is. Charles Coburn, as Hussey's father, gives a delightful performance as usual, but it is Douglas' film all the way. For many, the debonair actor runs a close second to Cary Grant in the screwball genre.

The same year as they made *The Lady Eve,* 1941, Henry Fonda and Barbara Stanwyck reunited for Columbia's *You Belong to Me.* Fonda plays Peter Kirk, a dilettante socialite who has married Dr. Helen Hunt (Stanwyck).

He has nothing to do all day but annoy his wife, being insanely jealous of the attention she gives her patients, many of whom are male. This premise gives the stars plenty of comic situations to work on, like Peter's showing up at Helen's office at inopportune times or his asking inane questions about her patients. Helen finally tells her husband that his idleness and behavior are ruining their marriage, that her work is important to her. He gets a job in a department store. In a funny scene, the owners of the store find out that he is rich and he is fired.

Because she really loves her husband, the doctor suddenly does an about face and quits her practice, but money saves the day. Peter invests in a hospital which is about to go under and makes his wife chief of staff. This is the perfect solution. She gets on with her career and he is also doing something worthwhile.

The supporting cast consists of Ruth Donnelly as Stanwyck's chatty nurse, Melville Cooper as Fonda's butler and Edgar Buchanan as a philosophical gardener. This trio gives the film some highly funny moments. *You Belong to Me* became *Emergency Wedding* in 1950. A Columbia release, this remake stars Larry Parks and Barbara Hale. "Lackluster" is a good word to describe it.

Like Barbara Stanwyck and Barbara Hale in the afore-mentioned films, Margaret Sullavan is an M.D. in *Appointment for Love* (Universal, 1941). Charles Boyer co-stars as a playwright. The two marry, but she thinks that he is having affairs with other women. He's not, but is equally mistrustful of her. They bicker and complain—they even get separate apartments, but as in all screwballs, the battle of the sexes is resolved and doctor and playwright kiss and make up. The supporting cast includes Eugene Pallette, Rita Johnson, and Reginald Denny, who move the screenplay along at a fairly brisk pace. The two stars so enjoyed working together that they co-starred again, this time in *Back Street,* a remake of the old Fannie Hurst drama of an illicit love. This film came out shortly after the release of *Appointment for Love.*

Suspicion and mistrust in a marriage is the theme of many other screwball comedies. Linda Darnell is leery of Tyrone Power in *Daytime Wife* (Fox, 1939); feeling neglected, she thinks that her hubby is having a little fling with his secretary (Wendy Barrie). When Power forgets their second wedding anniversary and doesn't show up for the surprise party she's arranged, she goes to his office—and he is not there. When he comes home, he tells her that he was working late. Now she's sure something *is* going on.

Her friend (Binnie Barnes) suggests that she find the answer to the age-old question of why a man's secretary can hold such charm for him. She gets a job as a Girl Friday to an architect (Warren William) who is susceptible to a pretty face. He tells his new employee to think of him as "an ineligible

eligible bachelor." It is clear that he's got more than shorthand on his mind. When she reminds him that he is married, he tells her, "After a while, a wife gets to be a sort of a solved crossword puzzle. A man likes to be intrigued, likes to fence with someone, someone who might say yes." Darnell takes all of this in.

The film's climax shows the four in a "business conference" at a nightclub which winds up in William's penthouse. There the wife "confesses" her true identity. The last scene has Power calling Barrie "an old watermelon." The latter exits in a huff, with the straying husband coming meekly back into the fold.

Loretta Young, originally scheduled to star in the film, turned the role down, not wanting to take second billing to Power. The part went to the 19-year-old Darnell, who subsequently married Peverell Marley, who did the photography on the film.

Like the wife in *Daytime Wife*, in *The Bride Walks Out* Barbara Stanwyck secretly takes on a job after her marriage. She wants more material goods than her struggling engineer husband (Gene Raymond) can give her on his $35-a-week salary. She becomes a successful model and is quite happy, but when her husband finds out the truth, he is incensed and leaves her to the tender ministrations of wealthy department store owner Robert Young.

When Raymond accepts a job in South America, Stanwyck admits that she still loves him and uses a rueful Young to help her keep Raymond from leaving the country. Love has triumphed over luxury.

The three principals are immeasurably aided by Ned Sparks and Helen Broderick, who have the best lines as a constantly bickering screwball couple.

As is to be seen in *Daytime Wife*, philandering husbands play a large part in the screwball genre, making up a goodly portion of the battle of the sexes so entertainingly entered into by consenting males and females. Another case in point is *Affectionately Yours* (Warner Brothers, 1941): Ace overseas roving reporter Richard Mayberry (Dennis Morgan) has a roving eye while on assignment. When playing around with several lovelies, including Irene Malcolm (Rita Hayworth), his stock phrase is, "I'd marry you in a minute, but I have a wife."

Returning home after a long absence, he is chagrined to find out that his wife Susan (Merle Oberon) has divorced him and will soon marry Owen Wright (Ralph Bellamy). He feels threatened by this turn of events and promises to quit his job.

The film ends with Morgan escaping from a plot hatched by his editor to see that Oberon marries Bellamy so as to keep his ace reporter on the job. (From the minute "poor" Ralph is seen on the screen, we know that marriage to him ain't gonna happen.) Morgan invents an injury and finds a room in

Two-Faced Woman (1941): How does a woman (Greta Garbo) keep her straying husband (Melvyn Douglas)? This film was Greta's "swan song" to Hollywood.

the hospital. Oberon rushes to him, sees through the hoax, but realizes that she still loves him, and they end up in a clinch. Other cast members include such well-known personalities as George Tobias as Morgan's sidekick, James Gleason as Morgan's crafty editor, Jerome Cowan as a fellow reporter and Hattie McDaniel as the sassy Mayberry maid.

Two-Faced Woman (MGM, 1941) refers to Greta Garbo in a pseudo-double role, the enigmatic star using a secret weapon to bring her straying husband back into the fold. In this, her last film, she is Karin, a ski instructor who meets and impulsively marries sophisticated man about town Larry Blake (Melvyn Douglas). She wants to stay on her beloved slopes; he says he will join her after winding up some business affairs.

Time goes by, but he does not appear. He is having too much fun with old flame Griselda Vaughn (third-billed Constance Bennett). In screwball comedy, it is left to the imagination of the audience as to how "innocent" the fun has been.

To hold on to her man, Karin resorts to subterfuge: She pretends to be her more scintillating (but imaginary) twin sister who flirts unashamedly with and grabs the attention of her husband. Initially, the implication is that the husband willingly succumbed to his "sister-in-law's" charms, but the Catholic Church intervened and an added scene discloses that Douglas has seen through the ruse.

Although *Two-Faced Woman* is often cited as the reason for Garbo's retirement from the screen, it does have its charm. With antics involving a wild rhumba, a bathing suit scene and a chase finale, the film (like Jack Benny's *The Horn Blows at Midnight* [Warner Brothers, 1945]) is not the "turkey" its reputation has made it out to be. Garbo retired, fame and beauty intact and with lots of MGM money in safe investments.

Are Husbands Necessary? (Paramount, 1942) stars Betty Field and Ray Milland as a happily married couple. Hubby's past catches up to him with the reappearance of ex-girlfriend Patricia Morison. Milland must and does prove that the sultry Morison is a fling of the past. In support of the trio are such screwball stalwarts as Eugene Pallette, Cecil Kellaway, Charles Dingle and Richard Haydn. This plot had been done the year before with much better results in *Love Crazy* with William Powell and Myrna Loy as the married couple and Gail Patrick as the femme fatale. This film will be discussed in our next chapter.

Money problems are another source of conflict in a marriage and Claudette Colbert takes this to a higher level in *The Palm Beach Story*. She is Gerry Jeffers, a restless wife who spends money faster than her inventor husband Tom (Joel McCrea) can make it. They are so far behind in their rent that their apartment is to be rented out to other tenants. One such prospect is the self-proclaimed "Wienie King" who gives Gerry $700. She obtains a divorce and sets out for Palm Beach, Florida, hoping to bag herself a millionaire.

Aboard a train bound for the Sunshine State, Gerry meets a group of zanies who, in a wild adventure, induct her into "The Ale and Quail Club." She also meets a stuffy millionaire named J.D. Hackensaker (Rudy Vallee) when, getting into her upper berth, she steps on his face. When she apologizes, he tells her, "It's quite all right, I rather enjoyed it."

Before they arrive in Palm Beach, he has taken quite a shine to his new acquaintance. He buys her a complete wardrobe and wants her to come to his mansion and meet his man-crazy, much-married sister Maude (Mary Astor). Tom comes to Florida and Gerry introduces him as her brother. But then jealousy rears its ugly head when she sees Maude making a play for her ex.

Moviegoers can always expect something different when Preston Sturges is directing and *The Palm Beach Story* does not disappoint. In the hilarious ending, Gerry and Tom reveals that they are both twins. We then witness a triple wedding scene wherein Tom remarries Gerry, J.D. weds Gerry's twin

The Palm Beach Story (1942) with Joel McCrea, Claudette Colbert, Rudy Vallee, Colbert (again), McCrea (again), Mary Astor and Sig Arno. Only Preston Sturges could get away with this ending.

and Maude walks down the aisle with Tom's twin. Cut to a sign which reads, "And they all lived happily ever—Or did they?"

Screwball veterans Colbert, McCrea and Astor all give delightful performances, but the surprise hit of this 1942 Paramount release is singer Rudy Vallee, the Vagabond Lover of the 1920s and 1930s. As the musical part of his career waned, he became a successful character actor, plying his trade both on stage and on the silver screen for several years.

In *Second Honeymoon,* a recently remarried Loretta Young is bored with her stuffy businessman husband (Lyle Talbot) and yearns for the crazy times she shared with her wealthy playboy first husband (Tyrone Power). While on vacation in Florida, she sees him again and the old feeling is still there—so—exit Talbot, hello, Ty. A typical screwball comedy of the Depression era when people needed a good laugh and satirizing the wealthy was fashionable, this 1937 Fox release was a box office winner. In support of the popular star team are Stuart Erwin and the vastly underrated Claire Trevor.

Two years later, Loretta starred in *Eternally Yours* (United Artists). At first engaged to Broderick Crawford, she's swept off her feet by a dashing magician–escape artist (David Niven). After a few exciting years on the road, he in the limelight and she willingly in his shadow, Loretta is ready for a more domestic way of life—house, garden, dogs and kids—but Niven is not. "I don't want to be chained to four walls," is the way he puts it. She divorces him and marries the solid Crawford.

Soon after, she realizes her mistake, but is too stubborn to admit it. Her ex tries to woo her back, but only when he leaps handcuffed from a plane at the New York World's Fair (an actual attraction in 1939) does she give in to her emotions. Young and Niven are aided in their efforts by a strong supporting cast which includes a zany Hugh Herbert as Niven's valet, C. Aubrey Smith as Loretta's grandfather, who is a bishop, Billie Burke as her aunt and Eve Arden as a receptionist.

Merle Oberon stars in *That Uncertain Feeling* (United Artists, 1941) as Jill Baker, who feels that she is being neglected by her husband Larry (Melvyn Douglas), a successful insurance executive. She feels that he is insensitive to her needs (like Loretta Young in the film just discussed).

Known to one and all as "The Happy Bakers," they have plenty of money and a Park Avenue apartment. There is one problem, however: Jill is suffering from boredom and a bad case of hiccups. Her psychiatrist Dr. Vengard (Alan Mowbray) zeros in on her marriage as the cause of these hiccups. She denies this and tells him there isn't a happier couple to be found on Park Avenue. As the doctor prods, she launches into a whole list of complaints about Larry and begins to hiccup.

When Larry yells "keeks" and pokes her in the stomach once too often, her reaction to this is a session of violent hiccups. Back to the shrink she goes, where she meets a zany (possibly certifiable) musician named Sebastien (Burgess Meredith in an over-the-top performance) who claims to be the greatest pianist in the world. She thinks she's in love with him because her hiccups have stopped.

The three go to a lawyer to get a divorce, but Larry cannot go through with it. The final riotous scene takes place in the couple's bedroom. Larry has banished his rival from the apartment and all bodes well for "The Happy Bakers." Larry has learned never to neglect his wife again.

Loretta Young in *Eternally Yours* is married to a magician and yearns for the quiet life. In a turnabout, she is a bored spouse in *Wife, Husband and Friend* (Fox, 1939). Her husband (Warner Baxter) is busy at the office. To occupy her time, she takes singing lessons and has delusions about her voice, egged on by her teacher (Cesar Romero), who sees dollar signs in the form of extra lessons. She appears in public and flops. Meanwhile, hubby is encouraged to sing by a flirtatious professional singer (Binnie Barnes) and has a bit of success. Trying his hand at opera, however, he makes a fool of himself. He says that he will leave singing to the pros, and his wife agrees. A familiar face in the supporting cast is Eugene Pallette.

Ten years later, the film resurfaced as *Everybody Does It* (Fox) with Paul Douglas, Celeste Holm (who in real life had a musical comedy background) and Linda Darnell in the Baxter-Young-Barnes roles.

The couple in an odd screwball comedy titled *Turnabout* (United Artists, 1940) have an argument about their respective jobs. They each wish they could change places. An Oriental idol on their mantel suddenly comes to life and grants them this wish.

The next day, he wakes up speaking like a woman and she like a man. "He" goes to the office. Of course, this creates havoc there and at home. They revert back to their God-given roles. Starred are Carole Landis and John Hubbard as Sally and Tim Willows. Looking on in perplexity are several familiar screwball players: Adolph Menjou, William Gargan, Mary Astor, Donald Meek, Franklin Pangborn, Marjorie Main and Polly Ann Young, the latter the real life sister of Loretta Young.

Screwball wives are not always bored or neglected; sometimes they are the "perfect" little helpmates who come upon the screen with a mission, that of furthering the interests of their husbands in every way possible. Rosalind Russell is a long-suffering secretary who marries Brian Aherne for business purposes. She is his *Hired Wife*. She goes for him in a big way, but he only has eyes for model Virginia Bruce.

When John Carroll enters the picture, Roz sees her chance and encourages the handsome young man to make a play for her "rival." The latter falls for him, which leaves the field clear for the wife to turn her marriage of convenience into the real thing.

Humorist Robert Benchley heads the supporting cast as Aherne's lawyer. While not on a par with *His Girl Friday,* Russell and the 1940 Universal release did well at the box office. It is interesting to note that in many of her movies, this actress played career women. In an interview she once stated:

> I played—I think it was 23 career women. I've been every kind of executive and I've owned everything—factories and advertising agencies and pharmaceutical houses. Except for a different leading man and a switch in title and pompadour, they were all stamped out of the same Alice in Careerland. The script always called for a leading lady somewhere in her 30s, tall, brittle, not too sexy. My wardrobe had a set pattern: a tan suit, a gray suit, a beige suit and then a negligee for the seventh reel in the end, when I would admit to my best friend on the telephone that what I really wanted was to become a dear little housewife.

The plot of *Hired Wife* concerns a marriage of convenience. Claudette Colbert finds herself in almost the same position as Russell in *She Married Her Boss* (Columbia, 1936). With a twist, however. Colbert plays Julia Scott, a secretary who has managed the business affairs of her boss Richard Barclay (Melvyn Douglas) so well that he thinks she will do the same for his domestic life. The fun begins when newlywed Claudette finds herself saddled with her husband's disagreeable sister Gertrude (Katherine Alexander) who doesn't think that her newly acquired relative is good enough to bear the family name; his daughter Annabel (Edith Fellows, who is so convincingly nasty for the better part of the picture that one critic called her "the perfect antidote to Shirley Temple"); and his tipsy butler Franklin (Raymond Walburn).

Our lovely heroine becomes increasingly unhappy as she feels her husband is neglecting her and is oblivious to her feelings. Only when she decides to end the union, leaves the house, kicks up her heels a bit making the tabloids and decides to take a trip abroad, does he realize how much he really cares for her and that she is the best thing that has happened to him in a long time. In a classically screwball finale, he virtually kidnaps her to tell her so.

Colbert and Douglas would continue to be major screwball practitioners for many years. As did another of Colbert's co-stars, Fred MacMurray.

The year 1937 marked the end of Carole Lombard's contract with Paramount Studios. Under the direction of Wesley Ruggles and with MacMurray as co-star, she made *True Confession*. By this time, the actress had lifted her comedic style into an art form. In this gem, she plays Helen Bartlett, a congenital liar. Her husband Kenneth (MacMurray) is a struggling young lawyer. To further his career along, she confesses to the killing of her boss, a murder she has not committed. The audience knows that she is not involved in the matter. Kenneth, however, is unaware of the truth and gets her off on a plea of self-defense amid much publicity and fanfare.

John Barrymore is third-billed as a zany criminologist which uses broad satire in the courtroom sequences. Helen promises to be more truthful. Supporting the three principals is a cast which includes Una Merkel, Lynne Overman, Hattie McDaniel, Porter Hall, Edgar Kennedy and Fritz Feld.

Paramount remade *True Confession* in 1946. *Cross My Heart* stars Betty Hutton in the Lombard role with Sonny Tufts and Michael Chekhov doing weak imitations of MacMurray and Barrymore.

Between the release of *Twentieth Century* and *True Confession*, Lombard's career had far eclipsed that of Barrymore. It is ironic that both stars died in 1942, she in her prime, he an alcoholic has-been.

Gary Cooper is a much-married bon vivant in *Bluebeard's Eighth Wife*, director Ernst Lubitsch's last Paramount film. Michael Brandon may be successful in business but he is a failure in his personal life. He meets his match in Claudette Colbert's Nicole de Loiselle, daughter of an impoverished nobleman. The opening gambit in their game of love (read: battle of the sexes) finds the two in a Paris department store. He is trying to buy a pajama top. He refuses to buy the bottom and both he and the sales clerk are becoming increasingly frustrated.

Nicole steps in and offers to buy the bottoms, and the delighted clerk remarks, "Voila! A lady in love." Michael sourly retorts, "You Frenchmen think the worst."

He, however, is intrigued and thinks she will be an interesting addition to his string of women. She, seeing that he is attracted to her, sets her cap for him, marries him and is determined to be the last Mrs. Brandon. She launches into her campaign, using handsome Albert de Regnier (third-billed David Niven) to make Brandon jealous. Her machinations cause him to have a nervous breakdown and he is committed to an institution.

The final scene sees Cooper in a straitjacket (*a la* Margaret Sullavan in *The Moon's Our Home*) and Colbert in the room with him. They begin to fight on the asylum floor until she kisses him. Suddenly he frees himself from the restraints and embraces her. Nicole will get her wish: She *will* be the last Mrs. Michael Brandon.

An early Warner Brothers screwball titled *Easy to Love* (1934) stars Adolphe Menjou and Genevieve Tobin as John and Carol Townsend, a wealthy society couple. Carol doesn't know it, but John is having an affair with her best friend, played by Mary Astor.

Carol, beginning to think that her husband is spending too much time away from home and hearth, hires a detective (played by the always hilarious Hugh Herbert) and discovers the truth. She then pretends to have an affair with John's best friend (Edward Everett Horton). The Townsend daughter, hearing about her father's fling, then announces that she and her fiancé will live together without the benefit of clergy. This "shocker" brings John to his senses and the elder Townsends get back together again.

In *Remember?* (MGM, 1939), Robert Taylor is an advertising exec and his best pal Lew Ayres is a scientist who meets socialite Greer Garson while on vacation. Taylor lures Garson away from Ayres and marries her.

After a while, bliss becomes blitz and the couple contemplates divorce. Altruistic Ayres, who realizes that the two really love each other, gives each a potion which results in both forgetting everything about their meeting and marriage. In this condition, Taylor and Garson fall in love again and, not knowing they are already married, decide to go through the ceremony. A bemused judge (Henry Travers), who has already married them, has to do it again.

Though old pros Billie Burke, Reginald Owen, Henry Travers and Sig Ruman are well cast and the film has a couple of amusing sequences, it was not well received and did nothing for the stars or for the studio. The lady-like Garson, three years away from her Oscar-winning role as Mrs. Miniver, was no Lombard or Colbert. And Taylor, though likable, was no Cary Grant.

In 1941, after a seven-year absence from moviemaking, silent screen star Gloria Swanson appeared in RKO's *Father Takes a Wife*. Co-star Adolphe

Menjou had been a bit player at Paramount when La Swanson reigned supreme at that studio.

Menjou is top-billed as Frederic Osborne, a middle-aged businessman who falls for and marries tempestuous actress Leslie Collier (Swanson). His first problem is to break the news to his stuffy son Frederic Jr. (John Howard) and the latter's wife Enid (Florence Rice). Arguments break out before and after the wedding, but are smoothed out on a honeymoon cruise. An even bigger crisis arises when Osborne and Leslie take on singer Carlos Bardez (Desi Arnaz), a stowaway they meet on the cruise, as their house guest and protégé. Soon Osborne feels that Leslie is more attentive to the younger man than she is to him, but matters are resolved when Junior and Senior arrange a long tour for the singer. A surprise ending which only a screwball could have has the wives of both Junior and Senior announcing their impending motherhood.

The venture was ill-advised for the aging Swanson and it lost money at the box office. Not until 1950 and *Sunset Blvd.* would her star shine brightly again.

Dick Foran, an actor in many "B" films, plays a banker married to Claudette Colbert in *Guest Wife* (United Artists, 1945). When his good friend, foreign correspondent Don Ameche, must produce a wife in order to keep his job, well, what the heck, what are friends for? Foran loans his wife to Ameche. In the screwball situations which follow, Claudette is accused of living with a married man (in reality her own husband) and Foran becomes increasingly annoyed when he thinks that his erstwhile pal is taking advantage of the situation.

The release of *Guest Wife* coincided with the end of World War II. Because the Golden Age of the genre was more or less over, the film is not as well-known as its predecessors. Genre expert Colbert, however, is comfortable with frequent co-star Ameche, the action is well-paced and the dialogue is witty, insuring an enjoyable 90 minutes for the viewer.

This Thing Called Love (Columbia, 1940) stars Rosalind Russell and Melvyn Douglas as a couple, wed three months, who have not yet consummated their marriage (Russell feels that they should start out as good friends). When she is finally ready to give in to her natural instincts and her love-starved mate, the latter contracts poison oak. The coupling of seasoned pros Russell and Douglas make this lightweight film work. They are immeasurably aided by Binnie Barnes, Allyn Joslyn, Lee J. Cobb and Gloria Dickson.

Laughable by today's standards, this film, considered risqué at the time, was banned by the Legion of Decency. The Legion could not have been too thrilled to see a Mexican fertility statue with a frown on its face throughout the film and then having it break into a smile as the film ends. In spite of the condemnation, or maybe because of it, the film did well at the box office.

In our next two films, horses are the main focus in each story. Barbara Stanwyck and Robert Cummings in *The Bride Wore Boots* (Paramount, 1946) are not the happy couple they'd started out to be. He feels that she is spending too much time on her horses. He loves her, but detests horses. They separate but come together when he wins her back by entering the horse racing scene. Also in the cast are Diana Lynn, Peggy Wood, Robert Benchley, Patric Knowles and seven-year-old Natalie Wood. It was a weak entry in the genre, in spite of the efforts of a good cast.

In a reversal of this situation, *He Married His Wife* (Fox, 1940) stars Joel McCrea as a racehorse owner who is paying more attention to the nag than he is to wife Nancy Kelly. Though he is still in love with her, his overriding concerns about his horse results in a divorce. His alimony payments are so steep that he and his lawyer scheme to have her marry again. When she plans to marry a man whom McCrea thinks would be an unfit husband, he remarries her. Also in the cast are Cesar Romero as the "unfit" suitor, Roland Young as McCrea's lawyer plus Lyle Talbot and Elisha Cook Jr.

After Alfred Hitchcock's initial success in America with the very dramatic *Rebecca*, RKO, at the request of Carole Lombard, signed the rotund moviemaker to direct a project titled *Mr. and Mrs. Smith*—his only foray into the land of the screwball. The signing had to go through David O. Selznick, who had an exclusive contract with Hitchcock.

The Norman Krasna script contains several screwball elements: Ann and David Smith (Lombard and Robert Montgomery) are forever fighting. During one of their quieter moments, she asks him if would he marry her if he had it to do over again. He answers in the negative and the fur begins to fly.

They are beginning divorce proceedings when they learn that due to a shifting state line boundary, their marriage is not legal. She goes back to being Ann Krausheimer (shades of *Twentieth Century*'s Mildred Plotka!) and begins dating Jeff Custer (Gene Raymond), who turns out to be David's law partner. She even becomes engaged to him, but when the three wind up in a ski lodge, she knows that her heart will always belong to David.

The comedy is well-paced and aided by its three stars, especially the radiant Carole. She is a sheer delight to watch as she shaves David in one scene and in another as she meets Jeff's parents (Lucile Watson and Philip Merivale) and tries to explain her former husband to them.

Lombard's real-life ex-husband William Powell may not have found happiness with her, but he did find the perfect on-screen mate in Myrna Loy. The two share a distinct place in any discussion of the screwball comedy, or for that matter, in any perspective on the film industry. In our next chapter, we will meet this delightful duo and discover the reasons behind their impact on the genre and their unparalleled success on film in general.

Chapter Eleven

William and Myrna: Nick and Nora et al.

William Powell and Myrna Loy were already screen veterans by the time they met professionally in the early 1930s.

Born eight years before the turn of the century, Powell had studied at the American Academy of Dramatic Arts. After several years in repertory and on Broadway, he came to Hollywood under contract to Paramount Studios, beginning a long and successful career in motion pictures. His debut film, a 1922 silent titled *Sherlock Holmes*, was the first of many detective stories in which he would appear, a portent of things to come. His other silent films include *Beau Geste* (1926), *The Great Gatsby* (1927) and *The Last Command* (1928).

For most of the silent era, Powell was mainly seen as a heavy, but as movies began to talk, his distinctive voice, mannerisms and increasing popularity allowed him to show his versatility via a potpourri of roles, heroic, villainous and comedic. He starred in Paramount's first talkie, *Interference* (1929), and went on to star in several other early ones including four films in which he played S.S. Van Dyne's elegant sleuth Philo Vance. By 1934, he had signed on at MGM; the result was a string of hits, some of the most fondly remembered in the history of film.

Myrna Loy also paid her dues during the silent era. A native of Helena, Montana, the lovely actress, 13 years Powell's junior, was discovered by silent screen star Rudolph Valentino and began making films in 1925. Relegated to playing Orientals and vamps, her earliest appearances include *Don Juan* (Warner Brothers, 1926), *Ben-Hur* (MGM, 1925), and *The Jazz Singer* (Warner Brothers, 1927). The young actress did not have to worry about being a victim of the talkie revolution as did so many Hollywood performers of the era; her unique voice served to enhance her career, leading the former Myrna Williams to get work at many of the major studios while on the road to bigger and better roles.

Among the first talkies she made were *The Desert Song* (Warner Brothers, 1929), *A Connecticut Yankee* (Fox, 1931) and *Love Me Tonight* (Paramount, 1932). More important roles began to come her way and she was soon getting the female lead in "A" films. The halcyon period of her career began when she was signed by MGM.

In 1934, Powell and Loy were two-thirds of the starring team in a production titled *Manhattan Melodrama*. Top-billed was the other part of the triangle, Clark Gable. This film gained a place in American folklore as being the last one seen by famed gangster John Dillinger just before he was shot to death by agents of the F.B.I. MGM had successfully teamed Gable and Loy before, but this was the first vehicle for Myrna and Powell. Studio executives, thrilled by the way the two worked together, paired them in several films. Most of them are considered screwball classics. Six are part of the *Thin Man* series.

In September 1936, a British columnist wrote that most of the moneymaking stars in Hollywood were working at MGM. There was not much exaggeration in this statement: William Powell and Myrna Loy were at the top of the list.

That year brought moviegoers *Libeled Lady*. A wacky, fast-paced screwball farce, the film also stars two other top MGM personalities in their prime, Jean Harlow and Spencer Tracy. The opening credits show the four walking towards the audience. With these potent performers, the story of an heiress who slaps a lawsuit on a newspaper was bound to be a box-office sensation.

Heiress Connie Allenbury (Loy) is out for blood: A newspaper has printed libelous things about her. Her lawyers inform the paper's editor, Warren Haggerty (Tracy), that she is seeking five million dollars in damages. To give Haggerty another headache, his fiancée Gladys Benton (Harlow) comes into the press room in a wedding gown (the nuptials have been postponed many times). He puts poor Gladys off for the time being, saying that they will tie the knot after the catastrophe has been averted.

He then seeks the help of reporter Bill Chandler (Powell). His scheme is to have Bill marry Gladys and then pursue Connie and make the charges of man-stealing that the paper has made against Connie ring true.

The scheme backfires because the reporter and the heiress find themselves falling in love. But before this happens, there are some very funny moments: Powell taking fishing lessons from an instructor (E.E. Clive) in a hotel room to impress Mr. Allenbury, Connie's father (Walter Connolly), and later, trying his luck as an angler with a different kind of angle on his mind.

The film ends with Bill and Connie married and Bill punching Haggerty in the nose and Gladys doing the same to Bill. The unanswered question after all this is whether Haggerty and Gladys will ever get married.

Libeled Lady (1936): In this film, Spencer Tracy (left) is Jean Harlow's (right) guy. In real life, it was William Powell (center) who held the key to Jean's heart.

Though Powell and Loy were romantically linked throughout the film, it was Jean Harlow to whom the actor's heart belonged off-screen. Their love affair lasted until the screen's favorite platinum blonde's untimely death in 1937.

MGM remade this classic film in 1946 and titled it *Easy to Wed* with Esther Williams, Van Johnson, Keenan Wynn and Lucille Ball in the Loy, Powell, Tracy and Harlow roles, with Cecil Kellaway as Esther's father. A musical update, it also features June Lockhart, Ben Blue, Latin singer Carlos Ramirez and organist Ethel Smith. It is a remake which boasts Technicolor and four popular performers, but it cannot compare with the magic of the original.

Completed in 1937, before the Harlow tragedy, was *Double Wedding*. As in *Libeled Lady*, Powell and Loy start the proceedings as adversaries, throwing insults and quips across the silver screen with abandon, but wind up in a clinch. Myrna plays Margit Agnew, a successful businesswoman who has no time for anything frivolous, like romance and love. Powell is Charlie Lodge, an avant garde artist with whom Loy's sister Irene (Florence Rice) imagines herself in love; she wants to marry him although there is a perfectly nice young man named Waldo Beaver (John Beal) who adores her.

No-nonsense Loy is infuriated at this turn of events and tries to buy Charlie off. He has never been in love with Irene, but when he meets big sister Margit, he is definitely intrigued and pretends to go along with anything she says. In the end there is a double wedding—Powell and Loy, Rice and Beal—and the sisters each go off with the right man. Powell and Loy, old friends by now, were in command of their art and the film was a real crowd-pleaser.

By 1940, the duo was known around Metro, and probably all of Hollywood, as the team that never failed. They proved it again in *I Love You Again* with Powell as amnesiac Larry Wilson, a bit of a fuddy-duddy, with a pretty wife named Kay (Loy) and a good business—in other words, the epitome of a model citizen. A blow on the head makes him revert back to his former self, George Carey, a smooth-talking con man. He sends for his henchman, Doc Ryan (Frank McHugh, in a sparkling performance) and together they plan to bilk the town. One problem, however: George has now fallen in love with the "wife" he married while in a state of amnesia. He decides to go straight, but an old "colleague" (Edmund Lowe) wants in on the scheme George has abandoned. With the help of Doc, George outwits his nemesis, is hit over the head for the second time and becomes Larry.

In *Love Crazy* (1941), Powell is caught in a situation compromising his marriage and he goes through all sorts of wacky schemes to have things become "normal" again. Stephen Ireland (Powell) and his wife Susan (Loy) have been married four years when all sorts of trouble begins. She wants to celebrate their anniversary by doing the same things they did on their wedding day. But complications ensue: Stephen hurts his foot, Susan's matriarchal mother (Florence Bates) arrives to his consternation, and Stephen encounters Isobel (Gail Patrick), a sexy former flame who has taken an apartment on the floor below. In a very funny scene, the elevator gets stuck and when Stephen tries to get out, the doors close on his head. The elevator suddenly begins to move and his head is bashed against the top of the doorway.

He then tells Susan about Isobel, mentioning that she has a husband. Susan retorts, "Oh yeah? Whose husband has she got?"

We now know that jealousy has reared its ugly head. Stephen is totally innocent, but Susan will not believe him and wants a divorce. He does not and, under the presumption that a divorce cannot be granted if one of the parties is insane, proceeds to feign madness. He crashes a party, says he is Abraham Lincoln, "frees" the black butler, throws some men's hats into a pond and for good measure pushes his mother-in-law into the same water.

Susan knows he is sane but, when he is examined by a group of psychiatrists, he is found mad and is to be institutionalized. Towards the end of the film, Powell shows up in drag as his own younger sister. He gets away with it until his "breasts," made up of two skeins of yarn, begin to unravel when they are caught on a record player's revolving spindle. Susan realizes all her husband has gone through and knows that she loves him, so the divorce will never take place. Jack Carson plays Susan's potential suitor, while Vladimir Sokoloff and Sig Ruman play the psychiatrists.

The four films noted above were quite popular in their time, but may not have been box-office giants. For playing two other lovable screwball characters, William Powell and Myrna Loy were, are and probably will be best-remembered.

The top brass at MGM saw something special in *Manhattan Melodrama*, the first teaming of the duo, and so did director W.S. "Woody" Van Dyke. When he was assigned to do a comedy mystery titled *The Thin Man*, he felt that the cinematic rapport established by Powell and Loy would serve his new project rather well. *How* well, no one at the time could foresee.

Based on a Dashiell Hammett yarn, the film was shot on the MGM lot in 18 days. Van Dyke was famous for working quickly and earned the nickname "One-Take Woody." No one suspected that this "little film" would become a monster hit and spawn sequels and imitations.

The leading characters Nick and Nora Charles, as played by Powell and Loy, were a sophisticated pair, attractive, wealthy and irreverent in outlook, but obviously very much in love with each other and also the best of friends.

Before he met Nora, Nick had been a private detective and a mighty good one too, but as the film opens, he explains that he has "retired" from his profession in order to manage his wife's money. This does not mean that he cannot dabble in crime and when he does, it is with a drink in his hand, a glint in his eye and a quip on his lips.

Nora, the personification of the "perfect wife," is right behind her husband every step of the way, egging him on, cheering him along and making sure that his ego is not inflated even after he has brilliantly solved the crime. (Loy said that she based her characterization on writer Lillian Hellman, Hammett's mistress.)

The third regular in the series is the beloved pooch Asta. The frisky wire-haired fox terrier not only holds his own in the comedy department, he even sniffs out an important clue every once in a while.

The *Thin Man* movies are a happy blend of sophisticated dialogue, screwball comedy and crackling good mystery. Each story is set in a different locale and has a different set of characters from which Nick must ferret out the culprit.

The first of the popular films set the pace and the mood of the series. It concerns the disappearance of inventor Claude Wynant, a former client.

The Thin Man (1934): William Powell, Myrna Loy and Asta.

(This character, played by Edward Ellis, gave the book and series their names.) Wynant's daughter Dorothy (Maureen O'Sullivan) recognizes Nick at a night club and asks for his help. Nora enters and sees Nick and Dorothy. After the latter leaves, this bit of screwball dialogue takes place:

NORA: Who is she?
NICK: Oh, darling. I was hoping I wouldn't have to answer that.
NORA: Go on.
NICK: Well, Dorothy is really my daughter. You see, it was spring in Venice, and I was so young I didn't know what I was doing. We're all like that on my father's side.
NORA: By the way, how is your father's side?
NICK: Oh, it's much better, thanks.
NORA: Say, how many drinks have you had?
NICK: This will make six martinis.
NORA: All right, will you bring me five more martinis, Leo? Line them right up here.

A bit of nonsense, but it sets the proper tone for the film.

Nick is reluctant to take on the case and explains his reluctance as follows: "I'm much too busy making sure you don't waste the money I married you for."

But he does go to work, prodded to do so by Nora. Before the case is solved, three murders have been committed, among them Wynant's, but in the end Nick gets his murderer by hosting a dinner party. Among the reluctant guests, besides O'Sullivan, are Cesar Romero, Nat Pendleton, Edward Brophy, Porter Hall and Minna Gombell.

The on-screen chemistry between Nick and Nora was such that some moviegoers, upon seeing the film, wrote fan letters to their portrayers, addressing them as "Mr. and Mrs. William Powell."

The Thin Man was the sleeper of the year. It received an Oscar nomination for Best Picture and Powell became a candidate for Best Actor honors. Neither won; 1934 was the year of *It Happened One Night.*

Two years later, acceding to public demand, Van Dyke, Powell and Loy combined forces on *After the Thin Man.* In between the two MGM releases, Powell starred in two comedy-mysteries for RKO: *Star of Midnight* with Ginger Rogers as his leading lady and *The Ex-Mrs. Bradford* with Jean Arthur in the title role. Both productions are similar in form to the Nick and Nora films and will be discussed in the next chapter.

In *After the Thin Man,* set in San Francisco, a tired Nick and Nora come home to an unwanted surprise party welcoming them back. Also welcomed home is Asta by Mrs. Asta and his progeny.

Nora and Nick are then "commanded" by Nora's imperious aunt (Jessie Ralph) to attend a family gathering. Nora's cousin Selma (Elissa Landi) is in trouble, suspected of killing her unfaithful husband Robert (Alan Marshal). Nick is called upon to clear the young woman.

With the blessing of the Golden Gate Police Department, represented by a baffled and confused Lieutenant Abrams (Sam Levene), Nick, Nora and Asta hunt for clues, with the canine hiding something important from the humans in a screwball scene. The duo "grill" several suspects, among them Dorothy McNulty (a.k.a. Penny Singleton), Joseph Calleia, George Zucco and a 28-year-old named James Stewart. As David Graham, in a role not at all characteristic of the later Stewart image, it is Jimmy who turns out to be the villain. The character is calm, collected and helpful, but when he is found out, all of a sudden he is snarling and vengeful in a somewhat over-the-top performance.

In a typical Charles scene, Nora is taken into police custody. She tells the officers that she's Mrs. Nick Charles. They telephone Nick to verify this and he says, "Throw her in the fish-tank 'til I get there."

They are playing games, and Nora will get even somehow.

A new fact of life in the Charles household is introduced in *Another Thin Man* (1939): Nick Charles, Jr. Parenthood, however, does not stand in the way of Nick and Nora having fun or delving into deduction. (In *Shadow of the Thin Man,* Nora tells the housekeeper that Junior takes after his father.

Another Thin Man (1939): C. Aubrey Smith, William Powell, Myrna Loy, Tom Neal and Virginia Grey.

The housekeeper answers, "Yes'm, he sure does. This morning he was playing with a corkscrew.")

In this third entry of the series, they are visiting an old family friend, Long Islander Colonel MacFay, the former partner of Nora's father. When murder ensues, the dynamic duo plus pooch do what comes naturally. Veteran character actor C. Aubrey Smith is one unfortunate victim. Other familiar faces in supporting roles include raucous-voiced Marjorie Main in a funny bit as a wacky landlady, Ruth Hussey, Tom Neal, Otto Kruger, Nat Pendleton, Horace MacMahon and Virginia Grey, who plays C. Aubrey's stepdaughter.

The film marked Powell's reappearance on the screen after an absence of two years due to illness and the shock of Jean Harlow's sudden death. Nick, Nora and Asta were welcomed warmly by audiences and the film was a box-office winner.

The setting for *Shadow of the Thin Man* (1941) is the world of horse racing and the characters who are part and parcel of the sport of kings: jockeys, touts, bookies and gambling syndicates. Upon reaching the track for a day's outing, Nick and Nora discover that a murder has been committed. The detective in charge says, "You know that jockey Golez? The one that was caught throwing the fourth race? He was shot." Nora remarks, "My, but they're strict at this track."

The duo is on the trail of a murderer who has killed more than once. Not until the last few minutes of the film does (Nick) or we know the identity of the arch criminal.

Barry Nelson makes his debut in the film as a reporter out to get the scoop of his career while Donna Reed, relegated to second leads at the time, plays his girlfriend. Sam Levene is the detective who enlists Nick's help with the line-up of suspects which includes Henry O'Neill, Alan Baxter and, from the New York stage, Stella Adler.

Myrna took time out from her film career to aid in the war effort, but she interrupted her patriotic duties in 1944 to appear in *The Thin Man Goes Home*. Richard Thorpe directed ("Woody" Van Dyke, the man who had guided the first four films, died in 1943). Though some of the series' initial charm had somewhat diminished, the public welcomed Nick, Nora and Asta with delight and responded to the film like a canine to a bone.

In this film, Nick, Nora and Asta leave Nick Jr. at his school and get aboard a train bound for Nick's hometown. As you might expect, the humans spend much of the trip in the animal car with the third member of their trio.

We get to meet Nick's parents, Dr. and Mrs. Charles (played by Harry Davenport and Lucile Watson). They have always looked askance at their son's profession, but when he solves a hometown crime which involves murder and art forgery, they take pride in him. The doctor even bursts a button on his shirt, he is so thrilled. The original story was written by Robert Riskin (on "leave" from Frank Capra) and Harry Kurnitz. Riskin also had a hand in the screenplay.

Powell and Loy made their sixth and last appearance as Nick and Nora in the 1947 release *Song of the Thin Man*. Against a background of pulsating jazz and smoke-filled night clubs, the two hunt for the vicious killer of a musician. The supporting cast (i.e., list of suspects) includes Keenan Wynn, Leon Ames, Patricia Morison (who would later score brilliantly on Broadway in *Kiss Me Kate*), Philip Reed, Gloria Grahame and Don Taylor. Nick Jr. is played by Dean Stockwell and Asta Jr. takes on the role made famous by the beloved original.

Not only was *Song of the Thin Man* the last time that Powell and Loy played Nick and Nora, the film marked the last time that the popular twosome appeared together on screen. Both, however, made several other films throughout their illustrious careers and always maintained the standard of craftsmanship that they had shown in earlier years. Powell's last appearance on screen was in *Mister Roberts* (Warner Brothers, 1955). Loy's last film was *Just Tell Me What You Want* (1980). In the early 1990s, she was a recipient of the Kennedy Center Life Achievement Award for her contribution to the arts.

William Powell and Myrna Loy are no longer with us, but their names evoke some wonderful memories of a bygone era among movie buffs and serious students of film. In spite of all the other films they made, together and apart, they will always be Nick and Nora, "The Thin Man" and "The Perfect Wife."

Chapter Twelve

Mixing Murder and Mayhem: Screwball Comedy-Mysteries

What do a lady poet, a spoiled heiress, a novelist, a mild-mannered clerk, a doctor, his ex-wife and two Greenwich Village couples have in common? Nothing much, except an affinity for cinematic crime. These are only some of the characters in the screwball comedy mysteries.

The screwball movie mysteries boasted some of the most popular and attractive stars in Hollywood, plus clever plot twists and enough zaniness to allow the armchair detectives in the audience the enjoyment of matching wits with the on-screen super-sleuths to see who would be the first to unmask the culprits.

Screwball sleuths are in the main well-dressed, well-spoken and, above all, well-heeled. Several dabble in detection just for the thrill of it and others because they or their friends, for one reason or another, have a vested interest in the skullduggery at hand.

The second *raison d'être* applies to William Powell in the two films he made while on loan-out from MGM to RKO in 1935 and 1936. In the first production, *Star of Midnight* (1935), he is a debonair lawyer who becomes involved with a missing actress and murder. Being the accused, he sets about trying to prove his innocence and, aided by girlfriend Ginger Rogers, he solves both the murder and the disappearance. Ginger, no stranger to the wisecrack or to screwball antics, acquits herself well, as does the able supporting cast which includes Paul Kelly, Gene Lockhart and Ralph Morgan.

Star of Midnight is an imitation of *The Thin Man*, as is *The Ex-Mrs. Bradford* (1936), in which Powell is a well-known surgeon who becomes entangled in a series of racetrack murders. Suspected by the police, he decides that the only way to clear himself is to play sleuth and catch the killer himself.

His ex-wife Paula, a mystery writer, is engagingly played by Jean Arthur.

Her obsession with real murders has led to a divorce. She is going to help her ex whether he likes it or not. As they combine their efforts, she is at times more of a hindrance than a help: She serves him a dinner in which every dish contains gelatin because that substance has been found on a dead jockey's body and she wants to see if it is what killed the man. It isn't, but it makes for good screwball logic.

In spite of her, the killer is found and by the end of the film, the audience knows that there is a re-marriage on the horizon. The strong supporting cast includes Eric Blore, a comic delight as Powell's butler Stokes, Robert Armstrong, Lila Lee, Ralph Morgan and James Gleason as a police inspector who is willing to accept any help he can get. These productions were more than reminiscent of the *Thin Man* series and contained nothing new, but Powell's sophisticated verbal sparring with Rogers and Arthur left both audiences and the RKO accounting department quite happy.

Nineteen thirty-six was a good year for Jean Arthur, and also a happy one. Besides *Mrs. Bradford*, the blonde actress starred in *Mr. Deeds Goes to Town, More Than a Secretary* and the film which concerns us here, Columbia's *Adventure in Manhattan*. She stars as an actress who meets up with a crime reporter-cum-criminologist (Joel McCrea). McCrea has been hired by a newspaper editor (Thomas Mitchell) to help catch a master burglar with caviar tastes: He steals art treasures and gemstones and has been outwitting the law for many years. The dapper criminal is portrayed by popular character actor Reginald Owen.

There is a twist: The reporter and the thief seem to display similar attitudes and tastes and the former is able to predict the latter's every move. With the help of Arthur, with whom McCrea has fallen in love, the miscreant is apprehended and the reporter gets the scoop and the girl.

The year before, Ms. Arthur had gone to work for John Ford. The latter, not noted for comedy, turned his not inconsiderable talents to screwball with *The Whole Town's Talking* for Columbia. The iconic director cast Edward G. Robinson, also not noted for comedy, in the role of Arthur Jones, a mild-mannered white collar clerk who just happens to bear an amazing resemblance to "Killer" Mannion, a notorious gangster (also played by Robinson) who has escaped from jail. The gangster finds it convenient at times to take on his lookalike's demeanor, with comical results. Jones is arrested, but the proper identification soon frees him. The resulting publicity incites Mannion, who sets out to murder his innocent double, but is thwarted by the latter's newfound courage.

Jean Arthur is the object of Jones' unrequited love and is the catalyst in his transformation from timidity to heroism. Others in the cast include Edward Brophy as Mannion's cohort and Etienne Girardot as Robinson's office manager, plus Donald Meek and Wallace Ford.

A film that precedes the "official" start of the screwball genre, yet deserves to be part of it, is the charming and sophisticated 1932 comedy thriller *Trouble in Paradise,* satirizing the gullibility of the rich.

The Paramount release, directed by Ernst Lubitsch, stars Herbert Marshall and Miriam Hopkins as Gaston Monescue and Lily Vautier, a jewel thief and a lady pickpocket. These two unconventional eccentrics meet and engage in witty dialogue as they practice "the tricks of their trade" upon each other. The two find a mark in Mariette Colet (Kay Francis), a wealthy widow who finds them so ingratiating that she hires them, Gaston as her private secretary and Lily as a typist. The trouble starts when Gaston falls in love with Mariette. Lily finds this maddening, but in the end their true nature defeats any decent emotion (Gaston sends Mariette flowers and charges them to her account) and the two sharpies take off with some "souvenirs" (among them a gorgeous necklace that Lily covets) from their former employer's home. The excitement of a life of crime is too much of a lure for them to give it up.

In the supporting cast are Edward Everett Horton and Charles Ruggles, who play bumbling rivals for Mariette's affections. They supply the screwball aspects of the film. To paraphrase *The New York Times,* it was an engaging and imaginative piece of work. Other critiques of the time were just as glowing.

Though Clark Gable had starred in and won an Oscar for his performance in *It Happened One Night,* the most famous screwball comedy of the decade, he is not considered a superstar of the genre. He did, however, make a few films in this vein. In the comedy-mystery *After Office Hours* (MGM, 1935), he is a newspaper editor (a step up from the previous year when he was merely a reporter) investigating a juicy crime story. Along for the ride is his "now you're hired, now you're fired" girlfriend, society reporter Constance Bennett, with whom he is always at odds. Their battle of the sexes is sparked by a literate and witty script and their own sharp performances. Seen in the supporting cast are Harvey Stephens as the murderer, the ever-present Billie Burke, Stuart Erwin and Henry Travers.

Joan Bennett did not make as many comedies as her sister Constance, but she did make her share of comedy-mysteries. Joan stars with Cary Grant in *Big Brown Eyes* (Paramount, 1936). Manicurist Bennett helps boyfriend detective Grant trap a gang of jewel thieves headed by Walter Pidgeon. With a bit of Nick and Nora thrown in, bolstered by a trio of big names and snappy dialogue, the film did well at the box office. Also in the cast are Lloyd Nolan and Alan Baxter.

Two years later, Bennett was at United Artists for *Trade Winds,* a film combining romance, comedy and mystery. It was produced by Walter Wanger, who later married his star. She plays the suspect in the murder of a man whose apartment she had visited. Co-star Fredric March, is a San Francisco Police Department detective assigned to the case.

"Aiding" him in the search for the missing girl are Ann Sothern as his ditzy Girl Friday and Ralph Bellamy as his bumbling detective sidekick. Sothern and Bellamy supply the screwball antics, she mangling messages, he mixing up clues and getting to the right place at the wrong time.

Finally March finds his quarry and falls in love with her. She has murdered no one; a jealous wife committed the crime. Bennett had wanted to get her sister out of the clutches of the man. The reader can guess at the finale. For this film, Bennett, in the early part of her career a blonde, became a brunette and, for the rest of her days in Hollywood, remained one.

The actress also starred in a comedy-mystery involving reporters, editors, gangsters and the law. In *The Housekeeper's Daughter*, a 1939 United Artists release, Bennett's tough-talking lady visits her housekeeper mother (Peggy Wood), falls for the son of the household (John Hubbard) and is instrumental in cracking a case involving the murder of a showgirl with the help of a womanizing, hard-drinking reporter (Adolphe Menjou).

Also in the cast are William Gargan as a photographer, Donald Meek as their apoplectic city editor, Marc Lawrence as a racketeer, George E. Stone as a weirdo murderer who kills by lacing his victim's coffee with poison and up-and-coming star Victor Mature as a gangster. Menjou, Gargan and Meek make this minor screwball enjoyable to watch.

For Barbara Stanwyck, Brooklyn-born chorus girl, Broadway actress turned movie star, playing an heiress in *The Mad Miss Manton* may have been a stretch, but as one of the more versatile performers of her era, she threw herself into the role with her characteristic professionalism and verve. She, co-star Henry Fonda and the 1938 RKO release garnered rave reviews from critics and fans alike.

Melsa Manton is a charming but slightly zany socialite who, while walking her dogs late at night, sees a man running from a building. Brimming over with curiosity, she runs into the building, investigates and finds a corpse. She tries to get out, but her cape is caught in the door.

She is not unknown to the law. According to the cops, she's "one of a bunch who once held a treasure hunt and stole a traffic light." She is a handful, as they ruefully note. One of the men in blue, motioning with his gun, asks, "Why can't I use this just once?"

The pack leader of a group of equally daffy friends, Melsa decides that they will catch the killer. Before the gals can accomplish this, Melsa meets reporter Peter Ames (Fonda). The two take an instant dislike to each other, an important element in screwball comedy, but this changes as he falls in love with her and she unwillingly falls for him.

Melsa's friends walk in on her as she is in danger of being killed by the murderer. One of the dizzy debs says, "If you kill her, you'll have to kill all of us." To which another retorts, "Oh, you're always talking communism." Melsa is rescued, the villain arrested and it is made abundantly clear that Peter will get used to his true love's nutty ways *and* all of her lovely money.

In the capable supporting cast are Sam Levene, again playing a harassed cop and Hattie McDaniel as Melsa's sassy maid. In one scene Hattie throws a pitcher of water in Fonda's face. She does so, saying, "It was orders, but I used distilled water." One of Melsa's debutante friends is played by Vicki Lester, an actress who took her name from the character portrayed by Janet Gaynor in the 1937 film *A Star Is Born*. Lester, an RKO contract player, faded from view in the early 1940s.

The foregoing was concerned with a group of zany socialites who think that catching a murderer is a lark. *Remember Last Night?* (Universal, 1935) has a somewhat similar storyline. After a night of carousing and heavy drinking, a free-wheeling couple (Robert Young and Constance Cummings) and a group of their zany society friends find themselves mixed up in murder and suicide. Edward Arnold plays the detective who solves the crime.

Supporting the stars are Reginald Denny, Robert Armstrong, Sally Eilers and Gustav von Seyffertitz as a hypnotist who seems to know the identity of the criminal, but is killed before he reveals it. Special mention should be made of Arthur Treacher, who in his perennial role as butler steals every scene in which he is seen. Though the scenario sounds like a horror story, there are enough comedy situations to give this minor film a place in the screwball mystery genre.

A product of the Broadway stage, Joan Blondell came to Hollywood along with James Cagney in 1930. For several years, she toiled in the Warner Brothers vineyards as a member of their now-famous stock company which included the likes of Cagney, her then-husband Dick Powell, Bette Davis and Pat O'Brien, among others.

By 1938, she had left Warners and was at Columbia. Within the next three years, the blonde star made a trio of comedies with Melvyn Douglas. Two of them, *There's Always a Woman* (1938) and *The Amazing Mr. Williams* (1939), fall in the category of the screwball mystery. (The third film, *Good Girls Go to Paris,* was discussed in Chapter Six.)

There's Always a Woman pairs Douglas and Blondell as Bill and Sally Reardon. He is a struggling gumshoe, she's his meddlesome wife. Mary Astor gets things going when she walks into Bill's office and offers him $300 to investigate a case that starts routinely enough, but winds up as a double homicide. Prominently involved in the goings-on are Jerome Cowan, Robert Paige and Thurston Hall. Up-and-coming star Rita Hayworth had a featured role in the film, but her scenes were cut out when Columbia thought they would have a series on their hands.

There's Always a Woman is another of the 1930s films which tried to emulate the success of *The Thin Man* series. It couldn't quite do it, but watching the sassy Blondell and the urbane Douglas being put through their paces is enjoyment enough.

In 1939, Columbia released the other film in which the Reardons were featured, *There's That Woman Again.* Douglas is back as Bill Reardon but gone is Blondell; Virginia Bruce plays Sally.

The new caper involves some stolen jewels with a couple of murders thrown in to complicate matters. Margaret Lindsay and Stanley Ridges are up to their eyeballs in the skullduggery while Gordon Oliver, Tom Dugan and Jonathan Hale wander in and out of the scenario to keep the action from lagging. Though an engaging film, *There's That Woman Again* did not fare as well at the box office as its predecessor.

The next year, Blondell and Douglas were a pair once more for Columbia in *The Amazing Mr. Williams.* Kenny Williams (Douglas) is a detective so hot on a case that his wedding to Maxine Carroll (Joan) has been postponed. He's out to get the Phantom Slugger, a violent masher. In one screwball scene, he puts on woman's clothes to capture this villain.

Aiding and abetting the two principals in this 1940 Columbia release are Ruth Donnelly as Effie, Joan's roommate, and John Wray as a parolee suspected of the crime.

There's Always a Woman and *The Amazing Mr. Williams* deserve to be mentioned in any look at the screwball comedy genre, not only for their storylines but because of the star quality of Blondell and Douglas. The two were always a joy to watch, separately as well as together. The longevity of their careers is ample proof of that.

An actress receives a box containing a dead body and two rival reporters are on the scene to solve the mystery of who sent it. Set in a Hollywood locale, this is the premise of *The Corpse Came C.O.D.* (Columbia, 1947). As the scenario develops, more murders are discovered. With a chase at the climax, the newshounds sniff out the nefarious one. This time, the zesty Blondell is teamed with George Brent and a cast including Grant Withers, Una O'Connor and Jim Bannon.

In the 1930s, MGM was busily engaged in making screwball mysteries. Case in point is the "Fast" trilogy consisted of *Fast Company* (1938), *Fast and Loose* and *Fast and Furious* (both 1939). The most interesting aspect to this threesome is that each film stars a different twosome portraying the same characters.

Fast Company stars Melvyn Douglas and Florence Rice as Joel and Gerda Sloane, rare book dealers not averse to some amateur sleuthing, especially when another dealer is murdered and a friend is the chief suspect. Also in the cast are well-known performers Claire Dodd, Louis Calhern, Douglass

Dumbrille, Horace MacMahon, Thurston Hall, Minor Watson and George Zucco.

The second film in the trilogy, *Fast and Loose* stars Robert Montgomery and Rosalind Russell as the Sloanes. This time around they solve the case of a stolen Shakespeare manuscript which leads to a double murder. Among the usual suspects are Ralph Morgan, Reginald Owen, and Alan Dinehart.

Last in the series is *Fast and Furious* which stars Ann Sothern and Franchot Tone. The Sloanes' last go-round involves murder during a seaside beauty contest. Among the beauties are Ruth Hussey and Mary Beth Hughes. This last film was directed by Busby Berkeley, famous for his choreography of the Warner Brother musicals of the 1930s.

Though the three may be considered "B" films by critics, they are well-paced, well written and well acted by each group of performers and contain many aspects of the screwball.

In the MGM production *It's a Wonderful World*, James Stewart is detective Guy Johnson, whose client Ernest Truex has been framed for murder, found guilty and sentenced to be executed. Johnson is on the lam, having been convicted of harboring Truex, who has offered him a lot of money if he (Johnson) can catch the real criminal. Johnson gets mixed up with poetess Edwina (Claudette Colbert) and several screwball scenes follow, including one in which a troop of Boy Scouts hunt for clues and another in which the two "adversaries" are in an orchard and she, climbing on his shoulders, drops apples down on his head one by one.

Edwina's efforts to "help" are not appreciated by Guy, but she does contribute and he, his partner Cap Streeter (Guy Kibbee) and their client are proven to be innocent. Guy gets the money and a bride. He celebrates with a poem of his own—he does not like Edwina's:

Roses are red,
Violets are blue,
I get a hundred grand for this
But I want you.

The two stars are surrounded by a cast of talented performers including Edgar Kennedy and Nat Pendleton as the not-too-bright minions of the law chasing Jimmy. The film was a great success with both critics and fans alike. How could it go wrong with Ben Hecht writing the script, "Woody" Van Dyke directing and the team of Claudette Colbert and James Stewart starring?

Like Clark Gable, Warner Brothers star Errol Flynn was not noted for his comedic prowess, but in 1941, after appearing in seven costume dramas in a row, he starred in the screwball comedy thriller *Footsteps in the Dark*. In the film, he is a successful investment counselor whose dream is to be an equally successful writer of mystery stories. He puts his theories to work when he is confronted with a real murder. Brenda Marshall (who that year married up-and-coming actor William Holden) co-stars as his wife.

The finale has Flynn answering a phone call from the police about an odd new case. He tells his wife he has some business to attend to, races to the front door—and finds his wife waiting for him. From now on, they will detect together.

A phony princess contending with a handsome bandleader and a case of murder on a trans–Atlantic voyage adds up to *The Princess Comes Across,* a delightful whodunit teaming a very successful pair of stars. In this 1936 Paramount production, Carole Lombard plays Wanda Nash, a Brooklyn showgirl who went to Europe third class and is returning via first class to the U.S. posing as Olga, a Swedish princess, hoping to be discovered by a Hollywood talent scout and becoming the next Garbo. Fred MacMurray is King Mantell, the music-maker who falls for her. (Fred, who began his lengthy show business career as a singing saxophonist and appeared on the New York stage, gets to sing in the film.) Before he knows the truth about her identity, he invites her to have cocktails with him and then asks her if she enjoyed the drinks. Says Wanda, "Oh, the first couple. After that I was bored."

The two become involved in the murder of a blackmailer and, in tandem, bumble their way to a solution of the crime. In support of the two stars are Douglass Dumbrille, William Frawley, Alison Skipworth and Porter Hall.

On a ship, in a plane, on the ground—murder is murder. It is also a staple in the lives of Pamela and Gerald North.

During the 1930s and the 1940s, the husband-and-wife team of Richard and Frances Lockridge delighted mystery fans with a series of novels in which the main characters are Mr. and Mrs. North, a publisher and his charmingly offbeat wife who live in Greenwich Village and have a habit of getting themselves involved in murder. The adventures of Pam and Jerry became a weekly series on radio during that medium's "Golden Age" and it was only a matter of time before the Norths made it to the silver screen.

In 1941, MGM released *Mr. and Mrs. North* with Gracie Allen as Pamela and William Post, Jr., as Jerry. When Pam opens their liquor closet, a corpse tumbles out. The Norths decide to help police lieutenant Bill Weigand (Paul Kelly) solve the case and Pam, in her convoluted way, comes up with the killer. The competent supporting cast is comprised of Tom Conway, Porter Hall, Felix Bressart, Keye Luke and Jerome Cowan.

The film made a poor showing at the box office: Gracie without her husband and show business partner, George Burns, was evidently not what the fans wanted to see. If a series on the Norths was in the planning stage, the idea was quickly dropped.

Two years before, Gracie had been at Paramount for *The Gracie Allen Murder Case*, also with a New York locale. S.S. Van Dyne, a popular author at the time, had written a series of mysteries starring his fictional detective Philo Vance. The debonaire sleuth was portrayed in the movies by many actors, among them William Powell, Basil Rathbone, Paul Lukas, Edmund Lowe and Warren William.

William, as Vance, plays second banana to Gracie in the film, as he tries to solve the murder of an ex-convict, "aided" by the ditzy comedienne. The detective even answers to the name Fido. It was a "B" film with an interesting premise, but again, without Burns. Fans did not come out in droves.

Greenwich Village of the 1940s was the locale of *A Night to Remember* (1942). Brian Aherne is a mystery writer whose wife (Loretta Young) wants him to write the Great American Novel. This charmingly screwball lady thinks that the arty atmosphere of the Village will awaken and inspire the muse in her husband.

Upon moving into their new digs, they find a dead body in the backyard. The two investigate amid shadows and creaking doors until the killer is unmasked. Seen in support are such worthies as Sidney Toler playing a police inspector, Miss Jeff Donnell as a young neighbor and Blanche Yurka as a nutty cleaning lady.

New York City is also the setting for *Lady on a Train,* a 1945 Universal release starring Deanna Durbin as a young lady who, while on her way to the city, witnesses a murder from her train window.

Trying to get the police to believe her is hard as she had been reading a mystery by her favorite author. The determined lady hunts down the writer (David Bruce) and persuades him to help her. They solve the mystery while becoming involved with the victim's nutty family, members of which include Ralph Bellamy and Dan Duryea. Also involved in the scenario is a case of mistaken identity: Duryea thinks Durbin is the murdered man's nightclub singer sweetheart, which gives her a chance to warble a couple of numbers and gives him a chance to chase her. It's a delightful film, one of the singer's best as an adult.

Jimmy the Gent, a 1934 Warner Brothers film, has a fascinating premise and features the always intriguing duo of star performers, James Cagney and Bette Davis. The feisty Cagney is seen as a cagey con man who sets out to find missing heirs to large unclaimed estates. If these heirs don't exist, Jimmy's character invents them.

The mystery lies in how he has gotten away with these capers. When he meets Bette, however, he falls for her. She is his Waterloo and he will, albeit reluctantly, go straight. The Runyonesque script contains showy roles for Allen Jenkins, Alice White and the interesting Mayo Methot.

A Warner Brothers contract player, Mayo was more famous in her off-screen role as the third Mrs. Humphrey Bogart. During their stormy marriage, the two were known as "The Battling Bogarts." While filming *To Have and Have Not* in 1944, Bogart met Lauren Bacall, divorced Mayo and married his young co-star.

Chapter Thirteen

Screwball Families:
The Mamas, the Papas, the Kids

Grandpa Vanderhof quit his job 35 years ago and has never looked back. He has not paid taxes and spends his time doing whatever grabs him at the moment.

His daughter, Penny Sycamore, is a writer only because a typewriter was delivered to the house by mistake. Her husband Paul, a fireworks enthusiast, spends much of his time in the basement along with a man named De Pinna who had come to the house years before to deliver ice. Between the two, it's a wonder that the house is still intact.

Their daughter Essie is a mediocre ballerina taking lessons from Kolenkhov, a wacky Russian émigré who thinks more about his stomach than he does of his pupil's feet. Ed, Essie's husband, is a xylophone player. Another of Grandpa's friends invents toys and party masks. Essie's sister Alice, the only "normal" one in the household, has a job and is being courted by Tony, the son of her boss, a wealthy industrialist.

But wait a moment. *Is* Alice the only normal one in the family? And how do we define the word "normal"? These are the questions explored in Frank Capra's *You Can't Take It with You*. The film was the director's sixth hit in a row.

Columbia mogul Harry Cohn paid $200,000 for the screen rights to the George S. Kaufman–Moss Hart Pulitzer Prize–winning play. This was a record amount for the notoriously cheap studio, but whatever Capra wanted in those days Capra got, and the feisty Frank justified this expenditure in every way.

Are Grandpa and the Sycamores screwy or are they a group of people living in harmony, beloved by friends and neighbors, who find peace and contentment as they pursue their own individuality? Are they considered offbeat because of their non-conformity to what is supposedly the norm?

You Can't Take It with You (1938) with James Stewart and Jean Arthur. This film about an endearingly eccentric family won an Academy Award, as did its director Frank Capra, his third in five years.

Tony, Alice's boyfriend, asks her to marry him. Grandpa Vanderhof is then pitted against Alice's boss and future father-in-law, Anthony Kirby, an already wealthy man who is obsessed with making even more money.

When a crisis involves the family's home, Alice runs away. Tony goes after her and Grandpa meets the industrialist, charms him and all turns out well for the family and the two lovers.

Moviegoers watching this example of "Capra-corn" cheered Grandpa on, probably envying him as he played his harmonica and let the rest of the world go by. Critics raved and the Motion Picture Academy of Arts and Sciences honored both film and director. (Capra's Oscar for direction was his third in five years.)

The success of the film was immeasurably helped by an ensemble cast, a who's who of Hollywood and screwball royalty: Lionel Barrymore as Grandpa Vanderhof, Spring Byington as Penny, James Stewart and Jean Arthur as young lovers Tony and Alice, Edward Arnold as Tony's father, Mischa Auer as the zany Russian Kolenkhov, Samuel S. Hinds as Penny's husband and Ann Miller as Essie.

There may be some question as to whether the Vanderhof-Sycamore clan is a true screwball family but there is absolutely no doubt that the Bullocks of *My Man Godfrey* (Universal, 1936) pass the test with flying colors. Its premise has Irene Bullock (Carole Lombard) picking up a tramp named Godfrey (William Powell) in order to win a society scavenger hunt. It is interesting to see the usually suave Powell playing against type. As Godfrey, he's a derelict with a difference—something about him intrigues Irene and she hires him as a butler. (Reel life had followed real life: Lombard and Powell were married from 1931 until 1933.)

There is an air of good breeding and erudition about Godfrey and no wonder: he had once been a prominent socialite himself but left that world because of an unsuccessful love affair. We find this out when he meets Tommy Gray (Alan Mowbray), an old friend, whom Godfrey swears to secrecy.

Godfrey sees only chaos in the Bullock home: Irene's mother is a self-centered, addle-brained woman, her harried father is only the nominal head of the household and her sister (Gail Patrick) is a scheming vixen of a girl. There is also a starving "artist" living off the Bullock clan, a "protégé" of Mrs. Bullock. The elder Bullocks are played by Alice Brady and Eugene Pallette, the freeloader by Mischa Auer (the character is similar to the one he played in *You Can't Take It with You*).

Before Godfrey leaves the Bullock household, he has given the inhabitants a lesson in humility and taught them that money isn't everything. By this time, Irene has fallen in love with him, he has thwarted Cornelia's attempt to portray him as a jewel thief, and he has helped Mr. Bullock out financially. He has also found a cause for himself: He builds a nightclub on the site of a dump. "The Dump" will provide jobs for the needy friends he has made and Irene will be at his side, whether he likes it or not.

The film is a devastating satire on the Depression, big business and the idle rich. Powell at the dump sarcastically remarks, "Prosperity is just around the corner." The scene cuts to the society types milling about the dump.

Lombard, Powell, Auer, director Gregory La Cava and the film were nominated at Oscar time. They went zero for five, but it has lost not one whit of its charm and, seen via television stations playing films of the Golden Era or on DVDs, it remains as fresh as ever.

It's a far cry from the 1957 remake starring June Allyson, David Niven, Robert Keith and Martha Hyer. *My Man Godfrey* is a film of the 1930s, the era of the Great Depression; bringing it into the era of the 1950s is a disservice to the original. In the remake, Niven plays an illegal alien hired as a butler. He and Allyson are good performers but lack the madcap qualities of the Powell-Lombard combination.

In the same vein as the previously discussed film is *Merrily We Live* (Hal Roach, 1938) with Constance Bennett as Jerry, the high-spirited daughter

My Man Godfrey (1936) with Carole Lombard and William Powell. Reel life followed real life: the two were married from 1931 to 1933.

of a screwball family, the Kilbournes. Her daffy mom (Billie Burke) hires Wade Rawlins (Brian Aherne), a man who seems to be a tramp, as the family chauffeur. Wade is actually a famous novelist, working incognito on a new project.

Animosity between author and heiress develops into love. Also, in true screwball fashion, the family indulges in childish whims and defies conventions, then learns a lesson in better living. Towards the end of the film, Aherne's character, presumed dead, turns up very much alive, prompting screwball reaction from the family and the household staff.

Billie Burke was nominated as Best Supporting Actress for her performance as the fluttery matriarch (she lost to Fay Bainter in *Jezebel*). The cast of characters also includes Alan Mowbray as Grosvenor the butler, Patsy Kelly as the cook, Clarence Kolb as head of the Kilbourne tribe and Bonita Granville as Marion, Bennett's younger sister.

Godfrey and Rawlins are not really servants in any sense of the word, but Marmaduke Ruggles (Charles Laughton) is in *Ruggles of Red Gap* (Paramount, 1935). He plays a proper butler who is lost in a poker game by his English employer (Roland Young) to a nouveau riche American couple, Effie and Egbert Floud (Mary Boland and Charles Ruggles), who are bewildered by their new status in life.

Ruggles is then transported to the western town of Red Gap. Laughs come fast and furious as he tries to teach the "niceties" of life to the Flouds. While engaged in this, he is affected by their somewhat crude but endearing behavior and settles down with their friend, played by ZaSu Pitts.

The film had a new incarnation in 1950: *Fancy Pants* stars Bob Hope as Humphrey, a poverty-stricken English actor who is brought to a small town in America by rich Aggie Floud (Lucille Ball) to serve as the family butler. Bob and Lucy clown around—the horse scenes are hilarious, but the film is not up to the standards of the original. There is too much of the slapstick, which we expect from Bob and Lucy, but not much of the gentility of Laughton's character.

Like Bob Hope's Humphrey, Ginger Rogers' Mary Gray is broke in the opening scenes of *Fifth Avenue Girl* (RKO, 1939). She is a down-to-earth working-class girl who believes that "rich people are just poor people with money." She meets rich but miserable Mr. Borden (Walter Connolly) in New York's Central Park and spends a night on the town with him during which he celebrates his birthday (his family has forgotten it and him). For the first time in a long while, he has really enjoyed himself, and invites the jobless girl to live in his mansion as a member of his family.

Mrs. Borden (Verree Teasdale), son Tim (Tim Holt) and daughter Katherine (Kathryn Adams) are shocked and very much upset at this turn of events. Mrs. Borden thinks the worst about her husband and this much younger "interloper." For years, however, she has been somewhat indifferent towards her marriage and the children have virtually ignored their father while freely spending his money. Ginger's perky presence changes all that and also the family's attitude on life in general.

By the final reel, it is evident that Ginger will live happily ever after with Borden's son. The two young people had taken an instant dislike to each other, a different kind of battle of the sexes, he thinking she is after his father's money, she of the opinion that he is spoiled and selfish, a typical rich man's son. But in a Central Park setting, each sees the other in a different light and they begin to have feelings for each other. Feelings are also rekindled in the older Bordens when they reminisce about the days when they had little money and she did all the household chores.

The heroine of *Fifth Avenue Girl* begins by being broke. This is not the case of Claudette Colbert and her family in Paramount's *Three Cornered Moon*.

This early example of the screwball concerns a family, once wealthy, needing to go out and get jobs after the Wall Street collapse. Though not so funny today, the trials and tribulations of this family made for many laughs in 1933, giving some respite to Depression-weary audiences. Starring with Colbert are Richard Arlen and, as the matriarch of the clan, Mary Boland.

Money problems of another sort are faced by Walter Connolly's family in *She Couldn't Take It* (Columbia, 1935). Connolly goes to prison on a charge of income tax evasion. He considers it a sort of vacation from the screwy antics of his impossible family. While in the slammer, he meets ex-bootlegger George Raft, who is aiming for the straight and narrow upon his release. The two become friends, whereupon Connolly makes Raft the executor of his last will and testament. The older man soon dies and Raft, now out of jail, is confronted with this family of loonies, Connolly's ditzy wife (Billie Burke) and his spoiled and selfish children. Seen in these roles are Joan Bennett and Lloyd Nolan. After the prerequisite battle of the sexes between Raft and Bennett, he marries into the family and helps its members to turn over a new leaf.

Speaking about turning over a new leaf brings us to the zanies in Mortimer Brewster's family in *Arsenic and Old Lace* (Warner Brothers, 1944). Cary Grant, in an over-the-top performance, is Mortimer, a theater critic. The only sane one in his family, he is saddled with eccentric aunts Abby and Martha Brewster (played by Josephine Hull and Jean Adair) who take borders into their home, proceed to poison them with elderberry wine and then bury the bodies in their basement. Unless committed, the old ladies will never turn over a new leaf. This is a screwball plot, if there ever was one.

Raymond Massey plays Jonathan, Mortimer's brother, a dangerously insane escapee from a mental home. As Mortimer puts it, "Insanity doesn't run in our family. It practically gallops." Before the ladies are sent to a "rest home" and Massey is captured, Mortimer learns that he is not a Brewster (he was adopted) to his immense relief and that of his fiancée Elaine (Priscilla Lane).

There are several very funny scenes, one of which has Grant tied up and a cop thinking that it is part of a play. Peter Lorre is hilarious as Massey's equally nutty sidekick. A well-known supporting cast includes Jack Carson, Edward Everett Horton and James Gleason.

Aided by the publicity garnered by the success of the stage play upon which it was based, plus the direction of Frank Capra and the casting of Cary Grant, the film was an instant hit.

Publicity is definitely *not* what the Lord family is seeking as MGM's *The Philadelphia Story* (MGM, 1940), a romantic comedy of unconventional people and humorous incidents, opens. Daughter Tracy is about to embark upon marriage number two and *Spy* magazine is on the premises to provide its readers with a first-hand view of the society wedding of the year.

Why are the *Spy* reporter and photographer at the mansion? A very good question. It seems that Father Lord has been indiscreet with a fan dancer, and the magazine will forgo covering that story in return for a wedding scoop. The real "scoop" turns out to be that Tracy goes back to husband number one, Dad returns to the bosom of his family and *Spy* is left at the starting gate.

The 1940 film, based on the play by Philip Barry, was a milestone in the career of Katharine Hepburn. She attained movie stardom in 1932, was an Oscar winner the next year and was labeled "box office poison" in 1938 by a group of film exhibitors—surely a roller-coaster effect on any young performer.

Undaunted, Hepburn went back to New York, appeared in *The Philadelphia Story* on Broadway to rave reviews, secured the screen rights to the hit play and returned to Tinsel Town in triumph.

MGM's deal with the canny Kate stipulated that she play leading character Tracy on screen. The studio added Cary Grant as the first husband C.K. Dexter Haven, James Stewart as reporter Macaulay "Mike" Connor and Ruth Hussey as photographer Liz Imbrie. (These roles were played on Broadway by Joseph Cotten, Van Heflin and Shirley Booth.) Also in the cast are John Halliday and Mary Nash as the elder Lords, John Howard as George Kitteridge (Tracy's intended) and, stealing every scene in which they appear, Virginia Weidler as Dinah, Tracy's younger sister, and Roland Young as the lecherous Uncle Willie, a glint in his eye and a hand ready to pinch.

From the opening scene, when Tracy throws Dexter's golf clubs at him and he responds by pushing her in the face, causing her to fall backward, to the end, when she is happy to return to him, the picture is a joy to watch. The critics agreed and so did the Academy. Hepburn, Hussey, Stewart, director George Cukor, the film and its screenplay were Oscar nominated. Only Stewart and the screenplay won.

An incident at that Oscar ceremony has gone down in Hollywood lore. Winning the coveted statuette for his *Philadelphia Story* screenplay, Donald Ogden Stewart jocularly announced to all gathered: "I am happy to say that I am entirely—and solely—responsible for the success of *The Philadelphia Story*." Not true, but it did get a big laugh and in these days with the "I need to thank" speeches going on ad infinitum, perhaps taking a lesson in brevity from Donald Ogden Stewart might be a good thing.

In 1956, the film was remade as the musical *High Society*. In the cast are a future princess (Grace Kelly in her last feature film) and two crooners by the names of Crosby and Sinatra. One of the few really good remakes, it benefits from a Cole Porter score and the appearance of the immortal Louis Armstrong.

Screwball families are not always as rich as the Lords. They can also be poor and on the make, like the Carltons in *The Young in Heart* (United Artists, 1938).

The Philadelphia Story (1940): Cary Grant, Katharine Hepburn and James Stewart. The trials and tribulations of the upper-crust Lord family.

The patriarch of the family is Colonel Anthony Carlton (Roland Young), a self-described member of India's Bengal Lancers. However, all is not what it seems, for not only has the "Colonel" never been to India, he's never been in the army. His scatterbrained wife Marmy (Billie Burke) and his two greedy, gold-digging children Georgie-Ann and Richard (Janet Gaynor and Douglas Fairbanks Jr.) round out the family.

The plot thickens when the family, traveling by train, meets sweet and very rich Ellen Fortune (Minnie Dupree). When the train is derailed, the con artists "save" the old lady and she invites them to live with her. The foursome moves in and take over the household. The fluttery Burke in charge of a bunch of servants is a highlight. The family's intent is to get their benefactress to leave them her fortune. While with the old lady, however, each has a change of heart.

The film, somewhat in the style of the Frank Capra films, features Paulette Goddard and Richard Carlson as the love interests of Fairbanks and Gaynor. It is a charming addition to the screwball genre and did well at the box office in 1938.

Speaking of fleecing the rich, we come to Gene Tierney in *Rings on Her Fingers* (Fox, 1942). The lovely lady is recruited by a pair of swindlers for the purpose of charming a millionaire out of his money. The "nefarious" duo, played by sweet-faced Spring Byington and Laird Cregar, are to pose as her mother and uncle.

As soon as Henry Fonda puts in an appearance with his talk of yachts, the "family" sets its sights on him. But things do not work out that way. Tierney falls for Fonda, who turns out to be penniless, himself out to snare a rich wife. This revelation fails to bother the smitten Gene, but "Mother" and "Uncle" are less than happy to be left to their own devices.

As in *The Lady Eve*, Fonda begins *Rings on Her Fingers* as a lamb being led to slaughter, but in true screwball fashion, he does not do too badly for himself in the end.

Joan Marsh, as Carolyn Page, is about to marry money (Reginald Denny) in *We're Rich Again* (RKO, 1934). This will help her once-wealthy family: her polo-playing grandmother (hilariously played by Edna May Oliver), her screwy, pampered mother (Billie Burke), her younger sister (Gloria Shea) and her put-upon father (Grant Mitchell).

Enter Marian Nixon as Cousin Arabella ("Ah'm from West Texas") with her down-home ways which hide a razor-sharp mind. She schemes to get millionaire Denny for herself and eventually does. She is not the villain of the piece, however: Carolyn is not in love with her intended bridegroom.

Cousin Arabella redeems herself by giving her uncle a good stock tip. She also encourages a marriage between Carolyn's sister and the man she loves (Olympic star Larry "Buster" Crabbe, doing some swimming in the film), who turns out to be quite a wealthy young man.

Into this merry mix comes a process server who tries to gain entrance into the house and is thwarted by the family. Even the butler has a turn at this "game." But the movie belongs to Oliver and Burke, who have been given the best lines, as witness the following exchange:

> BURKE: You shouldn't play polo on an empty stomach.
> OLIVER: What you need is a lesson in anatomy.

As in *We're Rich Again*, the family in *There Goes the Groom* (RKO, 1937) is trying to reverse their financial difficulties. Mama Russell would love to snare rich husbands for her daughters. She is overjoyed when Dick (Burgess Meredith), the boyfriend of the older girl, comes back to town after striking it rich in Alaska. The young man has come to claim Janet, the girl who promised to marry him if he's made something of himself. She's engaged to a doctor, but breaks it off when she finds out that Dick is rich. The younger daughter (top-billed Ann Sothern) does not share her family's motives; she has been in love with Meredith all along and gets him in the end.

Featured in this all-too-familiar story are Mary Boland as the grasping Mama, Onslow Stevens as the doctor and Louise Henry as the selfish older sister. In the film's funniest sequence, Meredith, pretending amnesia, is manic as he takes part in a football game his skeptical doctor has staged to "restore" his memory. The film gives the often serious actor another chance to show off his flair for comedy, which has been made evident by a couple of films discussed in this book.

Boland and Sothern again are mother and daughter in a minor venture titled *Danger, Love at Work* (Fox, 1937). Ann plays a much engaged girl who falls for a lawyer (Jack Haley) who wants her zany but wealthy folks (Boland and Etienne Girardot) to sign an important legal document. They do, once Ann has set her cap for the lawyer. Also featured in the cast are John Carradine as a screwy artist, Bonnie Bartlett as Ann's little sister, Edward Everett Horton, Alan Dinehart and Walter Catlett.

Two sisters from Ohio, Ruth, an aspiring writer, and Eileen, a wannabe actress, come to New York in search of fame and fortune in *My Sister Eileen* (Columbia, 1942).

First introduced in the pages of the magazine *The New Yorker*, the stories by Ruth McKinney formed the basis of a Broadway show. Seeing its potential as a film, Harry Cohn bought the screen rights and cast Rosalind Russell as Ruth and Janet Blair as Eileen. (The play had starred Shirley Booth as Ruth.)

The plot hinges on the lives of the sisters in their Greenwich Village basement apartment where they have a "foot-level view" of the world above and where they encounter some of the colorful characters who inhabit this part of the big city. The girls become part of what I would call a family, engaging in screwball antics, but lovingly protective of each other.

Roz meets editor Brian Aherne who buys her stories and, in the process, falls in love with her. While thus engaged with her writing and love life, she is also trying to rescue her younger sister from the vicissitudes of life in the Big Apple and also from the clutches of the two-footed wolves who come howling at the door.

The principals, especially Russell (who, in a hilarious scene, leads a Conga line of non–English-speaking Greek sailors), deliver their lines with skill and zest, the real flavor of the film comes from the girls' extended "family," the zany characters floating in and out of the scenario: George Tobias, their Greek landlord, Frank Sully, the janitor, Allyn Joslyn, a reporter, Donald MacBride, a pugnacious minion of the law, Richard Quine, a soda jerk with a crush on Eileen, Gordon Jones, a professional football player nicknamed "The Wreck," and Jeff Donnell, his adoring girlfriend. Also seen, very briefly, are the Three Stooges as workmen digging up the street to make way for a new subway.

A musical version of the McKinney story appeared on Broadway in 1951.

With music by Leonard Bernstein and lyrics by Adolph Green and Betty Comden, this version starred Rosalind Russell. The film's remake was released by Columbia in 1955. It stars Betty Garrett as Ruth, Janet Leigh as Eileen and Jack Lemmon in the role previously played by Brian Aherne. Although Garrett is a fine singer-comedienne, she is no Rosalind Russell, who made the role of Ruth her own on both stage and screen. Also, the characters in the remake are not as well defined as they are in the original and much of the comedy has been sacrificed to the musical numbers.

In getting involved with their village neighbors, Ruth and Eileen are part of an extended family. Also getting involved with their neighbors are Joan Bennett and George Brent. In *Twin Beds* (United Artists, 1942), the two star as newlyweds who would like to have some time alone. However, they are constantly being "visited" or annoyed by their extended "family" led by zany Russian Mischa Auer and his wife (Una Merkel) and also by Bennett's former boyfriend and *his* wife (Ernest Truex and Glenda Farrell). Things come to a head when the three couples decide to move away from each other, but in true screwball fashion, they find that they have moved to the same street. The "family" is intact once more.

Moving is the subject of our next film, but the Fullers are not newlyweds.

With the exception of *To Be or Not to Be,* Jack Benny always denigrated his films, but in reviewing many of them, they turn out to be not bad at all. A case in point: *George Washington Slept Here* (Warner Brothers, 1942), based on a play co-written by George S. Kaufman and Moss Hart. Benny plays the much put-upon husband of Ann Sheridan. The latter has bought a dilapidated Pennsylvania farmhouse for the family which includes her impressionable younger sister and a mischievous nephew. This house is rumored to have been one of the places in which General Washington slept during the Revolutionary War.

"Dilapidated" is hardly the word for the house: rotten floors, no water and poor roofing, among other things. Renovations begin and the Fullers learn that it was Benedict Arnold, and not our first president, who slept in their house. Benny and spouse go through several screwball moments involving Percy Kilbride's Mr. Kimber, a local handyman always finding things that will cost money, including digging for water in various places, Charles Coburn, the uncle who is thought to be rich but is not, and Charles Dingle as the local curmudgeon with an eye to getting the house, cheap of course, after the renovations have nearly bankrupted the Fullers. The end of the film has Kimber finding an old boot which contains a letter from General Washington. A threatened foreclosure is now an issue of the past.

In four of the five productions we will next look at, the action is dominated by ghosts and trick photography. *Topper,* Thorne Smith's whimsical novel about a henpecked husband and a ghostly pair who appoint themselves his guardian angel, had been on best-seller lists for several years before being filmed by MGM in 1937. Two superstars of the era and one of its most beloved character actors were assigned the principal roles: Cary Grant and Constance Bennett are the irascible "now you see them, now you don't" George and Marion Kerby and Roland Young is the meek Cosmo Topper.

George is the largest stockholder in a bank. He and his blonde wife Marion sail through life defying convention, with nary a care and with cocktail at hand. They are wealthy and they are irresponsible, but very happy and very much in love. Until ...

The Kerbys are killed in an automobile accident while under the influence. They find out that they can be accepted in Heaven, but first must perform a good deed. The daffy duo decide to win their halos by teaching their friend, staid bank president Cosmo Topper, how to live life to its fullest, Kerby style, defying convention and enjoying life. Unbeknownst to Mrs. Topper, they are now part of her family.

What follows is a wildly high-spirited hour and a half of fun, with Bennett and Grant in fine fettle, "toppered" only by Oscar-nominated Roland Young. The trio of laugh-getters are surrounded by a powerhouse cast of screwball veterans, among them Billie Burke as the befuddled Mrs. Topper, Alan Mowbray as the Toppers' long-suffering butler Wilkens, Eugene Pallette as a hotel detective and Arthur Lake in the role of an elevator operator, dazed by the sight of Topper laughing and talking to people who "ain't even there." As an added attraction, singer-composer Hoagy Carmichael makes a cameo appearance in a nightclub scene.

Two years later, with much of the world in chaos, United Artists released a second *Topper* film, again with Roland Young and Billie Burke as the Toppers. In *Topper Takes a Trip*, which takes place before the start of World War II, Mrs. T., bewildered by her husband's behavior, is contemplating a divorce and decides go to the French Riviera to think things over. Cosmo follows her in an attempt to save his marriage. And who decides to come to his aid but the invisible member of the Topper family, good old Marion Kerby, once more played by Constance Bennett. Cary Grant makes a brief appearance in a flashback from the first *Topper*, but as his price per film had soared in the two years between productions and Bennett needed a comic accomplice, the handsome actor was "replaced" by another handsome "gentleman," the top dog star of the decade, Asta, in the role of Mr. Atlas. Connie and the canine help "Toppy" salvage his marriage and get Clara Topper out of the clutches of a suave European fortune hunter, Baron de Rossi (Alexander D'Arcy).

Alan Mowbray, again playing the Toppers' faithful butler, Verree Teasdale and Franklin Pangborn helped to make this sequel a box office winner.

Topper Returns (1941): The lady (Joan Blondell) has been murdered. Why is Topper (Roland Young) always involved with ghosts?

The third and final *Topper* film, *Topper Returns*, was released by United Artists in 1941. This production would ordinarily have been part of the section on screwball mysteries, but I have placed it in this chapter because it completes the trio. *Topper Returns* is an entertaining spoof of an old-fashioned murder mystery, replete with old house, sliding wall panels, hidden passages and disappearing bodies. For the third time, the Toppers are portrayed by Billie Burke and Roland Young. Also featured is Joan Blondell as Gail Richards, who accompanies her friend Ann Carrington (Carole Landis) to the latter's family home. The girl has not seen her father since she was a child. Gail is murdered shortly thereafter. Why has she been killed? That is the riddle the newly deceased young lady, now a comely ghost, is "dying" to solve. To whom does she turn? Why, none other than Cosmo Topper, whom she met on the road to her friend's home. In the end, they get their man: Carole's father who turns out to be the dastardly evil-doer. But we find out that the man is not Carole's father but the father's business partner, out to steal her fortune.

Seen in support are Dennis O'Keefe as a cab driver who has fallen in love with Carole, H.B. Warner as the villain, Donald MacBride as a put-upon policeman and an unlikely comic duo, Eddie "Rochester" Anderson and Patsy Kelly, as Eddie and Emily, the Toppers' chauffeur and maid. Watching this duo is sheer delight.

The film was well received, but did not do as well as the previous two at the box office. Producer Hal Roach felt the series had run out of steam and no more *Topper* films were made.

Thorne Smith's Topper characters came to television in the early 1950s with Leo G. Carroll in the title role and, as the ghostly couple, the real-life husband-and-wife team of Anne Jeffreys and Robert Sterling.

A ghostly screwball family of two is the subject of *I Married a Witch* (Paramount 1942), taken from a novel by the aforementioned Thorne Smith. Veronica Lake portrays Jennifer, a 17th century witch who is transported to modern times by a bolt of lightning. Her aim is to bring chaos into the life of ambitious politician Wallace Wooley (Fredric March), a descendant of the Puritans who burned her at the stake in 1690. Her curse upon the descendants of the man who denounced her is that all of the future males in the family have unhappy marriages. Thereby begins a most unusual battle of the sexes.

Jennifer and Wooley "meet" when she materializes as a modern woman whom he rescues from a burning building (she's caused the fire); she follows him home. Cecil Kellaway is Daniel, her tipsy father. Father and daughter try all sorts of tricks, but the bewitching witch becomes mortal because she has fallen in love with Wooley and he with her. The two marry in spite of Daniel's efforts to revert her to her former self. Susan Hayward and Robert Benchley are also featured in this delightful fantasy.

Acting honors also go to Gary Cooper and Barbara Stanwyck as we come to the last film in this section, *Ball of Fire* (1941) from Samuel Goldwyn. Cooper plays Professor Bertram Potts, who lives in a Manhattan brownstone with his "family"—seven other academicians compiling an encyclopedia. Potts is doing an entry on slang. A garbage collector comes into the house on a "quizzola," a hunt for some answers to a quiz he wants to enter. Never having heard the term before, Potts realizes that he is out of touch with his topic and he decides to obtain some information straight from the horse's mouth. He visits a nightclub where drummer Gene Krupa's band is playing and finds a perfect filly in the person of Stanwyck, playing a stripper with one of the greatest names in screwball, Sugarpuss O'Shea.

At first reluctant, she tells Potts to "Scrow, scram, scraw." The professor is jubilant. "The complete conjugation," he marvels.

When Sugarpuss finds out that she is wanted for questioning regarding the whereabouts of her racketeer boyfriend Joe Lilac (Dana Andrews), she tells Potts that she will help him, but only if she can stay at his home. She reasons that the last place the cops would look for her would be in a house full of professors. She is also somewhat curious about this "square" and his

Ball of Fire (1941): Sugarpuss (Barbara Stanwyck) and the professor (Gary Cooper). And just what is "yum yum"?

quest for information. "This is the first time anybody has moved in on my brain," she tells him.

Once ensconced in the house, she charms the older professors and then proceeds to give "Pottsie" an unforgettable lesson in slang and also in the art of kissing. Her "yum yum" treatment is like a double whammy for the naive prof. He is in love—and Sugarpuss is quite surprised to find out that she is also smitten.

In a rollicking climax, some gangsters (one of them played by Dan Duryea) literally kidnap Sugarpuss as the professors look on helplessly. The plan is for her to marry her former boyfriend so that she will be unable to testify against him. After the gangsters leave with Sugarpuss, the angry professors regroup and go after them. At the end of the film, the "family" sees Sugarpuss and their "Pottsie" in a "yum yum" clinch.

The film, considered a delightful romp by both critics and fans, was directed by Howard Hawks. Barbara Stanwyck was Oscar-nominated for Best Actress and Billy Wilder for his original story. Neither won, Stanwyck losing to Joan Fontaine of *Suspicion* and Wilder to Harry Segall for *Here Comes Mr.*

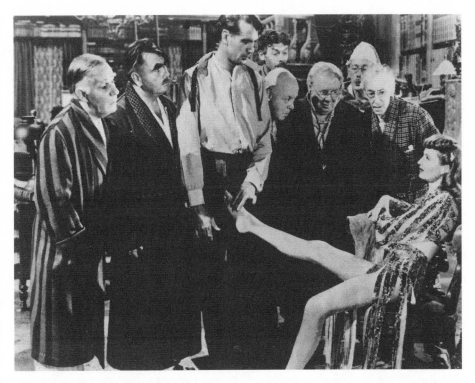

Ball of Fire with Henry Travers, Oscar Homolka, Gary Cooper, Leonid Kinskey, Aubrey Mather, S.Z. Sakall, Richard Haydn, Tully Marshall and Barbara Stanwyck: a grown-up version of *Snow White and the Seven Dwarfs*.

Jordan. Cooper, not nominated for *Ball of Fire*, did win 1941's Best Actor award for his portrayal of the World War I hero in *Sergeant York*.

Ball of Fire is a grown-up version of *Snow White and the Seven Dwarfs*. In a reversal of roles, Sugarpuss is Prince Charming and Potts is Snow White, while his fellow professors are the Dwarfs benevolently beaming down at him. The cherubic Cupids are played by Oscar Homolka, Henry Travers, S.Z. Sakall, Richard Haydn, Leonid Kinskey, Aubrey Mather and Tully Marshall.

In 1948 Hawks remade the film as the musical *A Song Is Born*, but though it featured a cast of well-known musicians and the talents of Danny Kaye and Virginia Mayo, it did not compare in any way, shape or form to the original. In this version, one of the professors is played by bandleader Benny Goodman.

Just a few weeks before the film was released, a peaceful America suddenly found itself in the conflict which had been engulfing much of the rest of the world for more than two years. After Pearl Harbor, Hollywood went to war and so did the screwball comedy.

Chapter Fourteen

Morale Boosters:
Screwball Goes to War

In the wake of Pearl Harbor, Hollywood geared up for the war effort, but in its own way. Many in the industry went into the military, including top stars James Stewart, Henry Fonda, Tyrone Power and, with the death of his wife Carole Lombard, Clark Gable. Also enlisting were some of the lesser known people who were instrumental in the making of movies, men behind the scenes: producers, directors, technicians and cameramen. Those filmmakers left at home distinguished themselves making films for the government, selling war bonds, visiting the wounded and entertaining the troops both on American soil and abroad.

The movie business continued non-stop as battlefront dramas began to proliferate. From the steamy jungles of the South Pacific and the hot sands of the African desert to the cold, chilling waters of the North Atlantic and the occupied areas of Europe, Hollywood gave the movie-going public a popularized version of the conflict.

On the lighter side, the screwball had begun to pale by the early 1940s, but conditions at home gave the genre plenty of material. The comedies of the previous decade, frothy cream puffs in the main, gave way to those of wartime, a tougher type of screwball, still very funny, but somewhat less sophisticated than its predecessors, satirizing real people and situations.

It Happened on Fifth Avenue (Allied Artists, 1947) pokes fun at the rich, in screwball style, while teaching a lesson in humanity. Victor Moore stars as elderly Aloysius T. McKeever, a hobo who solves his particular housing shortage in a unique fashion: He moves with the weather. He takes up residence in a fashionable Fifth Avenue mansion when the owner, Michael J. O'Connor (Charles Ruggles) goes to a warmer clime. When O'Connor comes back to New York, the two just exchange places.

McKeever meets and invites some homeless GIs to "share the wealth."

An "interloper" is found in the house: O'Connor's daughter Trudy, who has run away from finishing school. The squatters think she is homeless and take her in.

She falls in love with Jim, one of the GIs. When her father finds her, she begs him not to give away her identity. Instead she asks him to pose as a hobo, meet her young man and "join" the household. Against his better judgment, Dad agrees. And finds his estranged wife, who has become involved in the "plot," serving as the "cook."

Several screwball scenes are played out in the film: Jim, chained to his bed, being evicted from his apartment; O'Connor coming to his home and finding his living room has become a place for hanging clothes; and McKeever making him do household chores, even getting him a job shoveling snow. The ending has the millionaire reuniting with his wife, funding a housing plan for GIs which will become a reality, and the young couple on their way to matrimony.

McKeever has not been told of these events and takes leave of everyone. As he goes on his way, O'Connor tells his wife, "Remind me to nail up the board in the back fence. He's coming through the front door next winter." Also featured in the cast are Gale Storm as Trudy, Don DeFore as Jim and Ann Harding as Mary. The scenes between Moore and Ruggles make the movie.

Also using the returning GI premise, *No Room for the Groom* (Universal-International, 1952) stars Tony Curtis as a vet eager to resume married life with his wife, played by Piper Laurie. Our hero's got a problem on his hands: she's now living with her family, and has neglected to inform the folks that she has a husband. Mama (Spring Byington) wants her to marry another man (Don DeFore). This in itself is a screwball situation. All is straightened out with the GI moving into the picture and the erstwhile suitor moving out. It's a minor comedy, mostly to be enjoyed by fans of the young Curtis.

From the prolific pens of Charles Brackett and Billy Wilder came *The Major and the Minor* (Paramount, 1942), Wilder's debut as a director in America. As the plot unfolds, Susan Applegate (Ginger Rogers) has gone through 27 jobs. This last one is as a scalp masseuse whose customers want more than a hair massage from her. One such "client" is Mr. Osborne (Robert Benchley), who chases her around the room. He asks her, "Why don't you get out of that coat and into a dry martini?"

Deciding to return to her small town roots, she discovers that the cupboard is bare and that there is not enough money for the train fare back. Our plucky heroine is nothing if not resourceful and comes up with a screwball scheme: She will pose as a 12-year-old and pay half fare. (Wilder later rather gleefully stated that they bound Ginger's breasts for the scenes as a child.

He also maintained that the censors didn't say a word about this and he had gotten away with some sexy situations.)

En route, Susan meets Major Philip Kirby (Ray Milland), an officer-teacher at a military school. Seeing that the "youngster" is traveling alone, he takes her under her under his wing and brings her to his school where she proceeds to become the belle of the ball. "Su-Su," as Kirby calls her is found out by her roommate Lucy, played by 16-year-old Diana Lynn, who made a living playing sharp-tongued adolescents. (A grown-up Diana appears in Paramount's 1955 remake of *The Major and the Minor*, *You're Never Too Young*, a vehicle for Dean Martin and Jerry Lewis. The latter plays the Ginger Rogers role.)

Unbeknownst to the major, Lucy's older sister Pamela (Rita Johnson), whom Lucy calls a snake, has kept him back from being assigned to a real military post. Susan takes care of that. She poses as "the snake," phones an influential person and makes sure that Kirby will get the assignment he wants.

By now, the erstwhile juvenile has fallen in love with her "benefactor,"

The Major and the Minor (1942): Just why is Ginger Rogers playing a teen-ager?

but at a school dance, she sees her old nemesis Mr. Osborne, whose son is an academy student. Osborne unmasks her, much to the delight of her new nemesis, Pamela. Now aware of Susan's true identity, Pamela warns her away, saying that if her deception is found out, it will be detrimental to Philip's career. Susan leaves.

The major, unaware that Susan is a grown woman, is on his way to a real military assignment. En route, he tracks her down to the town in which she lives with her mother (played by Ginger's real mother, Lela). Susan appears to him as Mrs. Applegate and when he tells her he has not married Pamela, he then leaves. The last scene finds him at the railway station where he *finally* gets the point that Susan is there to go with him. Their first destination will probably be Washington.

The housing shortage was a real problem for this country during the war years and nowhere was it more pronounced than in Washington, D.C. With the nerve center of our war machine located in the nation's capital, the bustling city was full of transients, VIPs and constant movement.

No film caught the comedic nuances inherent in this situation with more panache than *The More the Merrier.* The 1943 Columbia release, nominated for six Academy Awards (including one for Best Picture), has an interesting premise: Government worker Connie Milligan (Jean Arthur), in a spirit of patriotism, rents half of her

The Major and the Minor with Ginger Rogers and Ray Milland: She is definitely not a teen in this shot.

apartment to elderly Benjamin Dingle (Charles Coburn), a wealthy industrialist who has donated his services to the war effort at a salary of a dollar a year. He, again in a spirit of patriotism, rents half of his half to handsome Joe Carter (Joel McCrea).

At first, Connie is not very happy with this turn of events. She makes up a schedule of what each of the three is responsible for and in a true screwball scene, the three try to stick to her schedule. Though Connie has been engaged to someone else for some time, Cupid Dingle thinks that his "boarder" is the right man for his "landlady." He aims his arrow straight at the young couple and scores a bull's eye: They fall in love to the delight of the cherubic match-maker.

The film is filled with screwball strokes and some not very believable situations, but the performances of the stars are as light as gossamer wings. They seem to be having a good time and invite the audience to do the same.

The picture, director George Stevens, Jean Arthur, her then husband Frank Ross (who wrote the original story) and Charles Coburn all received Oscar nominations. Coburn won the gold statuette as Best Supporting Actor, his first and only in a long and distinguished career.

Cary Grant playing the Coburn role? Unbelievable? Never, you say? But it did happen in *Walk, Don't Run,* Columbia's revamped version of the story, released 23 years later. With a change in location, Grant, who was 62 at the time and still as good-looking as ever, plays an English industrialist who rents half of Samantha Eggar's apartment in overcrowded Tokyo. He then turns around and offers half of his half to Jim Hutton, an Olympic competitor. Though the young woman is engaged to a rather stuffy embassy official, the older man decides to play Cupid to his apartment mates and is successful in this endeavor.

Eggar and Hutton are fine as the young couple, but fans flocked to see Cary Grant. This film was his last.

Standing Room Only (Paramount, 1944), a wartime screwball starring Paulette Goddard and Fred MacMurray, satirized the housing shortage in Washington, but with a different twist. It's the story of a resourceful secretary (Goddard) who is in D.C. on business with her boss (MacMurray). How does she get both herself and her boss living quarters? Simple: She hires them out as domestic servants in a luxurious household. And what do they know about being servants? Absolutely nothing. There are quips and comic situations as the erstwhile maid and butler get deeper and deeper into hot water, figuratively and literally. The executive eventually realizes that he is in love with his kooky secretary and both of them get out of the kitchen and back to business. An experienced cast, including Edward Arnold, Roland Young, Hillary Brooke, Porter Hall and Anne Revere add their considerable talents to the merriment.

The More the Merrier (1943) with Charles Coburn and Jean Arthur: Cupid shoots his arrow in wartime Washington. The film was Oscar-nominated in six categories, but only Coburn was a winner.

A minor film with a similar premise is *Make Your Own Bed* (Warner Brothers, 1944) which stars Jack Carson and, four years away from her Oscar-winning 1948 performance in *Johnny Belinda,* Jane Wyman. The two play detectives who hire on to a family as butler and maid to thwart a ring of Nazi spies. And what do they know about domestic service? Like MacMurray and Goddard in the previously discussed film, absolutely nothing. Zany situations follow, but they do get the job done. A cast including Alan Hale, Irene Manning and George Tobias make a valiant attempt, but the film was not a box office winner.

Broadway contributed a wartime screwball with Washington, D.C., as its locale. *The Doughgirls* (Warner Brothers, 1944) stars Wyman and Carson as newlyweds whose honeymoon is interrupted by friends of the bride who would like part of their hotel suite for their own forthcoming honeymoons. This makes for a truly frenetic situation. Most of the action takes place in the suite, with various characters coming and going, to Carson's chagrin.

Ann Sheridan and Alexis Smith are the conniving ladies, with John Ridgely and Craig Stevens featured in the roles of their prospective grooms. (Stevens and Smith were husband and wife off-screen.)

The film is well-acted by the stars and by a supporting cast which includes Alan Mowbray, John Alexander and especially by Charles Ruggles as Carson's boss. Eve Arden, as a Russian sniper in Washington on a government mission, steals every scene in which she appears.

Olivia de Havilland stars in *Government Girl* (1943), yet another screwball satirizing conditions in wartime Washington (sharing apartments, working crazy hours, over-crowded restaurants, etc.). Legend has it that the actress did not want to do the film, but was forced into it by an arrangement with Warner Brothers who loaned her to David Selznick, who promptly turned her over to RKO. At that time, studios were able to do this with their contract players.

In the film, a Detroit business executive (Sonny Tufts) is a dollar-a-year man who has been brought to wartime Washington by the government to speed up bomber production. Olivia, as his Girl Friday, shows him the hectic Washington scene as well as the ins and outs of departmental bureaucracy, resulting in several comical situations.

When hints of malfeasance and dealings in the black market surface with Tufts as a prime suspect, it's the loyal Olivia who gets him out of trouble and gets *him*, period. Supporting the two stars are well-known performers Agnes Moorehead, Jane Darwell. Sig Ruman, Jess Barker, Harry Davenport, James Dunn, Anne Shirley and Paul Stewart. The public bought the premise and the production made a nice profit for the studio.

Government Girl was not Olivia de Havilland's best effort in Hollywood. Neither was *Pillow to Post* Ida Lupino's finest hour. That the material of the

Warner Brothers 1945 release did not match the talents of its star is quite evident upon seeing this film.

The flimsy plot details the trials and tribulations of Lupino becoming a traveling sales agent for her father's oil refining company and landing in a town near an army base. The only accommodations she can get are at an auto camp which caters to the wives of men in the military. The saleslady puts her training to good use and sells a good-looking young officer (William Prince) on the idea of posing as her husband. Adding to the confusion are Prince's commanding officer, a rotund Cupid in the form of Sydney Greenstreet (light years away from his sinister portrayal of Caspar Gutman in 1941's *The Maltese Falcon*), Stuart Erwin, Johnny Mitchell and Ruth Donnelly. How the unmarried two manage to fool his superiors forms the basis of most of the film, but by the final reel, the mock marriage will become the real thing.

Lupino wisely went back to dramatic roles after this production, which was quickly forgotten by fans and critics alike. Later in her career, she became a top Hollywood director.

There are musical moments in *Seven Days Leave* (RKO, 1942) with the bands of Freddy Martin and Les Brown featured. Its stars, Victor Mature and Lucille Ball, however, were not noted for their singing and dancing abilities. The plot concerns a serviceman (Mature) who will receive a $100,000 bequest according to the terms of a will, but only if he will marry a certain young lady, whom he has never met. The zinger is that he has only one week to fulfill he terms of the will. Is this not a screwball premise?

Our hero meets the girl (Ball) and the two take an instant dislike to one another (yet another screwball battle of the sexes). With his buddies (Peter Lind Hayes and Arnold Stang) cheering him on and her sister (played by pert RKO contract player Marcy McGuire) egging *her* on, it is a given that the money will soon be theirs.

Lucy is not rich at all in *A Girl, a Guy and a Gob* (RKO, 1941). Silent screen star Harold Lloyd was the producer of this bouncy little entry, which concerns a secretary (Ball) who must choose between her rich boss (Edmond O'Brien) and a breezy sailor named Coffee Cup (George Murphy). After several screwball incidents, one of which involves Lucy on a ladder falling into O'Brien's arms much to the consternation of O'Brien's staid fiancée (Marguerite Chapman), and another, a nightclub scene involving O'Brien and a rhumba contest (he really can't dance), the end of the film has Murphy and O'Brien in a wild auto and motorcycle chase, the sailor rejoining the navy and Lucy again in the arms of her boss, this time romantically. Also in the cast are Henry Travers and Franklin Pangborn.

Money plays an important part in *Hi Diddle Diddle* (United Artists, 1943). Silent screen star Pola Negri, after an eleven-year absence from the film capital, returns in the role of Adolphe Menjou's temperamental wife. The two are the parents of a sailor (Dennis O'Keefe) who is about to marry a wealthy young lady (Martha Scott). Her mother (Billie Burke) suddenly announces that she has been swindled out of all her money. To get the money back, Menjou gets into various comical situations which includes investing in the stock market and doing some gambling. (Could it be said that the two are one and the same thing?) Everything goes back to normal when Burke comes clean and admits that it was all a ruse to prove that the daughter's fiancé is not marrying her for money. The young couple finally get married. June Havoc is also featured in this fast-paced screwball.

The Brothers Warner did quite well by Barbara Stanwyck in *Christmas in Connecticut*. In this 1945 romantic comedy with screwball overtones, she plays Elizabeth Lane, a columnist for a magazine called *Smart Housekeeping*. Her talents, to judge by what she writes, include cooking, motherhood and being an all-around good housewife.

There is, however, one catch to this lovely scenario: Not only can't she cook, she's not even married, has no experience in child rearing, and what she knows about being the compleat housewife would not fill a thimble. Her uncle Felix (S.Z. Sakall) has been supplying the delicious recipes for her columns.

Completely unaware of all this, her boss Alexander Yardley (Sydney Greenstreet—two screwballs in one year) asks her to entertain returning war hero Jefferson Jones (Dennis Morgan). Jones is a survivor of a Nazi submarine attack on an American vessel. He and another man had been adrift on a raft for several days. As they drifted along the raft, they could only envision different meals they would have if they were rescued. The next scene has them in a hospital being catered to by a nurse who sees stars in her eyes and marriage to Jones on her mind. To show him what wedded bliss would be like, she has penned a note to Yardley and then the fun begins.

All Elizabeth needs to do is find a husband, a home, a baby and a cook, in that order. Which she does. Reginald Gardiner is John Sloan, a pompous architect who has proposed to her several times—and been rejected. She does persuade him to be the "husband." His Connecticut home becomes "her" home, Norah the maid (Una O'Connor) supplies the baby and Felix does the cooking. Elizabeth trying to diaper the baby and also trying her hand at cooking are true screwball gems.

Things go fairly smoothly until Elizabeth realizes, on a moonlit sleigh ride, that she has fallen hard for her guest and he for her. But said guest still thinks she is married. While the two are on the sleigh, the real mother comes for her baby. The scene in which the befuddled Yardley sees the kidnapping and calls the police is true screwball.

By the end of the film, as the sun rises on the lovely Connecticut farmhouse, all has been straightened out. Elizabeth admits that she is not married. Yardley fires and then rehires her, Jeff now knows the truth and wedding bells are in the near future.

Arnold Schwarzenegger directed a remake for cable television in 1992. The stars are Dyan Cannon, country singer-songwriter Kris Kristofferson and Tony Curtis. Same title, same character names, similar storyline. This time, however, in the age of television, Elizabeth (Cannon) is the star of a successful TV cooking show. She has also written several books on the subject. Alexander Yardley (Curtis), her manager, has seen a program on which a forest ranger named Jones (Kristofferson) who has lost his home in a fire says that he would love a home-cooked Christmas dinner. Yardley arranges to have his client invite the ranger to a live show on Christmas Day, and she will do all the cooking.

But the "new" Elizabeth, like the "old" Elizabeth, can't cook (the cooking is done by her assistant) and her bio as the complete American housewife is untrue. As in the 1945 film, Elizabeth and Jones end up together.

Barbara Stanwyck and Dyan Cannon found love in Connecticut. Claudette Colbert finds love on a cross country train ride. The veteran Colbert co-stars with John Wayne in *Without Reservations* (RKO, 1946), a crowd pleaser due to the enduring popularity of its star duo and the appearances of guest stars Cary Grant, Jack Benny and gossip columnist Louella Parsons. The scenario follows somewhat along the lines of *It Happened One Night*: a woman traveling incognito and meeting a strong-willed man whom she will eventually marry.

A best-selling authoress (Colbert) is on a train to Hollywood to oversee the making of a movie based on her book. En route, she meets a Marine (Wayne) and decides he is perfect for the part of her hero. She follows him, trailing him all the way to the film capital—there is even a haystack scene (shades of the 1934 classic). When he discovers her identity, he wants no part of her until the finale.

A case of mistaken identity is the premise of *Pardon My Past* (Columbia, 1945) which stars another screwball veteran, Fred MacMurray. Fred plays Eddie York, an ex–GI who wants to be a mink farmer. His look-alike is Francis Pemberton, a ne'er-do-well who owes money to a gambler (Akim Tamiroff). Complications follow Eddie as he tries to prove his innocence, but as in all films of the era, good triumphs over bad, with our hero even getting the girl. William Demarest is Eddie's friend and Marguerite Chapman the girl.

MacMurray's character is looking to invest in minks. Don Ameche is looking for people to invest in rubber in *Girl Trouble* (Fox, 1942), a wartime screwball with topical references to rationing and civil defense. A young South American (Ameche) arrives in New York City on a business trip in

Without Reservations (1946) with John Wayne and Claudette Colbert: Shades of *It Happened One Night*. This was the last film in which Wayne received second billing.

search of investment for his father's rubber plantation. He runs into trouble when he rents the apartment of a society girl (Joan Bennett) who pretends to be a maid. This builds into an amusing situation. Both business and romantic complications are solved by the time the film comes to its conclusion. Featured in an interesting cast assembled to aid the stars are Billie Burke, Frank Craven, Alan Dinehart, Vivian Blaine and Dale Evans, better known to film fans as Mrs. Roy Rogers. It was a very minor vehicle for Ameche and Bennett.

While Dennis Morgan is a bona fide war hero in *Christmas in Connecticut*, Eddie Bracken definitely is not in *Hail the Conquering Hero* (Paramount, 1944), Preston Sturges' sharp, biting satire of small town Americana, flag-waving and hero worship.

Eddie had the part of his career as Woodrow Wilson Truesmith, as a rejected Marine. On a train bound for home, the asthmatic ex-recruit meets a group of boisterous Marines who invent a bogus story of heroism for him to tell to the townspeople. Upon his arrival, the "hero" is feted and fussed over by everyone and the celebration continues until he decides to make a clean breast of it and does, to a sadder and wiser group of friends and neighbors. As a result of his courageous stand, he becomes a real hero to the home town folks, winning their respect as well as that of Libby, the town beauty (Ella Raines).

Sturges surrounded his leading players with a cast of skilled screwballers, including William Demarest as the Marine sergeant who is the catalyst of the plot, plus Raymond Walburn and Franklin Pangborn as town muck-a-mucks. The film was "hailed" by fans and critics alike and Sturges received an Oscar nomination for his original screenplay.

Again in 1944, Paramount unleashed Sturges on the movie-going public. This time the filmmaker turned his iconoclastic pen and camera on American morals and chose the sanctity of motherhood as the target for his satirical barbs. The resultant film, *The Miracle of Morgan's Creek*, has come down through the years as one of the most original and well-known examples of the wartime screwball comedy.

Frenetic Betty Hutton stars as a small town girl with another improbable name of the genre, Trudy Kockenlocker. She goes to a wild party at a nearby military base and wakes up the next morning, hazy as to the events of the previous night. She thinks she has married a Private Ratskiwatski, but is not quite sure. One thing, however, quickly becomes clear: The patter of little feet is Trudy's future.

Eddie Bracken always was the little guy caught up in situations almost too big for him to handle. In *Bring On the Girls* (Paramount, 1945), he's a millionaire trying to fend off gold diggers and, in the aforementioned *Hail the Conquering Hero*, he plays a non-hero feted by his neighbors for being one. In *Miracle,* he is Norville Jones, Trudy's bumbling 4-F suitor. The schlemiel tries to help her out, but things become complicated due to her apoplectic father, superbly played by Sturges regular William Demarest. Trudy's sarcastic sister Emily, played by Diana Lynn, is sympathetic to her sister's plight and can put Dad down with one remark, which she does at frequent intervals.

Much to the delight of the townspeople, the little mother-to-be delivers sextuplets who become the focus of national attention. Norville is assumed to be the father and willingly accepts his new role.

Sturges then cuts to national figures—Hitler for one—who resent being thrown off page one of the newspapers. The writer-director also reprises his *Great McGinty* characters Brian Donlevy and Akim Tamiroff, political malfeasants who are hiding out in a "Banana Republic."

Though the multi-talented Sturges received another Oscar nomination for his work on this screenplay, he lost the coveted award to Lamar Trotti, screenwriter of *Wilson,* the biopic of President Woodrow Wilson.

The invasion of Russia is one kind of story that would knock even Trudy's sextuplets off the front page of every newspaper in the world. So what happens when the Moscow correspondent for Amalgamated News is

The Miracle of Morgan's Creek (1944) with William Demarest, Betty Hutton and Eddie Bracken. What "miracle" has pushed Adolf Hitler off the front pages of every newspaper in the world?

so busy dining on caviar that he does not file this story of a lifetime? He is called by his irate boss (Donald MacBride) and summarily fired. This is the comedic premise of *They Got Me Covered,* a 1943 swipe at news reportage. Produced by Samuel Goldwyn and released by RKO, the film stars Bob Hope as the inept newspaperman.

Back in Washington, Hope decides to get the kind of scoop that will win him back his job. He inadvertently stumbles upon a nest of Nazi agents headed by that arch villain of the silver screen, Otto Preminger. With the aid of his girl (Dorothy Lamour), our intrepid hero manages to break up the ring and get his scoop. The film features snappy dialogue about the wartime blackouts and rationing, plus screwball situations wherein Florence Bates, as a nutty fortune teller, tries to give him a message and sultry Lenore Aubert tries to seduce him.

Clark Gable plays the title role in MGM's *Comrade X.* The 1940 release, with a screenplay by Ben Hecht and Charles Lederer, stars the actor as a

Comrade X (1940): **When an American reporter (Clark Gable) meets a beautiful Russian streetcar conductor (Hedy Lamarr) named Theodore, sparks begin to fly.**

newspaperman whose beat is the land of steppes, samovars and spies, Mother Russia. Like Hope, he is stationed in Moscow. This film takes place just before the start of World War II.

Gable's character gets restricted information out of the country until he is found out by a porter in his hotel (Felix Bressart). The latter feels it is too late for him, but wants to get his overly indoctrinated daughter (Hedy Lamarr) away from the clutches of the Communists and into the United States. In a serio-comic scene arguing his case, he gives the newsman a choice. The latter is reluctant until he meets the gorgeous Hedy, a streetcar conductor who calls herself "Theodore" and spouts the "Party Line." She is adamant about staying in Russia until she becomes disenchanted by the duplicity of her party superiors. She, her father and the newsman (who is suspected of being the famous Comrade X, which of course he is) make a frenetic flight for freedom in a stolen tank which, they promptly find out, belongs to a Russian general. The troops are engaged in war games and they are in the lead tank. Needless to say, the three make it.

The last scene takes place in America and finds the trio at a baseball game. Says Hedy to Papa, "The Dodgers are murdering the Reds," to which her father replies, "Aha, the counter-revolution." The supporting cast of the *Ninotchka*-like film includes Eve Arden, Oscar Homolka, and Sig Ruman.

Cluny Brown (1946) is a sophisticated comedy with screwball elements, directed by the incomparable Ernst Lubitsch. Jennifer Jones stars in the title role as a plumber's niece who is working in an English country manor. There she meets and is intrigued by one of the guests, penniless writer Adam Belinski (Charles Boyer), a refugee from Czechoslovakia. He has been invited to the house by Andrew, the son of the owners. Peter Lawford plays this young man who is itching to get into the coming hostilities and is constantly asking the writer about conditions in Europe.

The writer soon becomes infatuated with the outspoken Cluny, but it seems that she has a gentleman friend, a pharmacist named Mr. Wilson. Belinski meets him and finds him quite dull, and remarks, "You couldn't have provided a better sedative for Cluny than yourself."

This fly in the ointment is soon disposed of and the Czech marries the girl to the amazement of her upper class employers. The finale finds Cluny the grand lady and her husband a successful writer of mysteries. Also featured in the cast are a few members of Hollywood's "English Colony," including Reginald Gardiner, C. Aubrey Smith and Richard Haydn.

The film is a delight and contains some true screwball scenes: Jones being mistaken by her employers for other than a parlor maid, a fight scene between Lawford and Boyer, and our heroine at a party given by her gentleman friend (hilariously played by Haydn), who looks on in sheer horror when there is a plumbing problem and his prospective bride begins to work on the pipes.

Released by Fox, the production takes place in England just before the start of World War II, with the country's population wondering what Nazi Germany's next move would be. Within a couple of years, America would enter into the fray and such things as rationing and the draft board would become realities.

Bob Hope is *Caught in the Draft*, a 1941 release from Paramount. The film came at a time before the attack on Pearl Harbor when draft evasion was still a topic for a comedian to make the most of. And old Ski Nose did. He plays a movie star who tries every trick possible, including a very funny medical exam, to avoid going into the army, but he is finally inducted.

Character actor Lynne Overman and soon-to-be star Eddie Bracken, as Hope's agent and valet, respectively, follow the boss into the army. The scene after the exam during which they are issued army uniforms and shoes is pure screwball.

The new recruit, who faints at the sight of blood, meets his colonel's daughter, played by Dorothy Lamour. Thinking he is a coward, she is not overly thrilled with him, but he proves, while on maneuvers (in a very funny scene), that he is not really as cowardly as she thinks he is. Besides she has fallen for him, and in true screwball fashion she winds up with him.

Hope also appears in one of two wartime screwballs spy spoofs released by Paramount in 1942. *My Favorite Blonde* casts him as a burlesque comic playing straight man to a penguin. During a train ride between theater jobs, he meets a beautiful British agent (Madeleine Carroll) who has vital information and secret orders in her possession. He is immediately attracted to her, but she has more than romance on her mind. This all changes when he agrees to help her elude the Nazi agents (played with sinister skill and gusto by Gale Sondergaard and George Zucco) pursuing her.

Man, woman and bird are chased across America by road, rail and air in the screwball tradition, but there is a happy ending: The Nazis are thwarted, the comic gets his blonde and the vital information gets into the right hands.

The second film, *The Lady Has Plans* (1942), is set in Lisbon, a World War II mecca for spies and for Hollywood scenario writers with a bent for satirizing the real threat of espionage. Paulette Goddard plays Sidney Royce, an American press correspondent stationed in the Portuguese capital. She is suspected of being a foreign agent but she is innocent; the real miscreant is Margaret Hayes as Rita Lenox, who has a tell-tale tattoo on her back, a set of plans which would do a lot of damage in the wrong hands. Goddard's frequent co-star Ray Milland is seen here as Kenneth Harper, a government agent assigned to find out whether or not Paulette is a spy. This case of mistaken identity has the Germans, headed by Albert Dekker, comically trying to disrobe Goddard and she trying to hand the plans over to Milland. The ending takes place in a Turkish bath with the two stars in a clinch. A good cast including Roland Young, Cecil Kellaway and Gerald Mohr help to keep the action moving at a fast clip.

The last two films to be discussed, both from 1942, are a radical departure from the usual screwball in that their several comic elements are played against the backdrop of a devastated Europe during the early years of World War II. The combination of screwball and black comedy in these two films was called "tasteless" by the critics of the era.

Once Upon a Honeymoon stars Ginger Rogers as Katherine Buchsmith, an American who has married a rich European, Baron Von Luber (Walter Slezak). Unbeknownst to her, he is an important Nazi official paving the way for the invasion of several countries.

At her hotel, she meets newspaperman Pat O'Toole (Cary Grant) who recognizes her as Brooklyn's own Katie O'Hara, ex–burlesque dancer (she thinks he's there to take her clothing measurements for her honeymoon trip).

O'Toole knows all about the baron and with difficulty makes Katie realize the truth and the enormity of her mistake. She goes away with him.

While the world is in flames, the two begin a love affair which ends on a ship getting out of Europe. Unfortunately the baron is also aboard and, in a screwball ending, is sent into the ocean by Katie while the ship's officers are engaged in a card game, not to be disturbed. Katie and O'Toole can continue their romance.

An interesting sidelight to the film is that neither Grant nor Rogers would agree to give each other top billing. A compromise was worked out wherein half the ads would feature Ginger's name first and the other half, Grant's name first.

Unlike the last film discussed, *To Be or Not to Be* had several formidable events working against it at the time of its release by United Artists: the brutal attack on Pearl Harbor, the Nazi control over much of Europe and the death of its lovely star, Carole Lombard. Ernst Lubitsch, who co-wrote the original story, co-produced and directed the project, was thought by many at the time "to have an odd sense of humor and a tangled script" when he made the film.

This is not the consensus of opinion among reviewers and students of film today. It is now considered a classic. It concerns the Nazi invasion and occupation of Poland. Comedian Jack Benny had the role of his career as "that great, great actor," Joseph Tura, whose troupe of Polish Shakespearean performers is put out of business by the Nazis until they find themselves knee-deep in intrigue and espionage.

Tura's wife Maria (Carole Lombard) is extremely beautiful and her husband is extremely jealous of her. Maria tells him, "You'll do anything to grab the spotlight. When I start to tell a story, you finish it. When I go on a diet, you lose the weight. If I have a cold, you cough. And if we should ever have a baby—"

"I'll be satisfied to be the father!" Tura responds.

He is also somewhat mistrustful of her. He needn't be, though she *is* engaged in a mild flirtation with young Polish airman Stanislaus Sobinski (Robert Stack). When Tura, on stage as Hamlet, utters the words, "To be or not to be," it is Sobinski's signal to go backstage and spend time with Maria.

All this changes as war breaks out. A Polish traitor, Professor Siletsky (Stanley Ridges), is returning to Warsaw from England with names of Polish Resistance members. Sobinski, in London with the Polish Squadron of the Royal Air Force, sees through the treacherous Siletsky and returns to Warsaw on a mission to kill him. He takes refuge in the Turas' apartment, and the actors become involved. Siletsky is killed and the actors become even more involved.

To Be or Not to Be (1942) with (posing for photographer, left to right) Charles Halton, Tom Dugan (made-up as Hitler), Lionel Atwill, Jack Benny, Carole Lombard and Robert Stack. Lombard's last film, and Benny's role of a lifetime.

Tura and his compatriots fool the Gestapo at every turn. One of the actors does such a good impression of Der Fuhrer that the troupe is able to escape to Scotland.

Screwball moments abound in the film: Benny's face when Stack leaves his seat at the beginning of Hamlet's soliloquy and then when he finds the airman asleep in his bed; Lombard's meeting with the real Siletsky; Benny masquerading as the notorious Colonel Ehrhardt when confronting the traitor and later meeting the real Gestapo chief; Lombard's fending off the traitor and then Colonel Ehrhardt towards the end of the film when "Hitler" appears. Benny and Lombard are ably supported by a superb ensemble cast including Lionel Atwill, Felix Bressart and Tom Dugan as members of the theatrical troupe and by Sig Ruman as Colonel Ehrhardt.

In 1983, Fox released a remake, produced by Mel Brooks, starring Brooks, his wife Anne Bancroft and Jose Ferrer. Much of the dialogue was taken almost word for word from the original, but does not compare to the Benny-Lombard film. To honor comedian Jack Benny, his given name, Kubelsky, is used in the film.

The end of the war heralded a new era in moviemaking. The public demanded realism, and this, more than anything else, led to less screwballs being made. Even so, they were still being produced in the years which followed and are still to be seen today.

In our final two chapters, we'll look at some which are fondly remembered and some which are not, plus several made in the last years of the 20th century.

Chapter Fifteen

Screwball Lives On: Part One

The early screwball comedies were a product of the times in which they thrived. They succeeded when the nation was at its lowest ebb, an escape valve sorely needed. Warm and healthy, yet often satirical, the genre lifted the spirits of the people, made them laugh and offered a brief respite from the realities of everyday living.

The growing maturity of the generation which had welcomed the screwball plus the advent of World War II brought a tremendous change in both the nation and in its moviegoing tastes. We had more to come to grips with than cross-country chases and nutty heiresses. The plight of returning veterans and the popularity of the neo-realistic films imported from abroad gave rise to new forms of filmmaking in Hollywood: adult westerns and comedies, socially significant dramas and exciting film noir—those grainy black and white forerunners of the anti-hero genre.

The screwball, for all intents and purposes, was no longer, but was this the case? There were several attempts made to emulate the genre's sophisticated lightness and it is these with which we will be concerned in the next few pages.

By the mid- and late 1940s, many of the stars who had pioneered the screwball genre were still making some, plus appearing in other genres. These old pros were still fan favorites and their films were eagerly anticipated.

Let's take a look at some of the highlights and also some of the lesser films of this body of films which has never truly given up.

The year 1945 brought us *She Wouldn't Say Yes* from Columbia. Rosalind Russell is top-billed as a psychiatrist who thinks people should keep their emotions under control. Lee Bowman, seen as second lead in several screwball comedies of the 1930s and 1940s, plays a successful cartoonist whose alter ego, a cartoon character, has different ideas. The two meet when he slams a door in her face, the battle of the sexes is on until they get together at the end. In the supporting cast are Charles Winninger as her doctor father, Percy Kilbride, Adele Jergens and Harry Davenport.

In *My Dear Secretary* (United Artists, 1948), Kirk Douglas plays a best-selling author who cannot keep his secretaries because he has the habit of being overly amorous towards them. This changes when he meets Laraine Day. She tames him, even marries him and then decides to write her own book, which becomes a bestseller. Thus begins the battle of man vs. woman, an important component of screwball, which ends with Douglas and Day in an equal partnership. Keenan Wynn is third-billed as Kirk's friend and his antics doing housework are in the screwball tradition. In support of the threesome are a cast consisting of several screwball veterans, among them Rudy Vallee, Alan Mowbray, Florence Bates and Irene Ryan, who would later star as Granny on TV's *The Beverly Hillbillies*.

Screwball alumnus Ginger Rogers stars in *It Had to Be You*, a 1947 release from Columbia. She is a young woman who has left three men at the altar and is about to do same to prospective husband number four. Her long-suffering parents (Spring Byington and Percy Warram) need not worry. Daughter Ginger meets handsome Cornel Wilde whom she at first thinks is an American Indian—he is not, but he exists in her vivid imagination as one. (As a small child, her first sweetheart was a little boy dressed up like an Indian.) Wilde disabuses her of this fantasy and winds up with a much wiser Ginger. If this is not a screwball plot, what is? Only dyed-in-the woods Rogers fans could find any merit in the film.

Our next tale is of a lady who seeks a rich husband and the method she uses to find one. Claudette Colbert stars in *Bride for Sale* (RKO, 1949) as Nora Shelley, an ex–WAC officer with a unique scheme to attain her goal: She gets a job at an income tax firm owned by Paul Martin (George Brent). The latter finds that his employee is combing his files for some hot prospects and prevails upon his wealthy friend Steve Adams (Robert Young) to woo and then dump her. This backfires when both realize that they are in love with the lady. Steve wins her. Watching the three pros at work is a lesson in making this sort of premise work.

Young stars, this time with Barbara Hale, in *And Baby Makes Three* (Columbia, 1949). The rather slim plot revolves around a recently divorcee, on her way to remarry, who suddenly thinks she is pregnant. Her former mate refuses to give her sole custody of the yet unborn child. All is resolved when the woman finds out that, not only is she not having a baby, but that she is still in love with Young. Taking part in this unbelievable mishmash is Robert Hutton, who is left at the altar, Billie Burke, Janis Carter and Lloyd Corrigan. Cast and crew deserved better.

Young made several films in the genre, but when one thinks of the top screwball performers, the name that first comes to mind is Cary Grant. Funny, yes, suave and sophisticated, definitely. So when he is being chased by a lovesick teenager, it is a given that the movie-watcher is in for lots of laughs. This is the premise of *The Bachelor and the Bobby-Soxer* (RKO, 1947).

Up on some minor charges before a judge (Myrna Loy), author-playboy Grant is the object of her young sister's (Shirley Temple) crush. Upon meeting him, the teenager envisions him as her knight in shining armor. Thereupon, the irate judge sentences him to be the teen's escort until the girl "sees the light."

This doesn't happen until Cary is subjected to jitterbugging, having ice cream sodas with a bunch of youngsters, running obstacle courses, etc. In the meantime, he is trying to romance Myrna who, at the beginning, isn't having any (again the battle of the sexes). But in the end, she, like her little sister, sees Grant as a knight in shining armor. Who can resist Cary Grant?

When television fans are asked to name their favorite small screen performer, five will get you ten that Lucille Ball will lead the parade. Lucy made several screwball films before catching the brass ring in *I Love Lucy*. Somewhat similar to the previously mentioned *Affectionately Yours*, Lucy's *Lover Come Back* (Universal, 1946) stars George Brent as a roving war correspondent who has a roving eye: There has been a dalliance with a photographer (Vera Zorina) in the two years he's been away. Brent's wife (Lucy), upon meeting her husband's wartime "companion," heads straight to Las Vegas. Brent follows and after several zany attempts to win her back, including fending off two of her admirers (Carl Esmond and Raymond Walburn) and dealing with his father who has come to "help" him, persuades her to leave Vegas and come back to him. In the cast are screwball veterans Charles Winninger as Brent's father plus Franklin Pangborn and Louise Beavers.

A year later, Lucy and Franchot Tone made Columbia's *Her Husband's Affairs*. Playing husband and wife advertising execs, they are trying to market a product brought to them by a screwball inventor (Mikhail Rasumny). The product is a potion that can do anything from growing hair to preserving flowers. The screenplay by Ben Hecht and Charles Lederer has Tone trying to interest a rich industrialist (Gene Lockhart) in the product and also trying to circumvent the problems posed by Lucy. Helping the proceedings along are Edward Everett Horton, Jonathan Hale, Mabel Paige and Nana Bryant.

In 1963, Lucy joined Bob Hope in the Warner Brothers production *Critic's Choice*. They play husband and wife, he a critic and she a fledgling playwright. Much of the running time is devoted to Hope denigrating Ball's ability to write a play. He is also jealous of her director, a much younger man. The fun begins when Bob faces the problem of whether or not he should review Lucy's play. When he does and gives it a devastating notice, war is declared. Before the situation leads to a satisfactory conclusion, Hope has been driven to drink and an analyst's couch. The lively supporting cast includes Marilyn Maxwell as Hope's first wife, Jerome Cowan, Jim Backus, Marie Windsor, and the improbably named Rip Torn as the director.

Like Lucy and her husband Desi Arnaz, Dick Powell saw his future in television and dove in head first, as a producer, a director and sometimes star. In between, he managed to make a few films, one of which is *Susan Slept Here*. This RKO 1954 production is the only one in Hollywood history thus far to be narrated by an Oscar statuette!

Powell plays an Oscar-winning screenwriter of a certain age who wants to write a script about delinquency. As a "Christmas gift," an obliging cop saddles him with a teenage hellion (Debbie Reynolds in the title role) for "research purposes." She'll be gone after the holidays, the cop promises.

A gentle battle of the sexes ensues, but to keep her from being put away, he marries her and, much to his surprise, he soon finds that he's in love with his young bride. In support of the leads are Anne Francis as Powell's green-with-envy ex-girlfriend, Glenda Farrell as Powell's secretary and Alvy Moore as his sidekick. Catch the newly married Susan speaking on the telephone to her husband's old flame, watching his home movies with accompanying smirks and grimaces, ordering pickles and ice cream (she always does) to the astonishment of Moore, etc. Improbable, yes. Entertaining, yes.

A more mature bride (Joan Fontaine) runs away from her stuffed shirt bridegroom on her wedding day and hires a good-looking pilot to take her to California in *You Gotta Stay Happy*, a 1949 film from Universal-International. The flyer is played by James Stewart. He is at first reluctant, thinking of her as a dizzy dame, but the money is good and she climbs aboard. After a crash landing on an Oklahoma farm, the pilot realizes that he's in love with this "dizzy dame." Supporting players include Eddie Albert as Stewart's friend, Willard Parker as the left-behind groom and the always funny Percy Kilbride as the farm owner.

Did the forgoing synopsis sound somewhat familiar? It should. Think *It Happened One Night* and *The Bride Came C.O.D.* Like its predecessors, the idea was taken from a story in a magazine, in this case *The Saturday Evening Post*. This production, however, does not compare to the earlier ones and has mostly been forgotten, even possibly by diehard fans of each star.

Three screwball comedies did do well at the box office around that same time. Two starred Cary Grant, the third Rex Harrison, a newcomer to the ranks of the screwball.

An aftermath of the war was the influx of war brides. Many in the armed forces married women they'd met overseas. Howard Hawks decided to turn this around and came up with *I Was a Male War Bride*, released by Fox in 1949.

Grant is Henri Rochard, a French officer assigned to a project in postwar Germany along with WAC Catherine Gates (Ann Sheridan). What starts out to be a battle of the sexes turns to love and, after a short courtship which involves a disastrous motorcycle ride and a night in a haystack, they marry. There is a lot of paperwork involved and when the Frenchman wants to come to America, he finds that he does qualify for entry, but the laws that govern this entry do not provide for husbands.

Catherine comes up with a scheme: Henri will become Florence, a war bride. Everything is eventually ironed out but not until Henri-Florence has gone through some humiliating experiences. These scenes were quite hilarious to those who flocked to theaters to see a favorite star in drag. They still are, when seen today on television.

In a 1952 Hawks venture for the same studio, Cary co-stars with Ginger Rogers in *Monkey Business*, a send-up of the science profession. He plays Barnaby Fulton, a brilliant research chemist who invents a formula for delaying the aging process. A laboratory chimp pours the formula into a water cooler. When the chemist takes a drink, he becomes an adolescent and when his wife Edwina (Rogers) has more than one drink, she behaves like a child.

In a very funny scene, Cary puts war paint on his face and joins some boys playing cowboys and Indians with war whoops and tries to "scalp" his lawyer. In another scene, Edwina begins to believe that a baby she sees is actually her husband.

Also affected is Barnaby's stuffy boss (Charles Coburn) who, upon taking a drink, reverts back to his childhood. They all recover and realize that what has happened is only temporary. Marilyn Monroe is featured as the office secretary. Coburn's line to her is a classic: "Find someone to type this." With a screenplay by veterans Ben Hecht, Charles Lederer and I.A.L. Diamond plus the screen magic of Cary Grant, how could the project fail? It didn't.

Another project that does not fail to get audiences laughing when shown on television is the first version of *Unfaithfully Yours*. The irrepressible Preston Sturges delivers his satirical barbs in this 1948 gem from Fox, which he produced, directed and wrote. It stars Rex Harrison as a British orchestra conductor imagining that his beautiful young wife (Linda Darnell) is having an affair with his male secretary, handsome Kurt Kreuger. This is not true, but during a concert, his mind wanders and he thinks of many forms of revenge, one of which is murder, another his suicide. All is forgiven, as the conductor soon realizes that his wife has been blameless, but not before he has made a complete fool of himself.

In the cast are Rudy Vallee and Barbara Lawrence as a wealthy husband and wife. She utters this classic line as she sees Harrison kissing Darnell: "You see, some men just naturally make you think of brut champagne, with others, you think of prune juice."

A very successful film in its day, it was remade by Fox in 1984 with

Unfaithfully Yours (1948): What can that look in Rex Harrison's eye mean? Should Linda Darnell be afraid?

Dudley Moore and Nastassja Kinski in the Harrison-Darnell roles. The original premise is intact, but in this version, the wife is imagined to be having an affair with a concert violinist, played by Armand Assante. The latter is the soloist in the composition Moore is conducting while picturing the "revenge" he will wreak upon his wife and her "Lovere." It's still funny, but Moore lacks the elegance and panache required for the role. Also, Kinski does not have the grace and beauty of Darnell and the film is missing the Sturges touch.

In *My Wife's Best Friend* (Fox, 1952), a husband tells his wife about his dalliance with her best friend. The wife, in her mind, seeks revenge and imagines how she would behave if she were Cleopatra, Joan of Arc and other such historical figures. She soon realizes that the "affair" was just a mild flirtation and the marriage is saved. Macdonald Carey and Anne Baxter play the married couple with Catherine McLeod appearing as the "best friend." Does this sound familiar? It should. Think Rex Harrison and Dudley Moore.

By the 1950s, films that would have been called "screwball" decades before were now known as "romantic comedies." But to paraphrase Gertrude Stein, a rose by any other name would still smell as sweet. Screwball veterans were still plying their trade in the 1950s. To wit: Rosalind Russell, Fred MacMurray, Claudette Colbert, and Gary Cooper.

In *Woman of Distinction* (Columbia, 1951), Rosalind Russell plays the dean of a small college. The last thing on her mind is marriage. Through some unwanted publicity, she meets an English astronomer (Ray Milland) visiting the U.S. on a speaking tour. The newspapers play up this meeting, much to the delight of his blonde press agent (Janis Carter).

The star-gazer seems ready for romance, but the dean is not. The battle of the sexes is in full swing. A series of screwball scenes, one with Milland riding with a group of women on an unsteady bike, eventually losing the wheels, another with Roz riding in a student's car (read: heap) trying to avoid seeing Ray and ending up in a drag race, make for much hilarity. But, as in all of these films, the antagonists wind up in a clinch.

Aiding in the merriment are Edmund Gwenn as Russell's father, who would like to see his daughter married, and Jerome Courtland as a bewildered student.

How does a legal secretary who wants to get married, accomplish her goal? *A Millionaire for Christy* (Fox, 1951) starring Fred MacMurray and Eleanor Parker takes you through the process one step at a time.

Step One: You get sent cross-country (in this case Los Angeles) to inform a lucky man that he has inherited a lot of money.

Step Two: You meet him and decide that you are going to marry him. But there is a problem: He already has a fiancée. You also learn that said fiancée is loved by a doctor.

Step Three: Meet the medic. The two of you devise a scheme wherein each of you gets the mate you want.

Step Four: Celebrate the happy ending.

The stars are supported by Kay Buckley and Richard Carlson as the fiancée and the doctor. A fast pace and snappy dialogue make this film a winner.

Miriam Halsworth (Claudette Colbert) in *Let's Make It Legal* (Fox, 1951) is not looking for a husband because she has just divorced one: Hugh Halsworth (Macdonald Carey), an inveterate gambler. Daughter Barbara (Barbara Bates) tries to reconcile the bickering couple, but to no avail. Enter Victor McFarland (Zachary Scott), millionaire politician and long-ago suitor of Miriam. He now becomes Hugh's rival.

Still in love with his wife, Hugh tries a number of schemes, including introducing Victor to a sexy mantrap named Joyce (Marilyn Monroe), digging up his rose bushes with help from his son-in-law Jerry (Robert Wagner) and getting arrested. The newspapers get hold of the story. This does not bode well for the Miriam-Victor nuptials. And when it's revealed that Hugh won Miriam in a crap game, all bets are off for both men, until Hugh confesses that he had played with loaded dice. The finale has the formerly divorced couple in a clinch.

In the 1950s, Billy Wilder was still at his best. The writer-producer-director, whose films were and still are considered by film buffs and critics to have the Lubitsch type of sophisticated comedy, came up with *Love in the Afternoon* (Allied Artists, 1957), a witty and charming story with overtones of screwball. In Paris, millionaire playboy Frank Flannagan (Gary Cooper) is being shadowed by private detective Claude Chavasse (Maurice Chevalier). The latter has been hired by an irate husband (John McGiver) to find out if there is anything going on that he ought to know about. If there is, the husband will go gunning for his wife's seducer.

Chavasse's daughter Ariane (Audrey Hepburn), looking in her father's files, becomes curious about Flannagan and decides to warn him. She goes to his hotel, where gypsies are playing the lovely song, "Fascination." He is intrigued and she falls in love, but before they wind up together, there are some screwball situations. One of the funniest is the seduction scene with the gypsies playing, which ends with Flannagan and the music-makers in a Turkish bath.

Though Wilder first wanted Cary Grant, Cooper proved that he could still have the fans flocking to see his films. And then, there *is* Audrey Hepburn.

The energetic Billy worked on two other blockbusters in the mid– and late 1950s. A few years before, in the late 1940s, Marilyn Monroe had exploded on the screen with a force that is still felt today, decades after her untimely and controversial death. She made love to the camera and it responded in kind. Wilder cast her in *The Seven Year Itch* (Fox, 1955). With his wife Helen (Evelyn Keyes) away for the summer, Richard Sherman (Tom Ewell) fantasizes about the sexy blonde (Monroe) who has moved into the apartment upstairs. A gentle "battle of the sexes" ensues, on his part alone. The young woman spends time with him, but does not realize the effect she is having on him. He is brought back to reality when his wife comes home. Also in the cast are Sonny Tufts, Robert Strauss and Oscar Homolka.

This is the film during which the famous scene of Marilyn's skirt billowing up was shot, to the consternation of her then husband, baseball superstar Joe DiMaggio.

As Marilyn's star power increased to incredible heights, she became increasingly insecure and difficult to work with. Even so, Wilder cast her in *Some Like It Hot* (United Artists, 1959). The story revolves around two musicians Joe (Tony Curtis) and Jerry (Jack Lemmon) who have witnessed the infamous St. Valentine Day massacre. To escape from the gangsters who know that they are eyewitnesses, the two join an all-girl band on its way to Florida. In drag, they are now "Josephine" and "Daphne." They befriend the band's vocalist Sugar Kane (Monroe).

While in Florida, Jerry, as "Daphne," attracts the attention of rich eccentric Osgood Fielding (Joe E. Brown). Joe is busy, as himself, attracting the attention of the sexy Sugar, using the millionaire's yacht to woo her.

The gangsters are unsuccessful in their attempts to get the two witnesses and Joe's life will be "sweetened" by Sugar, but what about Jerry? Still in drag, he is proposed to by Osgood. He accepts but then has second thoughts and confesses that he is a man. Osgood's reply is one of the most memorable in the history of film: "Well, nobody's perfect."

Others in the cast include George Raft, Pat O'Brien and Nehemiah Persoff. The film is considered one of the greatest comedies in the history of Hollywood, a combination of parody, romance and farce, a tribute to both the screwball comedies and gangster movies of the 1930s. Lemmon and Wilder were both Oscar-nominated, but lost to Charlton Heston and director William Wyler for *Ben-Hur*. The only *Some Like it Hot* Oscar went to costume designer Orry-Kelly.

On the subject of Marilyn's troubles off-screen, Wilder is said to have put it this way: "Difficult to work with? Yes. Late on the set? Yes. I could hire my grandmother for the role. She'd be on time, but who would pay to see her?" Succinct and to the point.

Another beloved lady of the fifties whom we lost all too soon (in 1965) is Judy Holliday. On Broadway, she scored a resounding hit as the not-so-dumb blonde Billie Dawn in *Born Yesterday*. Repeating her role in the film version, released by Columbia, brought her the 1950 Best Actress Oscar.

Billie is the mistress of vulgar Harry Brock (Broderick Crawford), who calls her "a dumb broad." When Brock goes to Washington to do a little bribing, he hires reporter Paul Verrall (William Holden) to "smarten her up a little." To show Billie up, Brock asks her what a peninsula is. Her answer? "It's that new medicine." Paul and Billie go to work and soon she is "smartened up" enough to fall in love with her teacher.

Catch Billie playing gin rummy with Brock, wriggling her pinkie when winning, giving Brock his comeuppance at she realizes that he is nothing but a two-bit crook and, at the end, envisioning a life with the reporter based on love and respect. The film garnered great reviews and was Oscar-nominated but lost to *All About Eve*.

A 1993 remake starred Melanie Griffith as Billie, John Goodman as Brock and Don Johnson as Verrall. As in most cases, it does not compare to the earlier version.

A soon-to-be Oscar winner, Jack Lemmon (for *Mister Roberts*, 1955) joined Holliday in *It Should Happen to You* (Columbia, 1954). Judy plays Gladys Glover, a small town nobody who has dreams of fame and fortune. New York is not waiting for her with bated breath, so she hits upon the idea of paying for a billboard with her name on it in lights. Upset by this is Pete (Lemmon), her smitten neighbor, a small-time documentary filmmaker. One billboard leads to another and she becomes an object of curiosity. After being taken advantage of by an unscrupulous promoter (Michael O'Shea) and a soap magnate (Peter Lawford) with anything but business on his mind, Gladys goes back where she belongs, a nobody to some, but a somebody to Pete.

Judy plays Laura Partridge in *The Solid Gold Cadillac* (Columbia, 1956), satirizing big business. She is a small stockholder (ten shares) in a large corporation who attends a stockholders meeting and, in an unmistakably Judy Holliday voice, asks some embarrassing questions. To keep her quiet, the board of directors gives her a job answering correspondence from small shareholders. Her answers to questions are wise, funny and to-the-point. She is also finding things out and not liking what she learns—for instance, that Edward McKeever (Paul Douglas), founder of the company and an honest businessman, has resigned to work for the federal government in Washington.

Laura now knows there is corruption within the board and tries to get McKeever to come back to the corporation. She puts him wise to the machinations going on in his absence, in the meantime falling in love with him. They team up and after several hilarious incidents, Laura becomes chief stockholder in the company due to the trust of the small stockholders who have given her their proxies. She faces the corrupt board and in her inimitable voice, yells, "You're fired." She and Douglas get the company back and also get together.

Judy's film debut had come in *Adam's Rib* (MGM, 1949), a winner with Spencer Tracy and Katharine Hepburn top-billed. Doris Attinger (Holliday) is on trial for the attempted shooting of her no-good philandering husband Warren (Tom Ewell). Adam and Amanda Bonner (Tracy and Hepburn) are lawyers at loggerheads (read "battle of the sexes") over the case, she defending Doris and he trying to convict her. She is acquitted.

Catch Judy on the witness stand, Tracy giving Hepburn a rubdown and, best of all, Tracy with a gun in his mouth trying to prove a point (the gun is made of licorice).

Tracy and Hepburn would continue to work together until his death in 1967. In 1945, MGM signed the duo to *Without Love*, the story of an odd battle of the sexes between a scientist and a widow who marry "without love."

Pat Jamison (Tracy) is working on an important project for the government and his new wife, Jamie (Hepburn) becomes his willing partner. Jamie is the first to undergo an emotional change, but soon Pat, seeing his wife being ogled by a foreign charmer, becomes jealous and realizes that his marriage cannot be without love. Keenan Wynn and Lucille Ball are in a secondary battle of the sexes, but are hindered by his bitchy ex-fiancée.

There are many funny scenes in the film. A drunk Wynn, Tracy sleepwalking and finding himself in Hepburn's bed (she acts like her husband's old flame) and the clever repartee make the production a lively one.

Another success for the duo is *Pat and Mike,* a 1952 MGM production. Pat Pemberton is a terrific all-around athlete. She dazzles, except when her domineering fiancé, Collier Weld (William Ching), is around. She is within reach of a golf championship until she sees him. He wants her to forget the whole thing and marry him.

She meets a somewhat shady sports promoter named Mike Conovan (Tracy) whose other client is a dimwit boxer named Davie Hucko (Aldo Ray). Mike takes Pat on, saying to a buddy, "There's not much meat on her, but what there is, is cherce." Without her fiancé, but with Mike at her side, she feels she can go far in the world and does. Screwball scenes include Pat taking on a few gangsters in defense of Mike and the latter facing a bewildered Davie, who is jealous of his growing attention to Pat. An extra added attraction are cameos by sports greats Gussie Moran, Babe Didrikson Zaharias, Don Budge and Alice Marble.

In 1959, Doris Day became part of a star team that would prove as popular as the Hepburn-Tracy duo. Doris, a former band singer, had begun her Hollywood career in 1947 with Warner Brothers and had made several popular films for that company during her time there.

Before signing with the company that would make her a superstar, she made *Teacher's Pet* (1958) with Clark Gable. The film showed that the aging actor still had charisma after 25 years in the business. Gable plays a self-educated city editor who reads a letter from a journalism teacher opposed to the old school of reporting. He visits the class and who is the teacher? None other than Doris. He enrolls in her class and the battle of the journalists becomes the battle of the sexes.

Third-billed is Gig Young who was Oscar-nominated for his role as Doris' former fiancé. Mamie Van Doren, Nick Adams and Jack Albertson head the supporting cast.

Universal signed Doris to a multi-picture deal and reaped a bonanza in the late 1950s and early 1960s, teaming her and Rock Hudson. Her first film for her new bosses proved to be a blockbuster.

Pillow Talk (1959) is the story of two people who are truly engaged in the battle of the sexes which, after many screwball situations, turns into love and marriage. Doris plays an interior decorator, while Hudson is a songwriter. What they have in common is a telephone party line. Any time she wants to make a call, he is on the line, crooning the same song to several different women.

She is irate and he thinks of her as a frumpy old maid. When he sees

Send Me No Flowers (1964) with Rock Hudson, Tony Randall and Doris Day. Is hypochondriac Rock really on his deathbed?

her, he changes his mind. To woo her, he pretends to be a shy, wealthy Texan and she falls for him, believing him different from the other men she's encountered. When she discovers the truth, it's too late, she's hooked.

Tony Randall is terrific as one of the lady's disappointed suitors and Thelma Ritter also shines as Day's alcoholic maid. Doris and Thelma were both Oscar-nominated, but Doris lost to Simone Signoret and Thelma to Shelley Winters.

Day and Hudson scored another bull's-eye in *Lover Come Back* (1961), a satirical look at the world of advertising. Carol Templeton (Day) is working to get business for her agency. Jerry Webster (Hudson) is her rival. She has never met Jerry, who then pretends to be a scientist at work on a product called VIP. No such product exists and much of the fun is in watching Doris trying to get an advertising contract for the "product."

A good supporting cast helps to make *Lover Come Back* a winner. Tony Randall is third-billed as a nebbish for whom Hudson works, with Edie Adams and Jack Oakie prominently cast.

Send Me No Flowers (1964) proved to be the last of the Day-Hudson ventures. This time Hudson is a hypochondriac who happens to overhear his doctor discussing another patient's fatal condition. He thinks that patient is himself and immediately sets out to find a replacement for his wife (Doris). Alarmed, she sees the medical man and finds out that her husband is perfectly well. She now believes that he has made up the story because he is having an affair. By the end of the film, Rock knows he will live a long life and Doris knows that there has been no affair.

Tony Randall, the third member of the previous Day-Hudson successes, is on hand again, this time as a nutty neighbor who is recruited to find a new husband for Doris. Other cast members include Clint Walker, Hal March and Paul Lynde as an aggressive but very funny cemetery plot salesman.

In between two of Day's films with Rock Hudson, she starred with the ageless and charismatic Cary Grant in *That Touch of Mink* (1962). Grant plays Philip Shayne, a philandering tycoon who sets his eye on chaste, job-seeking Cathy Timberlake (Doris). He invites her to go on a trip with him, he thinking that she will succumb to him. She goes away with him, but doesn't give in, and by the time he realizes that he is in love with her, she's gone. He finds her and, after a wild car chase, marries her and gets a rash on their wedding night. Gig Young and Audrey Meadows score, he as Grant's financial advisor and she as Doris' friend. It was a sure-fire money-maker for Universal, but the duo never made another film. Four years later, Grant made his last movie.

Down with Love (Fox, 2003) is reminiscent of the Doris Day–Rock Hudson films. Renee Zellweger, author of a book empowering women, meets up with Ewan McGregor, a macho reporter for a men's magazine. Like the Day-Hudson films, the battle of the sexes begins when the man, wanting to take the lady down a peg, takes on a different persona and like the Day-Hudson films, the two are together at the end.

It is time now to delve more into the last decades of the twentieth century and beyond.

Chapter Sixteen

Screwball Lives On: Part Two

Throughout this book, I have maintained that the screwball comedy still lives on, beyond the 1930s and the 1940s, contrary to the beliefs of many. To prove my point, I give you Cher, Goldie Hawn, Barbra Streisand, Bette Midler and Julia Roberts—four Oscar winners and one nominee. These stars let their hair down and made comedies during the last decades of the 20th century which have many elements of this delightful genre.

Gone are the days of the "studio system" which spawned the careers of some of Hollywood's greatest stars. The key word in the film capital of today is "bankable," and "bankable" is the word for the five ladies just mentioned.

Anyone who has seen *Moonstruck* (Palmer/Jewison, 1987) cannot help applauding the Oscar given to Cher, who has come a long way from her days with Sonny Bono. *Moonstruck* is a romantic comedy with screwball elements. Cher is Loretta Castorini, a young Italian widow who accepts a marriage proposal from somewhat nerdy Johnny Cammareri, well played by Danny Aiello. In a "screwballian" scene, she makes him get down on his knees, with funny commentary by both, to propose to her. When her intended goes to Italy to be with his dying mother, Loretta meets her fiancé's estranged brother Ronny (sexy Nicolas Cage) and sparks begin to fly.

Before this battle of the sexes is ended, Loretta, in love with Ronny, is in a quandary, but decides to go against Italian convention and wind up with the one she really loves. Vincent Gardenia and Olympia Dukakis play Cher's parents, with Dukakis taking an Oscar home as Best Supporting Actress. *The New York Times* called the film "an incredibly nourishing comedy filled with warmth, cheer and terrific snappy dialogue."

Goldie Hawn, like Cher, had spent the earlier part of her career on television. Not as dumb as the character she played on TV's *Rowan and Martin's Laugh-In*, she was tapped for the second lead in *Cactus Flower*, a Columbia release. Holding her own with Ingrid Bergman and Walter Matthau, she received a Best Supporting Actress Oscar.

Of the many films she's made in a career which has lasted over four decades, I've chosen two screwball Hawn films for discussion in this part of my narrative.

From the fertile brain of Neil Simon, *Seems Like Old Times* (Columbia, 1980) is the tale of a lawyer (Hawn), her nerd of a husband (Charles Grodin) and her ex (Chevy Chase) who comes back into her life while running from the law (he has been innocently involved in a bank robbery) and disrupts her seemingly happy marriage. After some funny scenes with Chase (and a "How did I get into this?" type of reaction from Goldie and Grodin), the lawyer settles her first husband's case and falls in love with him all over again. Needless to say, the current mate is no longer in the picture (pun intended).

Two years later, Goldie was at Warner Brothers for *Best Friends,* in which she co-starred with Burt Reynolds. They play two successful screenwriters who have a harmonious working and romantic relationship. They decide to get married. No more harmonious working relationship. As for "romantic"? Forget it. When the two sets of parents get together, true screwball reigns.

Catch Goldie and Burt in her parents' home. She doesn't want to sleep with Burt in her old room, saying, "This is my teenage room. It's not for sexual relations, it's for slumber parties." They later divorce. These and other choice bits of dialogue come from the pens of Valerie Curtin and Barry Levinson. The story was based in part upon their real-life relationship. In the supporting cast are Jessica Tandy and Barnard Hughes as Goldie's parents and Audra Lindley and Keenan Wynn as Burt's. Ron Silver plays a zany director for whom the team works.

Like Hawn, Barbra Streisand became an Oscar winner in her debut film. She had burst upon the screen in *Funny Girl,* a Columbia 1968 release. A native New Yorker, Streisand appeared in nightclubs and on television with Johnny Carson and Judy Garland. Her big break came via Broadway in *I Can Get It for You Wholesale.* After her appearance on the stage as Fanny Brice in *Funny Girl,* she again played the legendary performer in the film version of the play, winning the coveted award. Her Hollywood career was established.

She has become an icon, winning Oscars, Grammys and Tonys. During her lengthy career, she has sung, acted, produced and directed, insuring herself a place in show business history.

Considered temperamental, she calls herself a perfectionist. Movie fans couldn't care less: They have flocked to see her films, including three harkening back to the screwball comedies of yesteryear.

What's Up Doc? is filmmaker Peter Bogdanovich's homage to director Howard Hawks. The 1972 Saticoy Productions release casts Ryan O'Neal as Howard Bannister, an absentminded musicologist whose unwanted acquaintance with a kook named Judy Maxwell (Streisand) leads to him getting mixed up with underworld characters and four suitcases, one of which contains some stolen jewels, much to the annoyance of his fiancée (Madeline Kahn). Shades of paleontologist David Huxley and dizzy Susan Vance in *Bringing Up Baby* and also Sugarpuss O'Shea and Bertram Potts in *Ball of Fire*, both Hawks hits.

Bogdanovich was less successful with *At Long Last Love* (Fox, 1975), a screwball comedy with music. It stars Burt Reynolds and Cybill Shepherd as a rich couple who engage in a battle of the sexes, replete with songs by Cole Porter. The film wastes a supporting cast which includes Madeline Kahn, Eileen Brennan, John Hillerman and Mildred Natwick as a daffy old lady.

Two years after *What's Up Doc?*, Barbra moved over to Columbia and *For Pete's Sake*. In his book *The Columbia Story*, Clive Hirschhorn states that the company, then "in the doldrums," was saved by two Streisand films, one of which was the film under discussion. (The other: *The Way We Were*, released in 1973.)

For Pete's Sake is an old-fashioned screwball farce about a housewife named Henry, short for Henrietta (Streisand, whose talent for comedy is gloriously realized in this role), and her taxi-driving husband Pete (Michael Sarrazin). He would like to go back to college. In order to help him, she first goes to his brother (William Redfield) and the latter's condescending and thoroughly disagreeable wife (Estelle Parsons) whom she detests, but it's a no-go. She borrows the money they need, $3000, without telling her husband where she got it. On a tip, they invest in pork-belly futures and lose the money. The rest of the film is spent trying to pay back the people she owes, first a loan shark and then Mrs. Cherry, an elderly Jewish lady, wonderfully played by veteran actress Molly Picon, who just happens to be a madam. Hilarity ensues when Henry tries to be one of the madam's call girls.

The end of the film has the couple's pork-belly futures investment hitting an all-time high, but not before Henry gets involved with a judge, a bomb-sniffing dog and a group of cattle rustlers.

Once more, Barbra's leading man in *The Main Event* (Barwood Films, 1979) is Ryan O'Neal. Her character, Hillary Kramer, successful in the perfume business, finds out that her accountant has robbed her and gone to South America. What remains of her few assets is a small-time boxer named Eddie "Kid Natural" Scanlon, who has been making a living giving driving lessons. Hillary decides to recoup her fortune by putting Eddie back into the ring. Eddie resists, but the lady "owns" him and he helps her.

The boxing scenes are funny, including the one with the two stars in the ring together at the end of the film. It was not as funny as the other two films mentioned, but Streisand fans lined up at the box-office.

The Main Event (1979): Barbra Streisand "owns" Ryan O'Neal. Who will score the knock-out punch?

Bette Midler has, like Streisand, succeeded in every facet of show business. She may also be remembered as the last guest on *The Tonight Show* as Johnny Carson bid a fond adieu to his many fans.

Oscar-nominated in her first film, the dramatic *The Rose* (Fox, 1979) Bette has mainly stuck to comedy. In 1986, she starred with Nick Nolte and Richard Dreyfuss in *Down and Out in Beverly Hills*, a Touchtone Films satire based upon *Boudu, Saved from Drowning*, a 1931 French film directed by Jean Renoir.

The film tells the story of the nouveau riche Whitemans, Barbara and David (Midler and Dreyfuss), living in a posh Beverly Hills mansion. Wealthy, but not very happy, she does the things a society matron would do, while he is sleeping with the housemaid. The children are dysfunctional and totally spoiled.

Nick Nolte is Jerry Baskin, a homeless man who has lost his dog. He wanders into the Whiteman backyard and is almost drowned in their swimming pool. He is invited to stay with this mixed-up family and changes the lives of its members, young and old.

That Old Feeling (1997): **Dennis Farina and Bette Midler are divorced and have remarried. They wreak havoc at their daughter's wedding.**

That same year, Touchtone also starred the Divine Miss M in *Ruthless People* as Barbara, the obnoxious wife of Sam Stone (Danny DeVito). He is filled with hate for her and lust for Carol (Anita Morris), his gold-digging mistress. He plans to murder Barbara and go away with Carol. He is unaware of the fact that the mistress already has a boyfriend (Bill Pullman).

Barbara is first seen in a burlap bag, kicking and screaming. She has been kidnapped by the Kesslers (Judge Reinhold and Helen Slater), a couple who have it in for Sam. (Sam, a clothing manufacturer, has ripped off their designs.) At first Sam refuses to pay the ransom, but Barbara is such a nuisance that the couple releases her. Sam is then accused of faking the kidnapping. At the end, Barbara will stay with him, probably kicking and screaming all the way. DeVito and Midler are a joy to watch and they milk every nuance of the situation.

Bette got together with Dennis Farina for *That Old Feeling* (Buena Vista, 1997), an old-fashioned comedy directed by Carl Reiner. They play a movie star and a journalist, once married, now married to others, brought together after several years by their daughter's forthcoming marriage to a Senator's son. The groom would like a big wedding, but the bride-to-be warns against it: "My parents hate each other with a nuclear intensity."

She is so right. On the dance floor at the wedding reception, they cannot control themselves, yelling and screaming at each other. Their fighting is painful for Farina's new wife and Midler's new husband, but more disturbing to this scenario is when ex-wife and ex-husband engage in a short-lived affair.

Bette, as usual, is dynamic and Farina, known more for dramatic roles, is well-matched with her. In the excellent supporting cast are Paula Marshall as their daughter, Jamie Denton as their new son-in-law, Gail O'Grady as Farina's second wife, and David Rasche as Midler's husband.

Screwball scenes include O'Grady getting drunk with the groom, the bride locked in a room with a paparazzi trying to get attention by dropping fruit from the balcony, and the dialogue between the fighting Midler and Farina.

The star of the 1990s had to be Julia Roberts, who made her screen debut in a 1988 film titled *Blood Red*. Later in her career, as an established star, she won an Oscar for her role as the activist in *Erin Brockovich* (Jersy Film Productions, 2000).

Her break-out role came in 1990 with *Pretty Woman* (Touchstone/Buena Vista Productions) in which she plays a hooker who is hired by wealthy workaholic businessman Edward Lewis (Richard Gere). He has borrowed his aide's fancy car and winds up in the red light district of Los Angeles. Asking for directions, he meets Vivian Ward (Roberts), sees something in her and asks her to be his companion for a week. He takes her to a luxury hotel and buys her an expensive wardrobe. He wants to be seen at society events with a "pretty woman" on his arm as it doesn't seem right for a man of his "stature" to be seen going to these fancy functions alone.

At first, it is strictly business but then there are confrontations with the girl giving as good as she gets. The businessman is attracted to her feisty attitude as well her looks. Each goes through a metamorphosis: She has made him more human while he has seen an innate classiness about her and given her a taste of a life that some girls can only dream about. In the finale, Edward shows up in a limo (instead of a white horse), jumping out of the car and coming to claim his princess. (In the original story, the girl goes back on the street, but director Garry Marshall wanted a happy ending, so in the film, Cinderella does get her Prince Charming.)

Also in the cast are Ralph Bellamy as a business rival, Hector Elizondo as the hotel manager who falls under Vivian's spell and Jason Alexander as Philip Stuckly, Edward's smarmy aide. The scene with Alexander trying to grab Roberts is a screwball scene out of the past. The film became a megahit due to the chemistry between its two stars and its smart dialogue.

Not as successful as *Pretty Woman* is *I Love Trouble* (Meyers/Block, 1994).This time Roberts is paired with Nick Nolte, whom many critics felt at the time was too old to be sparring with her.

The Runaway Bride (1999): Julia Roberts has left three men at the altar. Will Richard Gere change this pattern?

Nolte is Pete Brackett, a smug veteran columnist on a Chicago newspaper who has just had a novel published. Roberts is Sabrina Peterson, a new reporter on a rival paper who meets Nolte at the scene of a train wreck. When she scoops him, he initiates a competition with her. Working separately at first, they each find out that the story is much more than just a train derailment—it involves corporate intrigue and greed. Eventually they come to the conclusion that they need to work together. All through their investigations, they insist it is only a business pairing, but at the end as in all battle of the sexes, they find a mutual attraction for each other.

The writers of this film tried to harken back to the newspaper stories of the 1930s and 1940 (like *His Girl Friday*) without too much success. Nick Nolte is no Cary Grant and Roberts does not have the brittleness of Rosalind Russell.

What could be a better idea for a screwball comedy than a girl who has left her prospective bridegrooms at the altar more than once? This is the premise for our last presentation in this chapter. The trio that made *Pretty Woman* a hit, struck gold again with *The Runaway Bride* (Touchstone, 1999). With Garry Marshall directing, Roberts plays Maggie Carpenter, a girl who obviously wants to get married, but cannot take that last step. Richard Gere is Ike Graham, a newspaper columnist who writes an uncomplimentary column about this interesting "phenomenon."

Maggie writes an irate letter to Graham's paper pointing out several misrepresentations and the guy is fired. He is, however, intrigued by the girl and travels to her home town to get a story which will vindicate him. The usual animosity between two opposites in a screwball takes place, but eventually, as we all know, this hostility turns to love. The popularity of the Roberts-Gere-Marshall team and the use of a theme popular in earlier decades, make for a delightful film. *The Runaway Bride* was a runaway hit with the public.

Supporting the duo are Hector Elizondo, Joan Cusack and popular television star Christopher Meloni (*Law and Order, SVU*), who plays prospective husband number four.

Epilogue

As long as there are men and women, there will be a battle of the sexes, therefore providing much fodder for the screwball comedy, i.e., romantic comedy movies. Whether this genre will, in this 21st century, achieve the luster of what has come before, is a matter of conjecture.

In many a film, there is a thread of familiarity coursing through its screenplay. Claudette Colbert cannot make up her mind in *It Happened One Night,* Ginger Rogers cannot make up her mind in *Tom, Dick and Harry* while Julia Roberts cannot make up her mind in *The Runaway Bride.* Different plotlines, released in different decades, yet there's that thread of familiarity.

Someone once said that there are only six or seven original plot lines that writers can use. I think that this can be seen from the foregoing. Moviemakers have always been aware of this and are constantly looking out for some new variations on a theme. This goes for any genre.

Let's hope the screwball comedy will be a part of this search. But in their search, filmmakers need to take another look at the comedies of an earlier era and produce motion pictures with the wit and sophistication that charmed the moviegoers of those bygone days.

The viewer can also look to television networks such as Turner Classic Movies, Fox Movie Channel and RetroPlex, go back in time and again watch the films that charmed America and other countries during the 20th century. DVDs of the films of an earlier era can be purchased or rented and enjoyed at the viewer's leisure.

Will the stars of today reach the heights of those who came before them? Only time will tell.

As in the Great Depression, we are in a period of turmoil, stress and strife. Whether in a movie theater or at home watching films on television or DVDs, what we all need now is a good laugh.

A well-made screwball–romantic comedy should be able to supply some laughter, at least for a little while.

Bibliography

Basinger, Jeanine. *American Cinema: One Hundred Years of Filmmaking*. New York: Rizzoli, 1994.

_____. *A Woman's View: How Hollywood Spoke to Women, 1930–1960*. New York: Alfred A. Knopf, 1993.

Bergan, Ronald. *The United Artists Story*. New York: Crown, 1986.

Blum, Daniel. *A Pictorial History of the Talkies*. New York: Grosset & Dunlap, 1958.

Boller, Paul F., and Ronald L. Davis. *Hollywood Anecdotes*. New York: William Morrow, 1987.

Canby, Vincent, and Janet Maslin. *New York Times Guide to the Best 1,000 Movies Ever Made*. New York: Times Books, 1999.

Capra, Frank. *The Name Above the Title: An Autobiography*. New York: Macmillan, 1971.

Cawkwell, Tim, and John M. Smith, eds. *The World Encyclopedia of the Film*. New York: Galahad, 1972.

Cook, David A. *A History of Narrative Film*. New York: W.W. Norton, 1981.

Dooley, Roger. *From Scarface to Scarlett: American Films in the 1930s*. New York: Harcourt Brace Jovanovich, 1979.

Eames, John Douglas. *The MGM Story*. New York: Crown, 1979.

_____. *The Paramount Story*. New York: Crown, 1985.

Hirschhorn, Clive. *The Columbia Story*. New York: Crown, 1990.

_____. *The Universal Story*. New York: Crown, 1983.

_____. *The Warner Brothers Story*. New York: Crown, 1983.

Jewell, Richard B., with Vernon Harkins. *The RKO Story*. New York: Arlington House, 1982.

Maltin, Leonard. *Leonard Maltin's 2002 Movie and Video Guide*. New York: New American Library, 2001.

Michael, Paul, ed.-in-chief, and James Robert Parish, assoc. ed. *The American Movies: The History, Films, Awards*. New York: Garland, 1969.

_____, and _____. *Movie Greats: The Players, Directors, Producers*. New York: Garland, 1969.

New York Times Directory of the Film. Intro. Arthur Knight. New York: Arno Press, 1974.

Quigley, Martin, Jr., and Richard Gertner. *Films in America: 1929–1969*. New York: Golden Press, 1970.

Shipman, David. *The Great Movie Stars: The Golden Years*. New York: Bonanza, 1970.
_____. *The Story of Cinema*. New York: St. Martin's, 1982.
Sikov, Ed. *Screwball: Hollywood's Madcap Romantic Comedies*. New York: Crown, 1989.
Thomas, Tony, and Aubrey Solomon. *The Films of 20th Century–Fox*. Secaucus, NJ: Citadel Press, 1985.
Vermilye, Jerry. *The Films of the Thirties*. Secausus, NJ: Citadel Press, 1982.
Walker, John, ed. *Halliwell's Film Guide*. New York: Harper Collins, 1994.
Wiley, Mason, and Daniel Bona. *Inside Oscar*. New York: Ballantine, 1996.

Index